Dr Peter Collett is a social psyc[...] he taught and conducted [...] Department of Experimental Psychology at Oxford University. He has co-authored two books, including *Gestures: Their Origins and Distribution* with Desmond Morris, and is the author of *Foreign Bodies: A Guide to European Mannerisms*. He has appeared in various television documentaries and is currently resident psychologist on the hugely popular Channel 4 series *Big Brother*. He lives with his family in Oxford.

www.booksattransworld.co.uk

Also by Peter Collett

Foreign Bodies: A Guide to European Mannerisms
Gestures: Their Origins and Distribution (co-author)
Driving Passion: The Psychology of the Car (co-author)

THE BOOK OF TELLS

How to Read People's Minds from Their Actions

PETER COLLETT

BANTAM BOOKS

LONDON • NEW YORK • TORONTO • SYDNEY • AUCKLAND

THE BOOK OF TELLS
A BANTAM BOOK: 0 553 81459 1

Originally published in Great Britain by Doubleday,
a division of Transworld Publishers

PRINTING HISTORY
Doubleday edition published 2003
Bantam edition published 2004

1 3 5 7 9 10 8 6 4 2

Copyright © Peter Collett 2003
Illustrations © Gino D'Achille

Photo credits: 49: Portrait of Henry VIII by Hans Holbein the Younger, Belvoir
Castle/Bridgeman Art Library; 81: PA/Martin Keene; 146: Matthew
Polak/Corbis; 148: John Sturrock/Network; 173: Ollie Atkins' photo 324–3–5,
Special Collections & Archives, George Mason University Libraries; 211:
PA/David Cheskin; 232–3: PA/Phil Noble; 270: The Kobal Collection; 295:
Reuters/Popperfoto; 319: Peter Collett; 344 top: © Pictorial Press; bottom left
to right: AP; Getty Images; John Springer Collection/Corbis.

The right of Peter Collett to be identified as the author of
this work has been asserted in accordance with sections 77
and 78 of the Copyright, Designs and Patents Act 1988.

Condition of Sale
This book is sold subject to the condition that it shall not,
by way of trade or otherwise, be lent, re-sold, hired out or
otherwise circulated in any form of binding or cover other
than that in which it is published and without a similar
condition including this condition being imposed on the
subsequent purchaser.

Set in 11/14pt Optima by
Falcon Oast Graphic Art Ltd.

Bantam Books are published by Transworld Publishers,
61–63 Uxbridge Road, London W5 5SA,
a division of The Random House Group Ltd,
in Australia by Random House Australia (Pty) Ltd,
20 Alfred Street, Milsons Point, Sydney, NSW 2061, Australia,
in New Zealand by Random House New Zealand Ltd,
18 Poland Road, Glenfield, Auckland 10, New Zealand
and in South Africa by Random House (Pty) Ltd,
Endulini, 5a Jubilee Road, Parktown 2193, South Africa.

Printed and bound in Great Britain by
Cox & Wyman Ltd, Reading, Berkshire.

Papers used by Transworld Publishers are natural, recyclable products
made from wood grown in sustainable forests. The manufacturing
processes conform to the environmental regulations of the
country of origin.

For Jill, Katie and Clementine

Contents

	Acknowledgements	9
1	*Tells*	11
2	Dominant Tells	36
3	Submissive Tells	71
4	Conversation Tells	104
5	Political Tells	127
6	Greeting Tells	163
7	Royal Tells	196
8	Anxiety Tells	219
9	Sexual Tells	244
10	Lying Tells	284
11	Foreign Tells	307
12	Smoking Tells	328
13	Tell-Tales	347
	Notes	357
	Index	381

Acknowledgements

I would like to thank my wife Jill, and my daughters Katie and Clementine, for their patience and loving support, without which this book would not have been possible. Thanks are also due to my agent Caradoc King, for his advice and encouragement, to Martha Lishawa and Linda Shaughnessy at A. P. Watt, to Brenda Kimber, Marianne Velmans and Sheila Lee at Doubleday, and to Beth Humphries, for all the help and support they have given me. In addition I would like to express my gratitude to my brother Tony and his wife Julia for their encouragement over the years, as well as to the following friends and colleagues for their valuable help and suggestions: Suzie Addinell, Max Atkinson, Rad Babic, Geoffrey Beattie, Steven Beebe, Giovanni Carnibella, Alberta Contarello, Tina Cook, Paul Ekman, Norma Feshbach, Seymour Feshbach, Mark Frank, Adrian Furnham, Tim Gardam, Doris Ginsburg, Gerry Ginsburg, Fergus Gleeson, Peter Henderson, Tim Horner, Brett Kahr, Christine Kuehn, Mansur Lalljee, Roger Lamb, Peter Marsh, Marie O'Shaughnessy, Sophie Ratcliffe, Monica Rector, Rachel Reeves, Bryan Richards, Dunja Sagov, Sandra Scott, Barry Shrier, Caroline Simmonds, Frank Simmonds, Mary Sissons Joshi, Charles Smith, Michael John Spencer, Oliver

Spiecker, Martine Stewart, Michael Stewart, Paddy Summerfield, Gaby Twivy, Paul Twivy and Peter van Breda. Finally I would like to record my special thanks to Peter du Preez, Michael Argyle and Desmond Morris, who taught me so much of what I know and encouraged my interest in human behaviour.

1. *Tells*

Let's imagine that you're talking to an old friend about your schooldays together. You casually ask him if he misses his days at school. 'Oh no,' he replies, 'I don't have any regrets. I'm glad that's all over.' As he's talking, he briefly wipes the skin under his right eye with his index finger. There's no reason why you should notice this tiny gesture, and if you did you'd probably think that he was just removing a bit of dust from his face. But he isn't. The gesture is in fact a *tell*, and it casts an entirely different light on your friend's true feelings. Although he says that he doesn't miss his days at school, part of his brain knows otherwise, and it instructs his finger to wipe away an imaginary tear. So, while the conscious part of his brain is saying, 'I have no regrets', another part is producing a *tell* which says, 'Well actually, I do have regrets!' Momentarily your friend might recognize his complicated feelings, but it's highly unlikely that he realizes what his unruly finger is doing, or what it reveals about his true feelings.

The friend who wipes away an imaginary tear produces an *autonomous tell* – in other words, a *tell* that has no purpose other than to reveal his true feelings. Because *autonomous tells* aren't intentional, they are hardly ever noticed by the people who produce them or the people who witness them. That's not necessarily the case with *attached tells*, which are connected to some other activity. For example, when two people are introduced to each other, the fact that they shake hands may be less informative than *how* they actually do so. How tightly they grip each other's hand, how they position their palm, how much enthusiasm they show, how much control they try to exert, the actual words they use to greet each other – these are *attached tells*. Within the greeting ritual they reveal what each person is really like, and what they're trying to achieve with the other person.

Whether a *tell* is an action or the way that an action is performed usually depends on how common the action is. Consider two societies – one where men regularly greet each other with a kiss on the cheek, and another where they hardly ever do so. When two men kiss each other in the first society they are simply doing what all the other men do. The fact that they kiss each other is therefore not very informative – it doesn't tell us anything about their relationship. However, *how* they kiss each other does tell us about their relationship. The situation in the second society tends to be reversed. Here, when two men greet each other with a kiss on the cheek they are doing something unusual. Now it's the kiss itself, rather than the way it's performed, that tells us what kind of relationship the two men have.

Poker Tells

The word *tell* comes from the game of poker, where it's used to refer to the signals that players unintentionally produce when they're trying to conceal what kinds of cards they're holding or the strategy they're employing. There are two essential skills in poker – one is the capacity to hide one's feelings, so that the other players have no idea whether you're holding a bad hand or a royal flush. This is the ability to keep a 'poker face' – to remain completely enigmatic. The other essential skill is the ability to read people's behaviour – to work out what kind of cards they're holding, simply by observing their actions and listening to what they say. While you, as a poker player, are looking for tell-tale signs in another player's behaviour, he's busy doing everything he can to mislead you. The reverse is also true – while the other players are trying to figure out what you're up to, you're doing everything in your power to ensure that you don't give them anything to go on, or if you do that it sends them off in the wrong direction.

One of the ways that poker players can improve their game is by learning to recognize the links between their opponents' actions, the cards that they're holding, and the moves they make. They can start to pay attention to little things, like the way someone holds his cards or the way he looks at them, the way he makes a call, what he does with his hands, how he fiddles with his glasses – the list of potential *tells* is endless. Mike Caro has made a life-long study of poker *tells* and the ways that players give themselves away by sighing, humming, tapping their fingers, playing for time, checking their cards and trying to lay false trails.[1] Several films, like *House of Games* and *Rounders*, have included scenes where the plot turns on someone discovering a poker *tell*. In *Rounders*, for example, there's a showdown game of poker between Mike, the hero (played by Matt Damon), and Teddy KGB, a Russian mobster (played by John Malkovich) who likes to break open Oreo cookies and eat them while he's playing poker. Mike eventually wins the game by working out the Russian's *tell* – when he splits the cookie beside his ear he's got a good hand, but when he splits it in front of his face it means that he's bluffing!

Poker players have lots to think about. Apart from deciding what to do next, they're constantly trying to undermine other players' attempts to understand them, while doing everything possible to see past the defences erected by the other players. It all seems very confusing, but in fact it's no more complicated than the things that we all do every time we relate to other people. In our daily encounters we're constantly trying to project an image of ourselves, and so are other people, and while they're trying to work out what we are thinking, we're doing the same to them. Our chances of success, like those of the poker player, will always depend on how sensitive we are to other people, and whether we can recognize and understand their *tells*.

Defining Tells

Everyday *tells* are highly informative. The way you stand when you're talking to someone – how you move your feet, hands, eyes and eyebrows – says a lot about your commitment to the conversation and your underlying attitude to the other person. It also affects how long you get to talk and how often you get interrupted. How you position your arms and legs when you're seated also provides a wealth of information about your mood and intentions, showing whether you feel dominant or submissive, preoccupied or bored, involved or detached. The way you smile – the facial muscles you use and how rapidly you enlist them – shows whether you're genuinely happy, faking it, lying or telling the truth, feeling anxious, miserable, superior or unsure of yourself. Speech disfluencies are also highly informative. The way you hesitate when you're speaking, how you 'um' and 'er', provides important clues to your mood. While the words you choose, the phrases you select, and the way you construct your utterances may convey an 'official message' to other people, your linguistic choices also contain 'disguised messages' which reveal your true intentions.

A *tell* needs to satisfy four conditions:

◆　It has to be some kind of activity – a feature of someone's appearance, a movement of their body, or something they say. Broadly speaking, *tells* fall into two categories – 'attributes', like height or weight, and 'actions', like folding one's arms, smiling or using certain giveaway words and phrases.

◆　The action needs to reveal something about the person that's not directly observable – it has to tell us about their background, their thoughts, their mood or their intentions. It follows that not every action is a *tell* – it's only those actions that convey information about someone that are *tells*. Of course there are some actions that we don't recognize as *tells* because we haven't yet discovered what they reveal about people. These are *undiscovered tells*. When we do learn how they are linked to people's internal states, they too will be added to the list of *tells*.

◆ The action has to be noticed. One factor that decides whether an action gets noticed is its size. Large, expansive movements of the body, for example, are more likely to attract attention, especially when they're visible for a long time. Small, fleeting movements, on the other hand, often get ignored, either because they're not in view for long enough or because they're obscured by other actions. Although large actions are more visible, it doesn't mean that we automatically notice them or that we understand their significance. As Sherlock Holmes remarked to Dr Watson, we may see but we don't always observe.

◆ The significance of the action needs to be recognized. It's not enough for us to notice that someone has adopted a certain posture or used an unusual expression. We also need to recognize what that posture or that expression tells us about that person.

When we look at the evolution of *tells* we find that there's a tendency for some *tells* to get bigger, and a tendency for others to get smaller. In areas like dominance and courtship, where there's a lot of competition between individuals, there's a natural tendency for the anatomical features that signal strength and reproductive fitness to get bigger, and for the displays associated with those features to become bolder and more eye-catching. This can sometimes be taken to extremes. In the animal world, for example, there are *macro-tells*, like the male fiddler crab's enormous red claw, which is even bigger than his body, and which he waves around whenever he wants to intimidate other males or impress the females. In our society there are men who pump iron and take body-enhancing drugs so that they look more muscular, and women who submit to the surgeon's knife in order to enhance their bum or increase the size of their breasts. Over-sized claws, large biceps and massive breasts are all weapons in the escalating war of dominance and attraction – they are designed to attract attention, to get the message across, to outclass the competition and ultimately to enable the individual to gain access to limited resources like food, shelter or sexual partners.

Micro-tells

There are two situations where signals get smaller. One is where there's a deliberate attempt to ensure secrecy, and the other is where there's unintended disclosure of what's going on in someone's head. By their very nature, secret signals are targeted at selected individuals – in order to remain secret it's essential that only certain people get the message and that everyone else doesn't. Very often this is achieved by using a miniature signal and by attaching it to an everyday action that doesn't attract attention. Lovers sometimes communicate in code, using special words or tiny signs when they're with other people – in this way they can exchange loving signals without anyone else knowing. In a similar fashion, members of secret societies often identify themselves to each other by the way they shake hands – for example, by scratching the palm or positioning the fingers so that the other person gets the message but nobody else can see what's happening. Detection is avoided by deliberately keeping the signal small. As a further safeguard, it's hidden inside an activity that's unlikely to arouse suspicion.

Miniature signals are also common when people are trying to hide what they're thinking. When people are lying, for example, or feeling anxious, the giveaway signs that expose their true feelings are often extremely small and short-lived. Unlike the signs exchanged by lovers or members of secret societies, these *micro-tells* are entirely unintentional. Psychologists have identified a special group of *micro-tells* called 'micromomentary expressions', which are confined to the face.[2] They are very brief and usually appear for no more than one-eighth of a second. When people are describing a painful experience while putting on a brave face, it's not uncommon for them to reveal their discomfort by briefly altering their facial expression. One moment they're smiling, giving the impression that the experience didn't bother them at all; the next moment their face is transformed into the briefest of grimaces. Then, before anyone notices anything, the smile is back, and all evidence of discomfort is erased from their face.

The distinguishing feature of facial *micro-tells* is their brevity – it's as though someone has opened the curtains, allowing passers-by to look into their home, and then immediately closed them again. The action is so rapid that people don't notice the curtains opening, let alone what's in the house. That's exactly how it is with *micro-tells*.

When we're concealing our thoughts, or a particularly strong image enters our mind, it sometimes shows on our face or in our movements. As soon as the wayward thought has managed to sneak on to our face, the processes that control our demeanour spring into action, remove it and reinstate the desired expression. In the meantime, however, the evidence is there for anyone to see – they just need to spot the *micro-tell* and be able to interpret it correctly.

In principle, *micro-tells* can appear anywhere on the body, but because of the fine-grained nature of the facial muscles, they're most likely to appear on the face. When a *micro-tell* does appear on our face, it shows that we're in a state of conflict – usually between a positive emotional state that we want other people to see, and a negative emotional state that we're trying to conceal. When the negative emotional state momentarily gains the upper hand, our facial control breaks down and the *micro-tell* appears. Most of the time we're completely unaware of the conflict that's taking place in us, and the fact that we're revealing our inner thoughts to the outside world. But even when we are conscious of our conflicting emotions, we still don't realize that our facial *micro-tells* are giving us away.

Facial *micro-tells* usually expose the emotions that people would rather conceal – like fear, surprise, sadness and disgust. There are times, however, when people are trying to sustain a serious expression and a *micro-tell* in the shape of a smile breaks through. Sometimes *micro-tells* appear on one side of the face; at other times they can be seen on both sides. Because they are so rapid, most *micro-tells* don't get noticed. When people are primed to look out for *micro-tells*, they're more likely to recognize them, although some people are much better than others. Those who are good at spotting *micro-tells* are generally more interested in other people, and they are better at identifying liars. However, everybody can be trained to be more sensitive to *micro-tells*.

Stealth Tells

Some *tells* are shy, giving the impression that they would rather not be noticed – they operate by stealth, pretending to be something other than what they really are. The *eye-wipe tell*, for example, tries to pass itself off as an innocent attempt to remove a flake of skin or a speck of dust from under the eye, but it's actually an unacknowledged sign that the person is feeling sad.

There are lots of other *stealth tells*. When people are lying, for example, they frequently feel an unconscious urge to stop themselves saying something that might give them away. They often respond to this impulse by touching their lips or by positioning a finger so that it stands guard over their mouth. These are unconscious gestures of self-restraint, and they would be quite easy to spot were it not for the fact that they manage to disguise themselves as other kinds of actions. Consequently, when we see people touching their lips we automatically think that they're just wiping them clean, and when we see people placing a finger beside their mouth we simply assume that they're being thoughtful or attentive. We don't recognize these actions as *tells* of self-restraint because the *tells* have succeeded in passing themselves off as something else.

It's the same when people pat each other on the back. If you watch people hugging you'll notice that one or both parties will sometimes pat the other on the back. To us as observers, to the person who's being patted, and even to the person who's doing the patting, this appears to be a gesture of affection. But it's not – it's actually a signal to release! Although people don't realize it, they always respond to being patted on the back by bringing the hug to a close. Although the person who's been patted on the back has silently been instructed to let go, there isn't any feeling of rejection. That's because the release signal operates by stealth, pretending to be a gesture of affection while it's actually giving a command.

Genuine Tells

Genuine tells show what's really happening in people's heads. They often reveal things about people that they don't want others to know, and in some cases are actively trying to conceal from others. However, there are some actions that pretend to be *tells*, but which aren't. These are not real *tells* – they're *false tells*. There are several differences between *genuine tells* and *false tells*. First of all, unintentional *tells* tend to be genuine. Blushing, sweating and pupil dilation, for example, operate outside conscious control. This means that there's no opportunity for bluffing – people cannot fake blushing or make themselves sweat or make their pupils dilate to order. Consequently, when someone's face reddens we can be sure that they're feeling self-conscious, and when we see someone sweating we can be certain that they're either hot or bothered, or both.

Similarly, when we see someone's pupils expanding, we can reasonably assume it's because there's less light around or that the person is emotionally aroused.

Although blushing, sweating and pupil dilation are all outside conscious control, there are nevertheless differences between them. For example, when we're blushing we're fully aware that other people can see our embarrassment and there's nothing we can do about it. Also, the people who witness our embarrassment are fully aware that they're drawing inferences on the basis of our blushing. However, the situation is very different with pupil dilation. When our pupils dilate, we are totally unaware of the information that we're providing about our emotional state. What's equally interesting is that people who see us, and who recognize our heightened state of arousal, don't know how they came to that conclusion – they know there's something attractive about our face, but they can't identify what it is.[3] In other words, when our pupils dilate we produce a *genuine tell*, but we don't know that we're doing it. At the same time, other people react to the tell, but they don't know why.

Genuine tells often appear when people are being deceptive – when they're trying to pass themselves off as more dominant or confident than they really are, when they're lying, when they're trying to conceal their anxiety or cover up their real intentions. Impostors, professional con men, expert liars and psychopaths often manage to produce convincing performances, with a minimum of revealing *tells*. Most people, however, feel awkward when they're being deceptive, and that's when they're betrayed by their *tells*. The pressure of trying to sustain a convincing performance is too much for them – their performance starts to fracture and very soon the *tells* are seeping out through the cracks. Paul Ekman and his colleagues at the University of California in San Francisco have shown that people differ widely in their ability to produce convincing lies, and that those who find it easy to lie produce fewer cues to deception or 'leakage'.[4] There are some experts who believe that there is no such thing as a consummate liar, and that, regardless of their ability, people always leave tell-tale traces of their deception. Freud, for example, believed that people ultimately cannot conceal their internal states from others – in the end there is always some outward sign of what they're thinking. As he put it, 'He that has eyes to see or ears to hear may convince himself that no mortal can keep a secret. If his lips are silent, he chatters with his fingertips; betrayal oozes out of every pore.'[5]

False Tells

A *false tell* appears to reveal something about someone, but doesn't. This may occur for at least two reasons – firstly because the *tell* is unreliable, and secondly because the person is faking the *tell*; in other words, deliberately trying to get other people to draw the wrong conclusion about their thoughts or feelings. These are *counterfeit tells*. *Tells* are unreliable when they fail to give us an accurate reading of someone's internal state. Sweating palms, for example, are a good indicator of a person's anxiety. But they're not completely reliable because 5 per cent of the population has hyperhidrosis, a genetic condition that produces chronic sweating, and which has nothing to do with anxiety.[6]

Counterfeit tells are everywhere. Every time a man puts on a jacket with padded shoulders or a woman wears high-heel shoes, they are deliberately providing misleading information about how broad or tall they are, and doing so in full knowledge of the impression they're trying to create. In other situations they may be less aware of what they're trying to achieve. When the man, for example, puffs out his chest or the woman walks on tiptoes, he seems broader and she appears taller, even though neither is fully aware why they are behaving in this way, if in fact they have noticed anything different about their own behaviour.

In the animal world vocal pitch serves as a genuine signal of size. The depth of the toad's croak, for example, provides a very accurate prediction of how large the toad is. This enables individual toads to publicize how big they are, and to assess how big their competitors are, and it's very difficult for toads to fake. Among humans there isn't a straightforward relationship between pitch and body size in adults, although everyone assumes that large people have deep voices. What's more, people find it relatively easy to lower their voice, and to give the impression that they're bigger than they really are. For humans, therefore, pitch isn't a genuine *tell* of size.

A *counterfeit tell* occurs when someone simulates a *tell* without having the attribute or the state of mind that normally goes with that *tell*. Take the case of crying, which of course is a *tell* of sadness and distress. When we're feeling this way we can either give in to the impulse to cry or else we can try to hold back the tears. One way we can do this is by biting our lower lip. This sends two messages. Firstly it shows that our feelings are so strong that they need to be brought under control, and secondly it shows that we're capable of reining in our emotions. The act of biting one's lower lip serves, not so much as a *tell*, but rather as a *tell-suppressing tell* – in other words, a *tell* whose purpose is to mask other *tells*.

As any actor will tell you, it's much easier to bite one's lower lip than it is to produce a false display of crying. When people want to pretend that they're in the grip of strong emotions it's much easier to produce a false version of a *tell-suppressing tell* than a false version of the *tell* itself. During his presidential campaign, Bill Clinton made a habit of biting his lower lip. He'd tell his audience that 'people are hurting all over the country', and 'you can see the pain in their faces', and then he'd bite his lip to show that he really meant it. Of course this could have been a genuine expression of Clinton's feelings, but it's much more likely that his lip-biting was a *counterfeit tell*, simply because it happened on more than one occasion, because he always managed to control his emotions, and because he stood to increase his popularity by giving the impression that he could be overwhelmed by feelings of compassion.

Signature Tells

Tells come in several varieties. Some *tells* are widespread, even universal. Others are restricted to groups of people, and some even appear to be unique to specific individuals. First there are *common tells*. These include blushing, shrugging and the genuine smile – wherever you go, blushing remains a sign of embarrassment, shrugging a sign of helplessness, and the genuine smile a sign of happiness. Next there are *local tells*. These are shaped by history and culture, and they are therefore confined to certain communities or groups of people. *Local tells* include different ways of standing, sitting, sleeping and eating. Then we have *signature tells* or *trademark tells*. These aren't necessarily unique, but because of their powerful association with certain individuals they appear to be unique to them, just like a signature or a trademark.

Several important historical figures have been identified with *trademark tells*. For example, the Roman writer Plutarch tells us that Julius Caesar had a habit of scratching his head with his index finger rather than with all the fingers of his hand.[7] This meant that he didn't have to disturb his carefully arranged coiffure any more than necessary, and it showed him up as a vain man. Adolf Hitler had a habit of standing with his hands clasped in front of his genitals. This is a defensive posture and it's commonly used by people who feel socially or sexually insecure. In Hitler's case it prompted the joke at the time that he was 'hiding the last unemployed member of the Third Reich'.

Whenever we think of Napoleon Bonaparte we imagine him with his right hand tucked into his waistcoat. In fact if you want to pretend that you're Napoleon, all you need to do is to slip your hand into an imaginary waistcoat and everyone will recognize you immediately. In spite of the universality of this image, there's very little evidence to show that this was Napoleon's favourite posture. Quite the contrary. It's said that his *trademark tell* was his habit of walking with his hands clasped behind his back, a practice that made him instantly recognizable to his troops, even at a great distance. The idea that Napoleon tucked his hand into his waistcoat comes from a famous painting by Jacques-Louis David, where Napoleon appears in his study in the Tuileries Palace, assuming this posture. What's interesting is that Napoleon didn't actually sit for this portrait – the artist did it from memory. It's quite likely that Napoleon's posture in the picture is a painterly conceit rather than a faithful depiction of how he actually stood. At the time it was customary for important men to be represented in paintings with their hand in their waistcoat, even when they didn't habitually adopt the posture. This convention was established in Europe and America long before Napoleon had come to power, and there's even a portrait of George Washington in which he's adopting this posture. Washington is remembered for many things, but not for standing around with his hand in his waistcoat.

We all know people with *signature tells* – for example, the guy who can't stop shaking his foot, or the woman who repeatedly curls her hair round her fingers in an unusual way. Most people recognize the *signature tells* of famous people today – like Princess Diana's 'head-cant', Margaret Thatcher's 'eye-flash', or President Reagan's 'head-twist' – but they don't understand what these *tells* reveal about the person concerned. In the chapters that follow we will look at these *tells* and uncover their true meaning.

Transposed Tells

When you see someone tapping their foot you can

reasonably assume that they're feeling impatient at that moment, and not that they were impatient some time ago, or that they anticipate being impatient in the future. Most *tells* relate to what's happening at that moment – in other words, they are 'time-locked'. There are two types of *time-locked tells* – one type reveals people's enduring traits, the other their current states. When someone who is chronically anxious bites his nails, it's because of his enduring traits, not because of any passing mood. On the other hand, when someone who's acutely anxious bites his nails, it's because of the current mood he's in, not because of his enduring condition. In each of these cases the nail-biting reveals what the person is feeling at that time, even though it's a permanent experience for the first person and a temporary one for the second.

There are a number of *time-locked tells* that reveal people's enduring traits. Some, like nail-biting and hair-pulling, are voluntary, while others, like tics, sweating, heavy or shallow breathing, are involuntary. Depending on their severity, some of these conditions may require medical or psychiatric treatment. A classic example of a chronic *time-locked tell* is hysterical paralysis, where the person is unable, for example, to use one of their arms, not because it's been physically damaged, but because they have experienced a traumatic event which has placed their arm beyond voluntary control. In such cases paralysis can be cured only by psychological treatment, not by any medical intervention.

There are also states that lie dormant, as it were, waiting to reveal themselves in people's actions. Phobias are a good example. People who jump up at the sight of a spider aren't in a permanent state of fear – it's only the appearance of a spider that makes them frightened. It's the same with 'memories in the muscles'. People who have experienced traumatic events sometimes lock their memories of those events away in their muscles. The effects of these locked-up memories can sometimes be seen in the way that people hold their bodies. Sometimes there's no external evidence – it's only when the muscles that retain these memories become relaxed that the memories are released. When this happens the person is usually overwhelmed by very powerful emotions.

While some *tells* are *time-locked*, others are transposed in time. They are *time-shifted* – that is, they reveal what the person was feeling earlier, or will feel later, and not what they are feeling at that moment. There are many everyday examples of *time-shifted tells*. If you watch people's hands while they're talking, you'll notice that they often use illustrative gestures to trace out the shape of the physical object they're talking about. The interesting thing about these gestures is that they tend to occur *before* the person utters the word that refers to the object. For example, someone who's talking about a spiral staircase will perform a spiralling motion with his hand before he actually says 'spiral staircase'. John Bulwer, the seventeenth-century student of gesture, recognized this when he described how 'the *Hand*, which is a ready Midwife, takes often-times the thoughts from the fore-stalled Tongue, making a more quicke dispatch by gesture; . . . For the gesture of the *Hand* many times gives a hint of our intention, and speakes out a good part of our meaning, before our words, which accompany or follow it, can put themselves into a vocall posture to be understood'.[8] This pre-emptive property of gestures shows that our thoughts can influence our actions before they inspire what we say – or, more controversially, that our gestures may actually shape what we think and say. On those occasions when we have trouble remembering a word, it's often only by performing the appropriate gesture that we can recover the word from memory.

There are other, equally revealing examples of *time-shifted tells*. George Mahl, a clinical psychologist, described an interview with one of his patients in which the woman was playing with her wedding ring while she was describing her symptoms. During this time she made no mention of her husband. It was only after she had stopped fiddling with her wedding ring that she started to complain about her husband, saying that he didn't help her round the house and that he made her feel inadequate.[9] There are two ways to understand what's happening when the woman plays with her wedding ring – either she had an unconscious image of her husband at the time, or it was the act of playing with her ring that brought her husband to mind and prompted her to complain about him. Either way, it's clear that while she was playing with the ring she was not consciously thinking about her husband – that only came later. Her manipulation of the ring is therefore transposed in time – it's a *time-shifted tell*. On the other hand, if we were to regard her complaint about her husband as a *tell*, we would consider it to be a time-locked tell, because it reveals what she was thinking about at that moment.

Predictive Tells

Some *tells* are predictive – they show what someone is about to do next or how a confrontation is likely to end. Imagine a situation where a young man and woman are talking to each other on a park bench, and she decides that it's time for her to leave. She doesn't just get to her feet, announce that she's leaving, and then disappear. Instead she does things by stages. To ensure that she doesn't upset the man, she starts by producing a series of 'intention movements', to show him that she's thinking of leaving. These may consist of tiny adjustments to her gaze or the way she arranges her arms and legs. The important point about these intention displays is that they aren't necessarily conscious, and the woman may not even be aware that she's producing them. Although the woman's signals are very subtle, the man is likely to pick them up and to alter his own posture accordingly. By responding to her displays and producing his own, he's able to show that he's understood her intentions. He may be unaware of the effect that her signals are having on him, and how he is responding – in fact the entire dialogue of *leaving tells* may be played out without either of them being conscious of what's happening.

There are other instances where people respond to *tells* without being aware of what's happening. When two people are talking to each other it's not uncommon for one or both of them to 'mirror' the posture of the other. One person may, for example, cross her legs and then turn her face, and a few minutes later her friend may perform exactly the same actions.[10] When we mimic other people's actions in this way we are usually oblivious of our own actions – it's only when it's been pointed out to us that we notice what we've been doing. Yawning operates on similar principles. We all know that yawning is highly contagious, and that when one person yawns other people nearby are very likely to follow suit. Research has shown that it doesn't require a complete yawn for one person to copy another – the mere sight of an open mouth, or the sound of a yawn, is often enough to get other people yawning.[11]

Our ability to read other people's intention movements is highly developed. We don't need to think about it – it happens automatically, very quickly, and usually with remarkable accuracy. Like other animals, we need to know whether other individuals are favourably disposed towards us. Instead of waiting to see what they do, we rapidly scan their behaviour for signs of intention movements that will help us to decide what they're likely to do next.

Intention movements play a central role in the resolution of confrontations. In the animal world threat displays are used to scare off the competition – in this way individuals can get what they want without getting involved in a fight and risking injury. If threat displays don't work, physical attack may be necessary. It's generally assumed that individuals who produce threat displays are likely to attack. However, research with birds and fish shows that threat displays don't necessarily lead to attack – in some cases individuals are bluffing and in others a threat is enough to achieve what they want.[12] Threat displays, it turns out, are not a very good predictor of who's likely to win in a confrontation. However, signs of uncertainty are a good predictor because they show which individual does not want to take the confrontation to the next stage. So, if you want to know which individual is most likely to win a contest you should look out for *retreat tells* rather than *threat tells*. For example, a middle-distance track athlete who takes the lead in a race may or may not dishearten the other athletes by continuing to look ahead. However, if he turns round to see where the others are, he's likely to expose his uncertainty and to reduce his chances of winning. During the presidential debate between George Bush and Bill Clinton in Richmond, Bush momentarily glanced at his watch. This fleeting action was a *retreat tell* – it showed that Bush had had enough and that he couldn't wait till the debate was over. Clinton didn't steal a glance at his watch. He didn't need to – he was in the ascendant and he wanted the debate to continue.

Telling Tells

As we can see, *tells* are everywhere. If you watch people talking to each other you'll notice that they are constantly moving their eyes, face, hands and body while they're speaking, and that they are just as active while they're listening. Every posture they assume, even the micro-momentary, almost imperceptible, expressions that dash across their face, carry messages about their thoughts and feelings. But *tells* aren't confined to conversations – even when people are alone they are constantly shifting their body, touching their face and providing clues to their state of mind.

Tells sometimes tell us things about people that they

don't even know themselves. Because certain *tells* are controlled by involuntary processes in the brain they are outside people's conscious control and therefore much more accurate indicators of people's emotions than the accounts that they might offer about their feelings. If you ever have to choose between believing what someone has to say about their feelings and what you can observe from their involuntary *tells*, you should always opt for the latter. In these instances the golden rule is always 'Trust the *tells*', and not what people say about themselves, or what other people say about them.

Some *tells* are easily recognized and widely understood – for example, when someone blushes, everyone knows that he or she is feeling embarrassed and self-conscious. Other *tells* aren't understood. That's because they're not recognized as *tells*, or because it's not clear what they mean, or because they seldom even get noticed. Even when people do notice other people's *tells* it doesn't mean that they understand them. This is especially noticeable in relations between the sexes. It's not unusual, for example, for a woman to make a friendly overture towards a man, and for the man to misinterpret her actions as a come-on. Equally, when we fail to notice the *tells* that other people produce, it doesn't mean that we aren't affected by them. It's still possible for their *tells* to slip under our radar, so to speak, and to influence us in ways that we don't fully understand. Psychologists have discovered that marriages are more likely to break down if one partner produces facial expressions of contempt, even if the other person is unaware that they're doing so.[13]

Tells are like the constituents of a language. But it's a very unusual language because, while we all speak it fluently, we often don't hear what other people are saying or understand what their *tells* are telling us about them. To become more proficient in the language of *tells* we need to be more observant – it's only by noticing what people say and do that we can begin to understand their thoughts and feelings. Concentrating on *tells* makes us more sensitive to other people, and ultimately it makes our dealings with them more rewarding. It also helps us to understand our own behaviour, and the impact that we have on others.

2. Dominant Tells

When we meet people for the first time we rapidly judge them in terms of whether they're dominant, friendly and sexually attractive.[1] Although we sometimes think that we're more interested in other issues, these three factors play a major role in the impressions that we form of other people. We share these concerns with our nearest relatives, the chimpanzees, who spend a lot of time sorting out their relative positions in the hierarchy.

In a chimpanzee troop the distribution of dominance displays, submissive displays and grooming creates a pecking order, which invisibly ranks individuals according to their rights to territory, food and sex. Individuals assert their dominance by adopting a posture which creates an impression of size, and which signals a readiness to attack. This may take the form of a facing orientation, fixed gaze, and heightening of the body. When there's a confrontation it may also involve stiffening of the limbs and erection of the ears and the hair on the back. A submissive chimpanzee, on the other hand, will turn away, avert its eyes, flatten its ears and hair, and create an overall impression of smallness. In most chimpanzee troops submissive individuals will even turn around completely, presenting their rear to the dominant individual, who will then go through the motions of mounting the submissive individual and producing a few non-copulatory thrusts. Through this ritual, individuals acknowledge their relationship to each other and the pecking order in the troop is affirmed.

We humans have inherited many of the postural signals used by our non-human relatives. Although we don't have mobile ears or erectile hair, we do use orientation, gaze, apparent size and posture as signals of dominance and submission in our dealings with each other.

Tall Tells

In most animal societies there is a strong connection between height and social status. In the case of humans the relationship is overwhelming. Statistics show that taller people are more successful than short people. They're also healthier, more intelligent, and they tend to live longer.[2] This is not a modern phenomenon: recent excavations of an old graveyard in Norfolk, England, have revealed that taller people were enjoying longer lives as far back as the ninth century.[3] In fact, the symbolic association between height and power is very primitive. It goes back to the time when armies on the high ground had a strategic advantage over those below, and settlements on the hill were able to defend themselves better than those in the valleys. The association now forms part of our language – we speak of the 'head' of the organization being 'superior' to 'those below', and of the need to 'rise above' or get 'on top of' our problems.

Women say that they prefer a man to be taller than them. It's also been found that tall men have greater reproductive success than short men, which shows that women are actively selecting tall men as their partners.[4] In the process, tallness has become an established ideal in men, and it's now rapidly becoming one in women. Tallness in men is linked to higher levels of the male hormone, testosterone, and to a more dominant personality.[5] In the history of the United States only three presidents have been shorter than the national average, and some, like Abraham Lincoln, towered over their contemporaries. The same association is found on Wall Street, where every inch in height above the norm is worth an additional $600 per month in salary.[6] Even in universities, where the staff are supposed to be appointed on the basis of academic excellence alone, we find that assistant professors are 1.24 inches taller than the national average, associate professors are 1.5 inches, and full professors are 1.94 inches taller than the average person for their age and sex.[7]

One way to appear more dominant is to increase one's apparent height by positioning oneself above other people. Another is to sit straight or to stand erect. Psychologists have found that people who adopt an erect standing posture tend to be seen as more dominant than those who adopt a slouched posture, and that those who are trained to stand erect feel more confident and optimistic than those who continue to stand in their customary fashion.[8] It has also been found that when people succeed at a task they tend to respond by sitting up straight, whereas those who fail at a task are more likely to respond by slumping forward.

But an erect posture isn't a cure for everything. It is widely assumed that people who feel depressed or defeated can improve their state of mind by sitting up straight. In fact it's quite the reverse. Research has shown that people who are given tasks involving failure show quicker recovery when they are allowed to adopt a slumped posture than when they are encouraged to sit up straight. Contrary to what one would expect, a slumped posture is actually an adaptive response to defeat – it enables people who feel dejected to gather their thoughts and to recover their confidence in their own time.[9]

Territorial Tells

Power is frequently linked to territory in the animal world. Among baboons, the dominant or 'alpha' individual usually occupies the highest branches in a tree, defending its position from the subordinates below and taking on the role of leader and protector. It also lays claim to more territory, both in the way it physically occupies the space around it and the way it keeps other individuals at bay. It's exactly the same with humans. High-status individuals occupy more space – they have bigger houses, cars and offices. They also use up more of the space around them, and other people usually acknowledge their claims by allowing them extra space. High-status people seem to create an invisible boundary around them – not unlike a military exclusion zone – which other people approach with caution. Indeed, it's often the hesitant way that people approach the invisible boundary around a dominant individual that provides the most telling clues about how important they are, and that serves to reinforce that person's feelings of superiority.

Dominance is also revealed and reinforced by where people sit around a table.[10] At a board meeting the Chief Executive Officer usually sits at the head of the table, with those who are next in importance sitting closest to him or her. People who sit at the head of the table attract more attention than anyone else. They also do most of the talking and get deferred to more often. This is not simply because people who occupy this position happen to be dominant, because when people are randomly assigned to different seats around a rectangular table, the person who's been placed at the head of the table still attracts most attention and does most of the talking. If you have a friend who's shy and retiring it's worth doing a little experiment: next time you have a dinner party, put him at the head of the table. It's likely that within minutes he'll be joining in, after half an hour he'll be interrupting other people, and within the hour he'll be dominating the conversation!

The importance that's attached to different positions is less evident with circular or square tables than it is with rectangular or oval tables. Rectangular and oval tables are fine for bilateral negotiations, where the two parties can occupy opposite and equivalent sides of the table. While this solution may not give rise to disputes about preferential treatment, it is likely to encourage conflict between the parties because of the opposing nature of the seating arrangement. Rectangular and oval tables are notoriously ill-suited for multi-party negotiations – one or more parties may threaten to walk out because they don't feel that the seats they're being offered reflect their importance in the negotiations.

Seating positions also influence relationships in other ways. Individuals sitting round a table are more likely, for example, to address their remarks to people sitting opposite them than to those sitting beside or at right angles to them. This may explain why, when they're seated with strangers, people usually choose to sit furthest from high-status and low-status individuals, and closest to those who have the same status as them.

Where people choose to sit in restaurants, pubs and bars also exposes issues of status and control. In pubs and bars courting couples tend to sit beside each other so that both of them can see what's happening. In a restaurant, where food is the focus, they are more likely to sit opposite each other so that each of them can keep the other in view. When a couple is offered a restaurant table beside the wall, the man usually tries to sit with his back to the wall. This way he can keep a watchful eye on what's happening around him – rather like a dominant male chimpanzee surveys the scene from the top of a tree.

Standing Tells

The way people stand is another good guide to their status or the status they are trying to claim. Dominant individuals frequently adopt a 'straddle stance', with their legs straight and their feet wide apart. Subordinate individuals, on the other hand, are more likely to adopt the 'parallel stance', where the legs are straight and the feet are close together. The straddle stance offers more stability than the parallel stance, and this appears to explain why men, who have a higher centre of gravity, are more likely to use the straddle stance than women. However, this is not the only explanation for this choice, because men use this posture much more frequently when they're with other people – in other words, in situations where they're using posture for the purposes of communication.

There are two basic messages conveyed by the straddle stance. One is a macho message, the other a threat signal. The macho message comes from the resolute immovability of the posture – when someone plants his feet apart he is literally and figuratively telling everyone that he intends to stand his ground, and that he won't be moved. The threatening aspect of the straddle stance comes from the fact that it is a loosely veiled phallic display – by standing with his legs apart a man is actually putting his penis on display. Phallic displays are widely associated with dominance. A dominant male baboon, for example, will frequently display its erect penis to remind other baboons of his elevated social position. Dominant men seldom expose themselves in this way of course, but they do try to draw attention to their penis and to inform others how big it is through the clothes they wear or the way they arrange their limbs. In the fifteenth and sixteenth centuries it was common for high-status men to wear a codpiece, a padded pouch on the outside of the breeches. Codpieces were frequently decorated and fashioned from eye-catching material; and the higher the man's status, the larger his codpiece.[11] The same principle applies in some traditional societies. In New Guinea, for example, men announce their position in the community by the size and decorative features of their penis sheath.

Although codpieces disappeared a long time ago, we can still find remnants of them in the shape of stonewashed jeans. Until fairly recently it was quite common to find young men wearing jeans where the crotch was almost entirely devoid of colour – a spectacle that was conveniently designed to draw the eye towards the crotch and to surreptitiously remind everyone what lies beneath. In Italy, young men would go even further. Having bought a new pair of jeans, they would wear them in the shower, furiously scrubbing the material over their crotch with a hard brush until it almost looked bleached. Sporting their new jeans with a faded crotch, they would then parade themselves in public, just as young Italian men have done for centuries, drawing attention to their manhood.

Not being content with their faded jeans, young Italian men have also developed another phallic display – 'the scrotch'. If you watch them in public, you'll notice that they are constantly readjusting their crotch and scratching their testicles, often when they are alone but typically when they are with other men. Although it is largely unintentional, this is clearly a phallic display which plays a significant part in competition between men. In terms of its function, it is very similar to what the alpha male baboon does when he displays his erect penis to his fellow baboons. When a young man performs the scrotch he is unconsciously trying to persuade other males that he is dominant because he's well endowed. The implication is that a large penis and testicles need special attention, and that without constantly adjusting himself he would soon become very uncomfortable.

The scrotch isn't confined to Italy – it's found in most societies where macho attitudes are encouraged – and it's certainly not the only form of phallic display. There's also the 'crotch-yank', where the hand is placed over the penis and testicles, and then yanked upwards. The purpose of this gesture is to publicize one's masculinity, which probably explains why it has become a favourite of various boy-bands and singers like Michael Jackson, who need to remind the public about their endowments. It's noticeable that the more feminine Michael Jackson's face has become, the more prominent the crotch-yank has become as part of his dance routine.

Sitting Tells

Sitting postures can also convey messages about dominance. Sitting postures are essentially about comfort, convention and communication. When somebody sits down they usually arrange their legs so that they feel comfortable, so that they don't violate any social norms, and so that their posture conveys a certain message. The message that a sitting posture conveys need not be intentional. In fact it's more likely to be motivated by unconscious desires. However, the fact that you aren't always aware of the messages that you're sending via your sitting postures doesn't mean that other people are impervious to those messages. Although they may not react consciously, it's often evident from their responses that they are affected by how you sit.

Three basic sitting postures can be identified on the basis of where people place their feet – 'straight-leg' postures, where the legs are extended, 'step' postures, where the feet are placed directly under the knees, and 'tucked' postures, where the feet are pulled back under the chair. When they get the opportunity, dominant people prefer to adopt 'straight-leg' sitting postures. By stretching out their legs, they symbolically place more of the public space under their personal jurisdiction, thereby reducing what's available to others and creating the impression that their own needs matter more than those of other people.

On their own, 'step' sitting postures don't necessarily offer any clues about dominance. However, the way that people position their knees does convey reliable information about whether they're feeling dominant or submissive. People who sit with their knees apart send clear, although usually unintended, signals that they are feeling dominant. This is most noticeable in the case of straight-leg sitting postures, where the legs are splayed and fully extended. A feeling of dominance is also conveyed by postures like the 'anvil', where the legs are bent, the thighs are splayed and both feet are planted firmly on the ground, and by the 'figure four' posture, where the ankle of one leg rests on the thigh of the other, so that the limbs look like the number 4. Both of these postures involve phallic displays. They are therefore used more frequently by men in parts of the world where there's a lot of emphasis on macho values, like the Latin American countries and the southern states of the US. Women don't like these postures, largely because they can create an impression of sexual availability. A fair amount of suppleness and stamina is required to perform the figure four, which is why the posture is associated with youthfulness. When someone adopts the figure four, they are more likely to be seen as youthful, relaxed and dominant.

Some sitting postures convey mixed messages – especially when the two legs are positioned differently.

Because they convey a strong impression of relaxation, asymmetrical sitting postures tend to be more dominant than symmetrical postures. But there are exceptions. For example, when someone extends his legs and crosses his ankles, his extended legs show that he wants to be seen as dominant. However, his crossed legs give the game away – they show that he is really quite reticent.

Relaxation is a key part of any dominance display because it suggests that the individual isn't concerned about being attacked and could easily respond if necessary. Relaxation is signalled by postural and movement cues – postural cues consist of low muscle tone, an absence of tension, and asymmetric arrangements of the arms and legs, while movement cues consist of less movement and slower movements of the body. As Balzac observed, 'slow movement is essentially majestic'. Submissive individuals display the opposite behaviour – they tend to adopt more symmetrical poses, to rearrange their arms and legs more often, to show more tension in their posture, and to move their body quickly and more often. Through their posture, dominant individuals show that they are unconcerned about being attacked and don't expect it to happen. Submissive individuals give the impression that they expect to be attacked – they're tense and defensive.

Elbow Tells

To appear dominant, people need to create an impression of physical strength, to look calm, and to appear unconcerned about any threats from others. One way to achieve this is by placing the hands on the hips. There are two main versions of this posture – the one-handed 'arm akimbo' and the two-handed 'arms akimbo'. The two-handed version is more spectacular, but the one-handed version can be pointed at other people in a way that the two-handed version cannot. There are three components that make hand-on-hip postures dominant:

◆ **THE EXPANSION COMPONENT**. When someone places a hand on their hip they appear to be larger and potentially more threatening. When both hands are used, the effect is doubled. Hand-on-hip postures also expand the territory that someone occupies – rather like straight-leg sitting postures.

◆ **THE THREAT COMPONENT**. Anyone who has ever tried to push through a large crowd knows how effective the elbows can be at clearing a path. Elbows are bony and sharp. They can be used to nudge, lever or prod people out of the way without causing the kind of offence that might arise if one were to use one's hands. In this respect the elbows are a 'second-grade weapon', but a weapon nevertheless. This makes it possible for the elbows to be used in an understated, almost subliminal way. With the arms akimbo the message is subtler – the elbows threaten people without them being fully aware of what's happening.

◆ **THE PREPARATORY COMPONENT**. The arms akimbo posture is half-way between having the hands down by one's side and having them raised and ready for attack. The posture is therefore a partial preparation for attack –

one where the intentions of the person are disguised by the fact that the hands have conveniently come to rest at the hips. In the case of people who are armed with a sword or a pistol, placing the hand on the hip often brings the hand closer to the weapon. This allows the hand to be at rest while it is preparing for attack.

During the sixteenth and seventeenth centuries the arm akimbo posture was an accepted part of upper-class male deportment. People in high office were frequently depicted in portraits with an elbow fully extended – Hans Holbein's famous painting of Henry VIII is a good example – and sometimes with their elbow pointing menacingly at the viewer. At the time the arm akimbo posture was intimately connected with the profession of arms – so much so that those who wanted to pass themselves off as having a military background would do so by adopting the posture.[12] In 1532 Desiderius Erasmus, the great Dutch philosopher, complained about those who 'stand or sit and set the one hand on the side, which manner to some seemeth comely like a warrior, but it is not forthwith honest'.[13]

The arms akimbo posture has caused offence on other occasions. For example, after accepting the surrender of the Japanese at the end of the Second World War, General Douglas MacArthur was photographed standing beside the Japanese Emperor. While the Emperor stood to attention with his hands discreetly by his side, General MacArthur had his hands on his hips. The Japanese saw this casual attitude as a sign of great disrespect. In Japan it is impolite to stand with one's hands on one's hips; to do so in the presence of the Emperor, regarded by many Japanese as a deity, was unforgivable.

The *Straddle Stance*. This is Hans Holbein the Younger's famous portrait of Henry VIII – legs apart and elbows firmly pushed out – a strong, vibrant-looking monarch who is very much in charge of his destiny and that of his people.

Superficially all hand-on-hip postures look the same. On closer inspection, however, we find that there are actually four main variants, each involving a different position of the hand or hands.

◆ **THE FINGERS VARIANT**. Here the fingers face forward, the thumb faces back, and the palm faces down. Men favour the 'fingers variant' because they feel better prepared for attack with their fingers facing forward. Men tend to adopt this posture in order to assert themselves – either when they are feeling dominant, or when they feel that their dominance is being threatened. For example, when a goal is scored in a soccer match, members of the losing side often assume the arms akimbo posture, partly to threaten their opponents, but also to reassure themselves. The posture can also be used as a gesture of defiance. When Mick Jagger was strutting his stuff in the 1960s, he frequently adopted an arm akimbo posture as part of his routine. This can be seen very clearly on recordings of the *Gimme Shelter* concert, when the defiant 'Jagger Swagger' was at its peak.

◆ **THE THUMB VARIANT**. In this version the thumb faces forward, the fingers face back, and the palm faces up. Women show a stronger preference for the 'thumb variant' than do men. The main reason for this is that women have a wider 'carrying angle' than men. This means that they can bend their arms further back at the elbow, which makes it easier for them to place their hands on the hips with their thumbs facing forward.

◆ **THE PALM VARIANT**. The 'palm variant' is the most

affected of all the hand-on-hip postures. This is the rather unnatural, flexed posture of the hand, where the back of the hand is in contact with the hip and the palm faces away from the body. It's the hand position that is commonly found in sixteenth- and seventeenth-century portraits of kings, Cavaliers and generals – in other words, individuals who needed to distinguish themselves from the rest of society by adopting artificial poses.

◆ **THE FIST VARIANT**. Here the fist is in contact with the hip. This is potentially the most threatening version of the hand-on-hip posture. Because men recognize the disruptive potential of this version, they tend not to use it. Women, however, do use it – occasionally to show their defiance, and sometimes as a gesture of self-mockery. There's a famous photograph of Bonnie Parker (of Bonnie and Clyde fame) where she has a foot on the front fender of their car, a cigar in her mouth and a revolver in her right hand. Her left elbow leans on the lamp of the car, while her right hand, holding the revolver, rests on her hip. When we look at the photograph, we see immediately that it's a picture of total defiance – not just because she's clutching a gun, but because she's showing her elbows!

Orientation Tells

How people orient their bodies towards others can also convey messages about dominance. When a man is talking to his boss he usually shows his respect by orienting his body towards his boss. The boss, on the other hand, is much more likely to orient his body away from the sub-ordinate. In their separate ways, the subordinate shows that he's totally focused on his boss, while his boss shows that he's dominant and keeping his options open.

There is, however, an entirely different set of messages conveyed by body orientation. For example, you'll have noticed that when two strange dogs approach each other for the first time, they usually circle each other. Making sure that they don't approach each other head-on, the dogs present their flanks to each other instead. The reason for this is that in order to attack, dogs need to be face-on. By presenting their flanks they expose a vulnerable part of their body, and this shows that they don't intend to attack each other. This process is called 'ritualization', and it's found throughout the animal kingdom, as well as among humans. It's Nature's way of settling disputes through displays of dominance and submission, rather than through fighting, which can easily lead to injury and death. Like dogs, we humans also present vulnerable parts of our body, including our flanks, when we want to show that we don't have aggressive intentions towards someone else. So when an aggressive-looking stranger approaches you in a bar, you're much more likely to present him with the side of your body than to face him directly. Standing face-on might suggest that you're ready for a fight, whereas exposing your flank shows that you're vulnerable and un-defended, and that you don't present a threat.

These two scenarios show that the same orientation can convey very different meanings in different situations. That's because the meaning of orientation depends on whether or not people know each other. When two people aren't acquainted and there's a lot of uncertainty, direct orientation is more likely to be interpreted as a prelude to attack. But when they do know each other, it's more likely to be seen as a sign of respect.

Face Tells

All five sensory modalities – sight, smell, hearing, taste and touch – are found on or near the face, and of these touch is the only modality also to be found elsewhere on the body. But the face isn't simply a location for housing all the sensory modalities – it's also the most important source of outgoing signals in the form of speech and features of the voice like accent and intonation, as well as myriads of expressions involving the eyes and muscles of the head and face. Some facial expressions, like the startle reflex, are entirely involuntary; others, like the smile, may be a genuine expression of pleasure or a deliberate attempt to create an impression of genuine pleasure. Because the face is partly under conscious control, it's a major weapon in our daily attempts to mislead and deceive each other. In spite of this, the face remains the prime source of information about our emotional states – it's by observing our faces that other people can tell whether we are feeling happy, sad, angry, surprised or frightened. Looking at our face, they can also tell whether we're feeling dominant or submissive.

The face conveys dominance signals in two ways. The first way is through 'facial attributes' – for example, whether the eyebrows are large or small, the chin is square or round, or the eyes are close together or set wide apart. The second way is through 'facial actions' – for example, how the eyes are widened or narrowed, the eyebrows raised or lowered, or the chin is pushed forward or pulled back. A person's facial attributes tend to last for decades, sometimes for most of their life. Facial actions, on the other hand, may change from one second to the next.

Several facial attributes are associated with dominance. People with square jaws are judged to be more dominant than those who have weak, receding jawlines. People who have prominent ridges above their eyes are also regarded as more dominant, and so are people with thin lips. Physiognomic attributes play a major role in how people are treated. Men who have a 'dominant face' are likely to have sex earlier in life and to have more sex. Research has also shown that men who have more dominant faces are more likely to attain high rank in the army.[14]

Non-human primates and humans share many signals of dominance. Several species of apes and monkeys, for example, lower their eyebrows as a dominance threat signal. It's the same with humans. People whose brows are set low, or who lower them, are seen as dominant, while those who have raised brows, or who elevate them temporarily, are seen as submissive.[15] This is one of the reasons why women pluck their eyebrows – by making them thinner and raising them, women create a semi-permanent submission display, which men are supposed to find attractive. The language of raised and lowered eyebrows is widely understood. However, there are parts of the world, including Africa and Asia, where raised eyebrows are not interpreted as a sign of submission.[16]

Jaw size also signals dominance. There are two reasons for this. Firstly, the teeth are a very primitive and effective weapon, and secondly the development of a large jaw is promoted by testosterone, which in turn is linked to dominance and aggression. People who have large jaws are usually assumed to be dominant, while those with small jaws are assumed to be submissive. It therefore helps to have a large jaw if you want to get ahead in business, or if you want to have a successful career in the armed forces. If your jaw isn't prominent enough, you can always resort to plastic surgery and get it augmented. Alternatively you can make a habit of sticking out your jaw. The 'jaw thrust', which involves raising the head slightly or pushing the bottom teeth out beyond the top teeth, is a common gesture of defiance, and it's widely used in confrontations by children.

People who have narrow eyes, or who narrow their eyes, are also seen as dominant. When the eyes are narrowed as a dominance signal, they take on the appearance of a visor – it looks as if the person is peering through a slit in their helmet. There are good examples of this in movies like *The Good, the Bad and the Ugly*, where Clint Eastwood and Lee Van Cleef narrow their eyes and adopt a 'visor eyes' posture to make themselves look tough. They also produce other revealing signs of dominance. One is the lowering of the eyebrows; the other is the narrow, resolute set of the mouth and the absence of smiling. Lowered eyebrows convey an impression of dominance because they create a more confrontational stare. Because facial expressions of anger include lowered eyebrows, someone who makes a point of lowering their eyebrows is likely to appear angrier. Recent research by Larissa Tiedens at Stanford University in California shows that displays of anger are frequently interpreted as a sign of strength.[17] This explains why so many people in positions of power affect an air of perpetual grumpiness – it makes them look dominant!

A good example of affected grumpiness may be seen in the TV series, *The Weakest Link*, in which the presenter, Anne Robinson, makes a point of not smiling. She also uses another *dominance tell*: looking over the top of her spectacles when she wants to make the contestants look stupid. This is in fact one of her *trademark tells*, and it fits very well with the role she's chosen to project of a rather dominant and cold-hearted presenter. Looking over the top of the spectacles works in this way because it draws attention to the eyes – it says in effect, 'Look at me, I'm lowering my glasses so that I can get a clear, unobstructed view of you; there's nothing you can hide from me!' The *overlook tell* is therefore a gesture of confrontation; it's a prelude to what zoologists call an 'agonistic stare'. The effect of the gesture is even stronger when it's accompanied by a slight dip of the head, because this makes the stare more threatening.

Thin lips are another sign of dominance because they show that someone is determined. As we shall see later on, smiling is a highly affiliative gesture – it's a sign of openness and acceptance, and that's why it doesn't feature in the roles played by Clint Eastwood and Lee Van Cleef. Researchers have found that men who are judged to be dominant, and who have high levels of testosterone, actually produce much smaller smiles, but that the same relationship doesn't hold for women.[18] Some dominant individuals never seem to smile at all. President Vladimir Putin of Russia is a good example of a national leader who's very sparing with his smiles. Although he's athletic, Putin isn't very tall, and he has a small chin. Not smiling gives him a way of making up for these deficits.

Of course there are times when dominant individuals need to smile. In these situations they often concede by producing a 'closed-mouth smile', where the lips remain together, instead of an 'open-mouth smile', where the lips are parted and the teeth are exposed. There are two types of closed-mouth smiles favoured by dominant individuals:

◆ **SEALED SMILES**. Here the lips are kept together while the corners of the mouth are stretched apart. The result is an elongated line across the face, and a strong impression that everyone is being excluded from knowing what's inside the person whose lips are sealed. Sealed smiles are a favourite of high-ranking businessmen and politicians – you'll often find them on the photographed faces of directors in corporate brochures.

◆ **CLAMPED SMILES**. Here the muscles around the mouth are tensed to show that the smile is being restrained. The actor Charlton Heston is the chief exponent of the clamped smile – it's one of his *trademark tells*. The clamped smile offers a way of smiling without actually smiling. In this respect it's a masked smile where the intention is not to conceal the smile, but to draw attention to the failed attempt at concealment. The clamped smile suggests that the person has a strong impulse to smile, but that they have managed to bring it under control. Quite often it's this aspect of control that forms the main message of this smile.

Yawning Tells

Everyone knows two things about yawning – that its purpose is to increase oxygen intake, and that it's very contagious. The first is wrong – there's no evidence that yawning actually increases our intake of oxygen – but the second is true. Why yawning is so contagious remains something of a mystery, although it's known that people yawn when they see someone else yawn, when they hear them yawn, when they read about yawning, and even when they just think about it. Why we actually yawn is also a mystery. Various explanations have been put forward, the most recent being the suggestion that yawning 'cleans the brain' by flushing out the cerebrospinal fluid. It's been discovered that yawning is controlled by very deep parts of the brain because there are some brain-damaged people who cannot move their mouth intentionally, but who open their mouth automatically when they yawn.[19]

Most of us think of yawning as a boredom signal. In fact there are four types of yawn, and they fall under the four 'Ts' – Tedium, Transition, Tension and Threat.

◆ **TEDIUM YAWNS.** These are triggered by monotonous tasks, inactivity, tiredness and boredom. If you watch someone who's engaged in a repetitive task, or who's waiting in a long line to be served, you'll notice that they often yawn. Tedium yawns are the most common type of all.

◆ **TRANSITION YAWNS.** These occur when people move from one kind of activity to another – for example, climbing out of bed and getting ready in the morning, or preparing to go to bed in the evening. Yawns also occur at social junctures – for example, immediately after someone has said goodbye to a close friend. Yawning can be used as an *activity tell* – in other words, when you see someone alone, reading a book, and they start to yawn, you know there's a good chance that they're about to do something different.

◆ **TENSION YAWNS**. Tension yawns occur when people are tense – usually when a dominant person is close and they feel awkward or embarrassed. Whenever people are anxious they are liable to yawn – it's even been reported in Olympic athletes who are waiting in their starting blocks, and paratroopers who are about to jump out of the plane. These yawns are responses to stress. They are examples of 'displacement activity', because they help to displace anxiety to some other activity.

◆ **THREAT YAWNS**. In human as well as animal societies, dominant individuals produce threat yawns. Yawning is found in a broad range of species, including fish, birds, reptiles, monkeys and apes. If there were a 'Yawning Olympics', baboons would be the outright winners. While other primates yawn about 10 times a day, male baboons produce 10–12 yawns per hour, and sometimes as many as 24 per hour! This is not because baboons are tired or bored; it's because life in baboon society is so threatening.

A large proportion of baboons' yawns are designed to assert dominance and to threaten potential rivals. As with other non-human primates, more yawning is produced by adult males than by adult females or by youngsters of either sex. Individuals with higher levels of testosterone also produce more yawning. The main weapon of baboons is their teeth. Male baboons have larger canines than females, and dominant males tend to have larger canines than other males. So it's usually the alpha male who produces most of the yawns, putting his large canine teeth on display. As his status increases, so does his yawning; when he looses his status, his yawning starts to decline.

Humans also use yawning as a dominance signal, although the basis is not exactly the same as it is for baboons. For one thing, men and women hardly differ in the size of their canines, which probably explains why there isn't a big difference in how often men and women yawn. However, when men do yawn they're much more likely to expose their teeth; women tend to cover their mouth with their hand.[20] This could be because women have better manners than men, but it might be a throwback to a time when there was a difference between the dental equipment of the sexes. Although our teeth are no longer our primary weapons, they are still used as a threat. If you observe dominant people you'll find that they often yawn at those moments when they need to assert themselves – for example, when they're feeling threatened and it looks as if someone else might try to usurp their position. This suggests that, for humans, the threat yawn is a *relic tell* – in other words, a *tell* that is left over from a time in our evolutionary past when our ancestors had larger canines and used them to intimidate each other.

Talk Tells

When people of different status are together, the most important person usually does most of the talking. This enables them to remind everyone else of their position. It also gives them a chance to hear the sound of their own voice, and to listen to their own opinions rather than those of other people. Dominant people are quicker off the mark when it comes to speaking. It's been found that when groups of people meet for the first time, the order in which they speak provides a fairly good guide to who will dominate the proceedings afterwards. The first person to offer his or her opinion invariably assumes the role of leader; the last person to make a contribution tends to be the person who ends up taking orders.[21]

Dominant people interrupt others more, and they are more successful at seeing off people who try to take the floor from them. They do this by continuing to talk over the other person, by raising their voice, and by using non-verbal signals to discourage the other person. As a result, interruptions initiated by the dominant person tend to show shorter bouts of overlapping speech than those initiated by the subordinate person. Dominant people are more confident in their speech, with the result that they use fewer hesitations and speech disfluencies like 'um' and 'er'. They often make a habit of talking loudly. This is especially noticeable in Britain, where old class divisions come into play and members of the upper class sometimes drown out the conversations of other people.

Dominance is also evident in other aspects of speech. One of these is what psychologists call 'accommodation' – that is, the tendency of individuals to modify their speech style so as to bring it into line with that of other people. This can be done through shifts in accent, speech speed, formality or pitch. Accommodation usually takes place between people who like each other, but it also occurs when there are differences in status. In these circumstances the subordinate person tends to accommodate his or her speech to that of the dominant person. A few years ago two sociologists, Stanford Gregory and Stephen Webster, studied a selection of interviews from the television chat show, *Larry King Live*.[22] Using an instrument that analyses low frequencies in the voice, they compared the voices of the host and his guests, to see who had accommodated to whom. They discovered that while Larry King accommodated to high-status guests like Elizabeth Taylor, people like Dan Quayle accommodated to him. These subtle changes in voice frequency operate outside of awareness – people don't know that they are modifying their voice to bring it into line with someone else's. It shows, nevertheless, how sensitive individuals are to the status of other people, and how eager they are to adapt to them.

Voice Tells

Vocal characteristics like pitch are often assumed to be a good guide to dominance and submission. It has been found that 'deep' sounds are associated with dominance and threat, while 'high-pitched' sounds are associated with submission and appeasement. This association is found throughout the animal world, from whales to shrews – a good example is the deep aggressive growl of a guard dog, as opposed to the high-pitched yelp of a submissive puppy.[23]

In the animal world, individuals with long vocal tracts produce much deeper sounds. Because large individuals tend to have longer vocal tracts, the depth of the sound they make provides a very good indication of how big they are, and how threatening they're likely to be. However, with humans there isn't a clear-cut relationship between body size and the depth of people's voices, so pitch doesn't provide a *genuine tell* of someone's size. Nevertheless, when people are presented with recordings of deep and high-pitched vocalizations, they consistently express the opinion that the deep voices belong to dominant individuals and the high-pitched voices to submissive individuals. Why pitch should provide a *genuine tell* of size among animals, but not among humans, is something of a mystery. It may be due to an 'evolutionary lag' – in other words, the association between body size and pitch, which was present in our evolutionary ancestors, may have installed a set of assumptions in our minds, which are still at work even though the association has long disappeared.[24]

If vocal pitch doesn't provide evidence about body size in humans, it does offer significant clues about dominance. It does this in several ways. Firstly, it's been discovered that men who have deep voices have high levels of testosterone – for example, male bass and baritone singers, who have deeper voices, tend to have higher levels of testosterone than tenors. Secondly, it's known that testosterone is linked to dominance in men. Thirdly, vocal pitch often shows whether people are in a dominant or submissive state of mind. Individuals who are attempting to be dominant usually lower the pitch of their voice – that's why John Wayne advised men to 'talk low, talk slow, and don't say too much'. On the other hand, people who are trying to appear submissive usually raise their pitch. When mothers are talking to their babies they instinctively adopt a higher pitch than normal.[25] This has the effect of calming the baby. Of course mothers may not know it, but the reason why they raise their pitch is that babies are most sensitive to higher vocal frequencies.

The vocal pitch that individuals adopt often reflects their social standing. Members of subordinate groups often speak with a higher pitch than those who belong to more powerful groups in that society. We can see this very clearly in the USA during the heyday of Motown, when African-American singers like The Stylistics sang in a high-pitched, falsetto register that is normally reserved for women. The same kind of self-emasculation could be seen at work among the so-called 'Coloureds' of South Africa during the apartheid era. The Coloureds are people of mixed race. Some are the descendants of Malay slaves, others the progeny of relationships between Blacks and Whites. Under apartheid they lived in a political no man's land between the Blacks and the Whites, and of all the racial groups in South Africa they were the most insecure. Their marginal position was very evident in the high-pitched speech style they used. It became their badge of oppression, a way of showing that they didn't represent a threat to the White establishment.

Rising and falling intonation also carry important messages. Falling pitch is associated with statements, certainty and dominance, whereas rising pitch is a characteristic of questions, uncertainty and submissiveness.

However, that's not always the case. When you talk to Australians, for example, you'll notice that they frequently make their declarative statements sound like questions by ending with a rising intonation. This has the effect of making their opinions appear less certain and less contentious, which in turn reduces the chances of conflict. However, in other respects Australians are becoming more assertive – or rather, Australian women are. Comparisons show that over the past five decades the pitch of women's voices in Australia has got deeper. The voices of Australian men and women are converging, and it's all because women are abandoning their submissive tones and starting to speak more like men.[26]

Touching Tells

If you watch people at an office drinks party, you'll notice that their position within the organization is often reflected in whom they touch and who touches them. Most of the touching that you'll see is between people who are at roughly the same level in the organization. One person pats his friend on the back, another rubs her colleague on the arm, and yet another plants a playful punch on someone's shoulder. All of these are 'horizontal' touches because they're between notional equals. They're about friendship, camaraderie or light-hearted provocation, and they can be mutual or reciprocal – in other words, it's quite acceptable for people of similar status to have their arms around each other's shoulders, or for one of them to pat the other on the back and for that person to respond with a similar gesture.

Looking round the party you'll also notice 'vertical' touches, that is, touches between people of different status. You'll see that, as the boss circulates among the staff, he places his hand on the shoulder of the young man who's just joined the company, or he squeezes his secretary's arm as she walks past looking for a drink. These touches are one-sided – neither the young man nor the secretary responds by touching the boss. In fact it's the non-reciprocal nature of each touch, rather than where the hand makes contact, that identifies it as a vertical touch – one that allows the boss to exercise his symbolic right to impose himself, however affectionately, on his staff.[27]

Most vertical touches consist of a dominant person touching a subordinate person, but the reverse does happen. If the young man who'd just been touched responded by putting his hand on his boss's shoulder, it would suggest that they are more equal than they really are, and this could threaten the boss's authority. There are some situations, like walkabouts, where high status people don't mind being touched by other people. But as a rule, they don't like it because they know it can reduce their authority. It can also cause offence. For example, when the Queen was in Australia in 1992, the Australian Prime Minister, Paul Keating, thoughtlessly put his arm around her. Many Britons found this deeply offensive, and the British tabloid press nicknamed Paul Keating the 'Lizard of Oz'. Most Australians couldn't see what all the fuss was about. They didn't realize that, for the British, this is a very touchy subject.

Looking Tells

The dominance hierarchy in a chimpanzee troop is reflected in the 'attention structure' of the troop, so that subordinate individuals spend more time watching their superiors than vice versa, and all the attention is on the alpha member of the troop.[28] Business firms operate on the same principle. Here again, subordinate individuals spend more time watching their superiors than vice versa, and everyone's attention is focused on the boss.

The similarity between chimpanzee troops and business firms goes even further. When a dominant chimpanzee meets a subordinate chimpanzee, the subordinate individual goes through an appeasement display by lowering its body, averting its eyes, and sometimes presenting its backside. Subordinate chimpanzees avert their gaze because staring is likely to invite an attack from the dominant individual. The greeting rituals in business organizations are similar to those in a chimpanzee troop. Although employees don't present their backsides to their boss – at least, not literally – they frequently try to make themselves appear smaller and less threatening by lowering their head and keeping their hands and feet close to their body.

Patterns of gaze are regulated in a similar way. When two people are involved in mutual gaze, they are visually 'locked together'. When they are of unequal status, the person who averts gaze, or 'unlocks' first, tends to be the subordinate. The issue of who 'out-looks' whom can have far-reaching consequences. It has been found, for example, that when two people meet for the first time, the person who 'out-looks' the other is likely to be more talkative and influential when they go on to work together in a group.[29] In a business firm, if the boss and a subordinate happen to look at each other at the same time, it's usually the subordinate who breaks off first. Veiled challenges to the boss can, however, be delivered through the eyes. For example, instead of openly disagreeing with the boss, a subordinate can simply engage him in a subtle bout of 'ocular arm-wrestling', holding his gaze for slightly longer than he would normally do. If carefully timed, this can have the desired effect, without appearing to be disrespectful.

In conversations between people of unequal status, dominant individuals usually show 'visual dominance' – that is, they spend proportionately more time looking at the other person while they are talking than they do while they are listening.[30] There are several reasons for this. First of all, because talking is a more controlling activity than listening, dominant individuals like to hang on to the speaker role. To do this they watch the other person closely, making sure that they're listening and that they're not about to try and take over. The opposite happens when dominant people find themselves in the listening role. Now, by reducing the amount of time they spend looking, they can show that they're not prepared to flatter the other person and that they don't expect to remain in the listening role for much longer.

Subordinate people, on the other hand, spend proportionately more time looking while listening than looking while talking. By being more attentive in the listening role they manage to reinforce the dominant person's feelings of self-importance, which may of course only encourage the dominant person to talk even more.

The reason why subordinate individuals look less while talking is probably due to their sense of insecurity. The listener is always judging the speaker. Dominant people don't mind this aspect of the speaker role – it doesn't upset them to know that a subordinate person is judging them. Subordinate people, however, are understandably anxious about how they appear when they are talking to dominant people. To reduce this anxiety they simply look at the dominant person less.

Relaxation is an essential feature of dominance.[31] It's displayed by sinuous and slow movements of the body. That's because the actions of dominant people are governed by the 'principle of economy', whereas those of subordinate individuals are governed by the 'principle of effort'. Subordinate people tend to be unsure of themselves when they're in the presence of dominant people. Like low-ranking chimpanzees, they're constantly on the lookout for trouble. This shows itself in their general demeanour and in rapid, jerky movements of the eyes. Dominant people are much more sure of themselves, so their eye movements tend to be smooth and unhurried.

Many years ago, when I was in the West African state of Burkina Faso, I was fortunate to have an audience with the Emperor of the Mossi. I was ushered into a reception room, where the Emperor sat, surrounded by his courtiers. The Emperor was a large man, with a very imposing presence. What struck me was how little the Emperor actually did for himself – actions that most people would normally do for themselves, like pouring a glass of water, were performed by the courtiers and servants who fussed around him. When he shifted his body or spoke, it was with enormous economy of movement. At times the only things that appeared to move were his eyes. When someone addressed him, he didn't switch his attention immediately, as most people would do. Instead, after a suitable delay, he would allow his head and eyes to drift towards the person, almost as though he'd been filmed in slow motion. The Emperor's actions were executed without the slightest hint of urgency. Every glance, every gesture, was performed at an imperial pace, in his own time. It reminded me of what Nietzsche, the German philosopher, said when someone asked him, 'What is aristocratic?' 'The slow gesture and the slow glance,' he replied.

3. Submissive Tells

In many ways, submission is the flip side of dominance. In his famous book, *The Expression of the Emotions in Man and Animals*, Charles Darwin described how the relationship between dominance and submission is governed by what he called the 'principle of antithesis'.[1] Darwin pointed out that when a dog is in a dominant and hostile state of mind it walks upright and stiffly, and its head is raised. The tail is erect, the hair on its head and back begins to bristle, the ears are pricked and pointed forward, and the eyes assume a fixed stare. As the dog prepares to attack it bares its teeth and the ears are pressed back. When the same dog is in a submissive frame of mind its appearance is almost exactly the opposite. Now, instead of walking upright, it lowers its body and crouches. The rigidity of the back and legs gives way to a more flexible posture. The tail, instead of being stiff and held upright, is lowered and wagged from side to side. The hair becomes smooth, the ears are depressed and relaxed, the teeth are no longer exposed and the lips hang loosely. With the drawing back of the ears the eyelids become elongated and the eyes no longer appear round and staring.

Shrugging Tells

When Darwin came to apply the principle of antithesis to humans he selected the shrug. 'With mankind,' he wrote, 'the best instance of a gesture standing in direct opposition to other movements, naturally assumed under the opposite frame of mind, is that of shrugging the shoulders.' According to Darwin, the natural contrast to the feelings of helplessness associated with the shrug is the frame of mind associated with displays of indignation. In the case of the shrug, he tells us, the shoulders are raised, the elbows are pulled inwards, the hands are raised and the fingers are extended. In contrast, displays of indignation are characterized by a squaring of the shoulders. The chest is expanded, the limbs are held rigid and the fists are clenched.

This all seems very convincing, but it is in fact mistaken, because displays of indignation are not the opposite of the shrug. Indignation, as Darwin calls it, involves a raised head, with the shoulders thrown back, whereas in the shrug the shoulders are raised and the head is typically placed to one side. The opposite of raising the head is lowering the head, and the opposite of throwing the shoulders back is curling them forward. What Darwin saw as the act of indignation was really a display of dominance. In man, raising the head and drawing the shoulders back signals dominance, while lowering the head and drawing the shoulders forward signals sub-mission. In the shrug, however, the head is placed to one side and the shoulders are raised. Neither of these actions has 'an opposite' – it's not possible to lower one's shoulders or to do the opposite of placing one's head to the side. In this respect the shrug is a 'wallflower action' – it doesn't have a partner and it's destined to remain on its own. In contrast, displays of dominance and submission are like inseparable dancing partners – neither can exist without the other. Each, by definition, takes its shape and movement from the other.

Although the shrug is forced, as it were, to sit on the side, watching the action, it is much closer to submission than it is to dominance. There are several reasons for this:

◆ **SHOULDERS**. Raising the shoulders is an integral feature of the shrug, which owes its origins to the innate 'startle response'. When we're exposed to a loud, unexpected noise we instinctively raise our shoulders and pull our head down. This enables us to protect our head and neck from injury. Raising the shoulders as part of the shrug is also self-protective, but in this context it's more symbolic. Because self-protection is such an integral part of submission, it means that the shrug has more in common with submission than with dominance.

◆ **HEAD**. When people shrug they frequently place their head to one side. As we shall see later, 'canting' the head is a submissive gesture. By adding this action to the shrug, the shrug is made more submissive.

◆ **EYEBROWS**. Another feature that is often added to the shrug is raised eyebrows. When this is done without the eyes being opened as well, the message is one of appeasement. Consequently, shrugs that are performed with raised eyebrows are much more submissive than those produced without this addition.

◆　**MESSAGES**. The message of the shrug is one of helplessness. Someone who shrugs is saying, 'I can't do anything about it', 'I don't know' or 'I'm not responsible'. These messages of impotence are obviously much closer to submission than they are to dominance.

The shrug is the gestural cop-out *par excellence*. It's hardly surprising, therefore, that it's so popular in close-knit communities where people are constantly making demands on each other for favours or information, and where they need to find a way of refusing these demands without causing offence. The shrug can be performed in several ways, depending on how the various components of raised shoulders, raised arms, exposed palms, raised eyebrows and canted head are combined. The way people combine these components has a lot to do with their cultural background. In his famous study of Italians and Jews in New York City, David Efron noted that while Italians tended to gesticulate with a wide circumference of movement, Eastern European Jews have a habit of keeping their elbows tucked in.[2] These differences are also discernible in the way they shrug; Italians tend to shrug with raised shoulders as well as raised arms, whereas Eastern European Jews tend to raise their shoulders while keeping their shoulders tucked in. The Italian shrug is much more expansive, relying on the self-protection provided by the raised shoulders. The Eastern European Jewish shrug is doubly defensive because it relies on the protection provided by the raised shoulders as well as the elbows being tucked in close. The fact that the elbows are not on display also reduces the likelihood of the shrug appearing dominant.

French shrugs, on the other hand, tend to be economical. They often consist of nothing more than a 'mouth-shrug', where the mouth is forced into an inverted 'U' by dropping the jaw, keeping the lips together and simultaneously drawing the sides of the mouth down. The classic French mouth-shrug is accompanied by the expression *Boff!*, an ejaculation that neatly summarizes the bored, disdainful tone that the French have added to the basic message of the shrug.[3] In fact, French shrugs frequently have a dismissive tone, almost as if the shrugger were saying, 'I'm helpless to comment, I'm bored and uninterested, and anyway it's irrelevant!' This contrasts with the messages conveyed by other ethnic variants of the shrug – while the Italians, for example, seem to be saying 'What's it got to do with me, I'm innocent!' the message conveyed by the Eastern European Jewish shrug is something like 'What can I do, I'm powerless.'

Defensive Tells

If strength and threat form the basis of dominance displays, then weakness and defensiveness form the basis of submission displays. Individuals who want to signal submission need to show that they aren't a threat and that their main concern is self-protection rather than attack. This can be done in three ways – by being inactive, by appearing smaller and by looking vulnerable. Inactivity reduces the threat to others because it's linked to the 'fear response'. When individuals are in danger they frequently 'freeze'.[4] This reduces their chances of being seen, but it also sends a very clear message that the individual is not preparing to attack – especially when it's combined with postural adjustments that are designed to make the person appear smaller. There are several ways that people try to look smaller than they actually are. One is by slouching; another is by squatting or sitting down. Wearing dull colours and avoiding padded shoulders and hats also helps.

The most potent messages of submission are those associated with vulnerability, especially in the way that people arrange their arms and legs. Standing and sitting postures are full of *tells* because dominant people tend to adopt 'open' postures, while submissive people tend to adopt 'closed' postures. There are several submissive standing postures. One is the 'parallel stance', where the legs are straight and parallel. Schoolchildren adopt this posture when they're talking to their teacher; soldiers use it when they're addressing a superior officer, and employees assume it when they're talking to their boss. In less formal settings, subordinate people sometimes stand with their legs crossed, adopting a 'scissors stance', where the legs are straight and one is crossed over the other, or the 'bent blade stance', where all the weight is on one leg and the other is bent, with the foot positioned either in front or behind, with just the toes touching the ground. People who are shy or lacking in confidence also adopt these postures.

Submission is revealed in two aspects of sitting posture. One involves drawing back the feet and even concealing them so that they don't invade the public space and impose themselves on other people. The other feature involves keeping the knees together and/or crossing the legs, either at the thigh or at the ankles. These postures are the antithesis of 'open legged' postures, where the genitals are put on display. With the knees together and the legs crossed, the genitals are symbolically placed out of sight and out of bounds, and other people are prevented, again symbolically, from getting between the person's legs. The other important function of crossing the legs and keeping them close together is that this increases the amount of 'auto-contact' – that is, the extent that the body is in contact with itself. When people feel threatened, as they tend to do when they're being submissive, they often feel the need to reassure themselves by increasing auto-contact. Again, this is not something that people consciously decide to do. Most of the time it happens without them being aware of what they're doing and why they're doing it.

Self-comforting Tells

When we're talking to someone in a position of authority we tend to assume that our own actions, rather than those of the other person, are being judged, and this makes us feel self-conscious and insecure. There are several ways that we cope with these feelings. One is by engaging in auto-contact actions where we touch, hold or stroke ourselves. These self-comforting gestures serve to reassure us – just as they do when someone else touches, holds or strokes us. In this sense auto-contact actions are really *substitution tells* – they're comforting and reassuring things that we do to ourselves when there isn't anybody else around to do them to us.

The potency of auto-contact actions lies in the fact that physical touch is the best way to comfort someone. It's the most primitive and it's also the most effective. The importance of touch is reflected in the composition of our skin, which has millions of receptor cells that are sensitive to the slightest change in pressure, and in the structure of our brain, where it's been discovered that the area in the prefrontal cortex that's devoted to touch is much larger than the areas devoted to any of the other senses. Touch forms the basis of the initial contact between mother and child; it's touch that comforts the baby and makes it feel secure. That's why touch is so reassuring throughout our lives – it recreates those feelings of love and security that we once experienced as a baby. The sad part of this is that if you watch people who feel dejected, lonely or vulnerable – people lining up for benefits, people waiting in accident and emergency, people appearing in court – they frequently touch themselves in a way that is reminiscent of how their mother comforted them. The same applies to people who are being submissive.

When people are feeling submissive they frequently stroke their hair, especially the hair at the back of their head. These actions can be traced back to the time when their mothers caressed their hair to comfort them, and when they supported them by cradling the back of their head. When people feel submissive they also touch their face, frequently placing their fingers on their lips. These self-comforting gestures also owe their origins to the way that mothers caress their baby's face, play with its mouth and kiss it on the lips. Mothers also hug their children when they're distressed. Consequently, when adults are feeling insecure or submissive they often try to recover these reassuring feelings by performing actions that enable them to hug themselves. One example of this is the 'arm grip', where the hand stretches over the chest to grab the bicep of the opposite arm; another is the 'bandoleer', where the arm is extended over the chest to grip the opposite shoulder. In the 'double bandoleer' both arms are crossed on the chest and each grips the opposite shoulder. These actions recreate the experience of being embraced. Other self-comforting actions recreate the sensation of being held by the hand. One is the 'palm press', where the palm of one hand faces upward, holding the palm of the other hand. Another is the 'dovetail', where the fingers of the two hands are intertwined. In both these actions the palms of the hands are either pressed together or kept loosely apart, creating a sensation that is very similar to holding hands, or having one's hand reassuringly held by someone else.

These submissive hand postures are in marked contrast to dominant hand postures like 'steepling', where the arms usually rest on the elbows, with the palms facing each other and the tip of each finger lightly touching its opposite number, making the whole arrangement look like the roof beams of a church. The steepling posture is used by people who want to put their hands on display but who don't need to use them to comfort themselves. While submissive hand postures attempt to maximize auto-contact, the steepling posture tries to keep it to the bare minimum.

Head Tells

Charles Darwin noticed that when people feel submissive they have a natural tendency to lower their head, making themselves look smaller and less threatening. Darwin also suggested that the habit of nodding to signal 'yes' was linked to submissive lowering of the head. Unfortunately for this theory, not every society signals affirmation by nodding or dipping the head. In India, for example, people roll their head from side to side to signal 'yes' or to show agreement. This movement is quite different from the headshake, because in the head-roll the head is rocked from side to side in the same plane as the front of the body. The head can either be rocked repeatedly from side to side or the head-roll can be performed with a short, sharp movement of the head towards one of the shoulders. Although there are cultural differences in the head movements that people use to signal 'yes' and 'no', the habit of lowering the head as a sign of submission appears to be universal.[5] In fact, the head is used to signal submission in several ways:

◆ **HEAD-DIP TELLS**. When individuals walk between people who are having a conversation, you'll notice that they frequently 'duck' their head down in order to make sure that they don't get in the way and to apologize for any inconvenience they may have caused. Some people produce an involuntary dip of the head when they approach someone who's important, especially when that person is unfamiliar to them or is involved in a conversation with someone else. By watching people's heads when they approach high-status individuals, it's possible

Head-canting. Here Jerry Hall sends a clear message of appeasement to Prince Charles by tilting her head to one side.

to identify how they feel; those who are relaxed about status distinctions don't usually produce any submissive tells at all, whereas those who feel that they are intruding on an important person are likely to reveal their discomfort by dipping their head very slightly.

◆ **HEAD-NOD TELLS**. Repetitive nodding is also an integral part of conversation. You often see people who are in the listener role nodding slowly while the other person is speaking. They do this both to show that they are listening and to demonstrate that they don't want to take over the speaker's role. Fast nodding also shows that the listener understands the speaker, but because it contains a sense of urgency, it shows either that the listener supports the speaker wholeheartedly or that the listener wants to take over the speaker's role. So while slow nodding sends the message, 'I understand what you're saying and I want to continue listening', fast nodding sends one of two messages – either 'I totally agree with you' or 'I understand you, but hurry up, I want to say something now!' The distinction between these last two messages usually depends on where the listener is looking – at the speaker when he or she is being supportive, and away from the listener when he or she wants the floor.

◆ **HEAD-CANT TELLS**. As we've seen, submissive people frequently lower their head or cant it to one side. Head-canting serves as an appeasement display because it exposes the neck, which is a vulnerable part of the body, and because it makes the person look shorter and therefore less threatening. It also makes the person look helpless, rather like a baby with its head to one side. It's very likely, in fact, that head canting owes its origins to the innocent feelings of helplessness that we experienced as a baby, tilting our head to one side and resting it on our parent's shoulder. We also find remnants of these early experiences in the shrug, which is often performed with the head tilted to one side. Head-canting tends to be used by people who want to appear submissive or sexually attractive, or both. There are several reports suggesting that women use head-canting more than men, but this has not been consistently supported by research.[6] A research project in Italy, conducted by Marco Costa, Marzia Menzani and Pio Ricci Bitti, looked at examples of head-canting in paintings from the thirteenth to the nineteenth century.[7] It was discovered that commissioned portraits of powerful men seldom include head-canting, but that depictions of religious or pious figures frequently do. In this study the researchers also found that head-canting is more pronounced among female figures than among male figures. Whether this is a case of art mimicking life remains to be seen.

Eye Tells

For territorial and solitary species, flight is the natural solution to a conflict where it looks as if one's going to lose. For these species it's better to run away and live to fight another day than to risk being injured. In a social species like ours, flight isn't really an option because our lives are based on co-operation. This means that we can't simply run away when there's a confrontation – we need to find ways of living together. One way to do this is through the ritualistic medium of submissive displays. These enable us to resolve conflicts without damage or loss of life, and they allow us to continue working together.

When we look more closely at submission displays we discover that they contain symbolic elements of flight. This is noticeable in the way that members of social species use their eyes. When they meet a dominant individual, they engage in what the zoologist Michael Chance called 'cut-off' – that is, they avert their gaze so as to visually remove the dominant individual from view.[8] This has several important effects for submissive people. Firstly, by removing the dominant person from view, the subordinate person is better able to reduce their sense of fear. Cut-off is like a psychological form of flight – it enables individuals to remove potential attackers from their mind. Secondly, cut-off shows that the subordinate person has no intention of attacking the dominant person. That's because looking at the other person could be a prelude to attack, whereas looking away is a preparation for defence. Thirdly, the act of looking away and demeaning oneself actually serves to 'cut off' any aggression from the dominant person. That's because submission displays are hard-wired. When we are confronted with someone who's trying to look small, defenceless and weak, our aggressive impulses automatically switch off.

There are several ocular *tells* associated with submission:

◆   **THE EYE-DIP**. People frequently avert their gaze downwards in order to appear submissive. This is usually a deliberate action, and it is designed to placate someone who's more dominant. The Eye-dip is also used as a flirtatious signal.

◆ **THE EYE-SHUTTLE**. Submissive people frequently flick their eyes from side to side, often without moving their head. This is designed not only to try and take in everything that's happening around them, but also, instinctively, to search for possible escape routes.

◆ **THE EYE-PUFF**. Here the eyelids are pulled back to make the eyes look bigger. This conveys an image of innocent attentiveness, and when the other person doesn't recognize what's happening it can be very disarming. The eye-puff relies on the fact that babies have disproportionately large eyes, relative to the rest of their face.[9] Large eyes are an 'innate releaser': we feel protective and nurturing whenever we encounter someone who has large eyes, or who has enlarged them to look more appealing.

It's worth noticing that all of these submissive ocular gestures are symmetrical – in other words, both eyes do the same thing. Asymmetrical movements of the eyes tend to be associated with more informal types of exchange, like friendship. There are, however, ways that these submissive ocular gestures differ from each other. Both the eye-dip and the eye-shuttle are motivated by negative feelings, like fear or shame, whereas the eye-puff gesture is designed to be disarming and solicitous.

Another way that people try to appear disarming is by wearing their spectacles or their sunglasses on the top of their head. Elevating the glasses in this way is rather like lifting the visor on a helmet – it shows that no threat is intended. When the glasses are placed on the forehead they create a 'four-eyed' spectacle, with the 'eyes' of the glasses above and the real eyes below. Because the eyes of the glasses are larger, they take on the signalling role normally performed by the eyes. They become 'super-normal stimuli', creating the impression that the person has extra-large eyes – in other words is like a baby. All along the French Riviera – in fact anywhere where people are carefree and on display – you'll see women strolling along, looking confident, well dressed and with their sun-glasses perched on their head. If you were to ask them why they are wearing their glasses on their head they'd prob-ably say it's a convenient place to put them. However, the real reason why they do it is to make themselves look youthful, unthreatening and attractive.

Eyebrow Tells

In adults, eyebrow position can convey several messages, depending on what's happening with the eyes. There are four basic postures involving the eyebrows and the eyes: (1) Eyebrows in repose and eyes in repose – this is the expression of the face at rest; (2) Eyebrows in repose and eyes widened – this is the threatening facial expression of anger, sometimes involving lowering of the brow; (3) Eyebrows raised and eyes widened – this is the facial expression associated with the prototypical fear response; and (4) Eyebrows raised and eyes in repose – the facial expression of submission.

The ancient Romans used the term *super cilium*, literally

'raised eyebrows', to refer to the facial expression where the eyebrows are raised and the eyes are slightly closed. This is, of course, not the gesture of submission – it's the exact opposite, an expression of haughtiness or, to borrow from the Latin, superciliousness. The fact that this gesture and the facial gesture for submission are distinguished on the basis of whether the eyes are in repose or slightly closed shows how very complex facial expressions can be. Although the difference between the two gestures is a matter of millimetres, nobody confuses an expression of superciliousness with one of submission.

When people want to demonstrate that they are not a threat, they frequently raise their eyebrows. This makes them look attentive and impressed. When the eyebrows are pinched together at the centre they create an impression of concern. Of course the eyebrows can be raised with or without being pinched. When they are raised and pinched the result is a hybrid gesture that conveys submission and concern.

Several movie stars have performed successful double-acts with their eyebrows. If there were Oscars for eyebrows, Woody Allen's would certainly be up for nomination. In movies like *Annie Hall*, his eyebrows seem to take on a life of their own, sometimes emphasizing his own confusion, at other times rising to defuse antagonism towards him. But in the eyebrow 'Hall of Fame', it's Groucho Marx's eyebrows that are king. We all remember Groucho for his enormous greasepaint moustache, his cigar and his rolling eyes. But what really carried the performance was his *signature tell* – the Groucho Marx 'eyebrow flutter'. Having delivered a punch line, Groucho would flutter his eyebrows up and down, to show that he'd completed what he was saying. Here the eyebrows acted as a pair of full stops, or rather exclamation marks, allowing Groucho a moment of triumph and giving the audience the opportunity to be appreciative.

A few British actors have also used their eyebrows to good effect. The pre-war actor Basil Rathbone's eyebrows were virtually typecast for the role of superciliousness. Roger Moore's trademark *tell* is the single raised eyebrow – actually his left eyebrow – which he regularly enlisted in order to appear quizzical, seductive or all-knowing in his roles as the Saint and James Bond. Whenever a villain needed to be put down or a pretty lady needed to be impressed, his eyebrow would spring into action, sometimes even upstaging Roger Moore himself.

Smiling Tells

How people smile at each other can provide useful clues to their power relationship.[10] Darwin noticed that smiling and laughter often occur together. He concluded therefore that they have the same origins, and that smiling is just a weak form of laughter. This idea seems very convincing, especially when you consider how easy it is to shift between smiling and laughter, and how close happiness is to amusement. In many languages the words for smiling and laughter even have the same root.

However, this theory has been challenged by the discovery that chimpanzees have two quite distinct facial expressions that correspond to human smiling and laughter – a 'submission face' where the lips are retracted and the teeth are exposed, and a 'play face' where the lower jaw is dropped and the corners of the mouth are pulled back.[11] The chimpanzee's play face is very similar to human laughter because the mouth is opened wide and it's accompanied by rhythmic vocalization. At the same time the chimpanzee's submission face is very similar to the human smile because both are silent and the teeth are fully exposed. These two chimpanzee expressions serve very different functions. Yet human laughter and smiling often appear together and seem to serve the same purpose. This suggests that, during their evolution, human laughter and smiling have converged. For our distant ancestors they were quite different, but for us they are very similar.

If the chimpanzee submission face is designed to appease dominant individuals, does smiling serve the same function for humans? The answer is 'yes', but it depends on how friendly the situation is and what kinds of smiles people produce. Take the case where two people are together and one has higher status than the other. When the situation is not very friendly, the subordinate person is likely to smile much more than the dominant person. Here, smiling performs the role of appeasement. However, when the situation is friendly, the dominant person may actually smile more than the subordinate person. The difference between these two situations, it turns out, is not that the subordinate person smiles less, but that the dominant person smiles more in the friendly situation. In other words, subordinate individuals produce similar amounts of smiling, regardless of whether the situation is friendly or unfriendly, but dominant people smile far less in unfriendly situations and much more in friendly situations. Marvin Hecht and Marianne LaFrance, who have studied this phenomenon, point out that while a subordinate person needs to smile to appease a dominant person, the dominant person is 'licensed' to smile when he or she likes.[12] The clue to why the dominant person smiles more in a friendly situation becomes clear when we look at the different ways that people compose their facial features into a smile.

We all know that some smiles are genuine and others are false. That's because we see people pretending to be happy, and we know what it feels like to smile when we're feeling miserable. Although we're constantly exposed to fake smiles, and spend a great deal of our time producing them for the benefit of other people, it's only since facial expressions have been studied in detail that we have come to understand what distinguishes a genuine smile from a false smile.

One of the first scientists to tackle this issue was the French anatomist, Guillaume Duchenne de Boulogne, who published his *Mécanisme de la physionomie humaine* in 1862, ten years before Darwin's book on the face appeared. Duchenne was fascinated by the musculature of the face – an interest he reputedly developed while examining heads chopped off by the guillotine. He was also the first person to apply electrical currents to the face to see how the muscles worked.[13]

Duchenne discovered that genuine smiles involve two sets of muscles. The first is the *zygomatic major* muscles, which run down the side of the face and attach to the corners of the mouth. When these are contracted the corners of the mouth are pulled up, the cheeks are puffed up, and the teeth are sometimes exposed. The second set of muscles, the *orbicularis oculi*, surround the eyes. When these are contracted the eyes become narrow and 'crow's feet' appear beside the eyes. Duchenne recognized that the critical clue to a genuine smile was to be found in the region of the eyes, because while the zygomatic major muscles are under conscious control, the *orbicularis oculi* are not. As he put it,

> The emotion of frank joy is expressed on the face by the combined contraction of the zygomaticus major muscle and the orbicularis oculi. The first obeys the will but the second is only put in play by the sweet emotions of the soul . . . The muscle around the eye does not obey the will; it is only brought into play by a true feeling, by an agreeable emotion. Its inertia, in smiling, unmasks a false friend.

If you watch how subordinate people behave towards dominant people, you'll notice that most of their smiles involve the muscles above the mouth instead of those around the eyes – in other words, they're 'mouth smiles' rather than 'mouth&eye smiles', or what are known as 'Duchenne smiles'. Strictly speaking, mouth smiles are 'false' smiles because they pretend to show enjoyment but they're really only motivated by the desire to appear sociable and unthreatening. But if you watch how dominant people behave towards their subordinates, you'll notice that they smile far less, but that their smiles are more likely to be 'mouth&eye smiles'. This difference arises because subordinates use smiling for the purpose of appeasement, whereas dominant people have the licence to smile when and how they wish. Smiles that are designed to appease may differ from genuine smiles in other ways. They may, for example, involve the corners of the mouth being pulled sideways rather than up, so that the resulting expression looks more like a grimace than a smile. In more extreme situations the corners of the mouth may momentarily be drawn down, thereby incorporating fleeting evidence of the fear-face into the smile. In these and other ways, the smile may reveal what lies behind its façade, and therefore what someone is really feeling.

It has been found that women smile much more than men.[14] This may have something to do with the sub-ordinate position that women occupy in society, although it doesn't explain why baby girls smile more than baby boys as early as two months. Investigations of the portrait photographs in school yearbooks show that as they get older, girls continue to smile more than boys, and that the difference is most pronounced after puberty. When women occupy positions of power they don't auto-matically abandon their smiling habits in favour of men's. It's been discovered that women who are in high-power roles don't smile any less than women in low-power roles, but that men who are in high-power roles do smile far less than those in low-power roles. Testosterone plays a part here, because men with high levels of testosterone tend to produce smaller smiles, with less activity round the mouth and eyes, whereas men with low levels of testosterone smile more frequently and produce larger smiles.[15]

These differences are reflected in the inferences that people draw on the basis of smiling. When men and women smile, they are both seen as happy, contented and relaxed. Unsmiling men, on the other hand, are seen as dominant, whereas unsmiling women are simply seen as being unhappy. These inferences may have something to do with the fact that women smile much more than men, so that while an unsmiling man appears to be fairly normal, an unsmiling woman can look quite unusual. Consequently, to appear normal a woman needs to smile much more than a man. A man, on the other hand, doesn't need to smile a lot because other men aren't smiling that much.

When people are asked to look at a smiling face and to decide whether the smile is genuine, they automatically look at the crow's feet areas on the outside of the eyes. They seem to know, instinctively, that genuine smiles wrinkle up this part of the face, and so that's where to look. However, although people clearly know where to look when they're deciding about the authenticity of a smile, they are quite happy to accept fake smiles instead. For example, when someone has committed a misdemeanour, other people are more likely to treat that person leniently if he or she offers an apology in the form of a smile. What's interesting is that it doesn't matter very much whether the smile that the person produces is genuine or false – provided it's some sort of smile, people are prepared to be lenient. This suggests that although we are capable of distinguishing a genuine smile from a false smile, we don't always exercise this ability – there are even times when we actively seem to suppress it. What's important to us is that other people smile at the right time. The fact that their smiling is a pretence doesn't seem to bother us at all.

Blushing Tells

For Charles Darwin, it was the blush, not laughter, which distinguished man from the other animals.[16] Darwin's opinions about blushing were very much in line with attitudes that had developed during the previous century and were still in circulation in Victorian times. In the eighteenth century the English developed the idea that embarrassment and blushing are the outward signs of sensitivity to others. They reasoned that it was only possible for someone to become embarrassed if they were capable of feeling shame, but incapable of concealing it. The English realized, of course, that this could not be said of foreigners. As Christopher Ricks has pointed out, it was 'part of the Englishman's objection to foreigners that they are "brazen-faced", unembarrassable, and therefore untrustworthy. Especially the French ... How can you trust a people whose very language does its best to conceal the existence of the blush?'[17]

The Victorians had an ambivalent attitude to blushing – they regarded it as a sign of sensitivity, but they also felt that it was inappropriate for men to show their feelings by blushing in company. Women, on the other hand, were actually expected to blush when something embarrassing happened. For example, if a young lady happened to be present when a gentleman mentioned the subject of sex, she was expected to show how shocked and innocent she was by blushing. Here blushing carried a double message, because in addition to declaring the lady's innocence it also showed that she was sufficiently informed about sex to be shocked. This double message of the blush – the fact that it admitted what it tried to conceal – fascinated the Victorians. So did the fact that blushing could not be brought under conscious control. The principles of order and self-control were central to Victorian society. Blushing represented a complete negation of those principles and therefore challenged the things that society stood for. That is why people found blushing so intriguing – it showed that genuine feelings could not be disguised, and that the emotions could triumph over reason.

Victorian scientists were fascinated and perplexed by blushing. Darwin himself recognized that certain animals redden when they become impassioned, but that there were no animal species that became embarrassed. Darwin concluded that only humans are capable of embarrassment because only they possess the sort of self-consciousness that gives rise to blushing. This, as he pointed out, represents much more than the capacity to think about oneself: 'it is not the simple act of reflecting on our own appearance, but the thinking what others think of us, which excites a blush'.

Self-consciousness and a concern with other people's opinions seem to be central to blushing. We often blush when we know that we've done something wrong or when we've violated other people's expectations of us, but we also blush when we've attracted the attention of other people by doing something positive. That's why we're as likely to blush when we've been caught out as when someone offers us a compliment. However, it's not just the recognition of our own failures and achievements that make us blush; we also blush when we see other people getting embarrassed, especially when we identify with them closely.[18]

Blushing involves the autonomic nervous system and it takes the form of increased blood flow to the cheeks of the face, and sometimes to the neck and chest. How blushing actually works is still something of a mystery, although there's lots of evidence to show that it's associated with unexpected and unwelcome attention from others. The individuals who are most prone to blushing are those who are most concerned about how other people see them, and who are most eager to behave properly and not do the wrong thing. When individuals do make a social gaffe or say something embarrassing, traitorous blushing often exposes them. Paradoxically, they can usually rely on blushing to get them off the hook, because blushing functions like an apology, showing that they adhere to the norms of the group. This can be seen in the responses that blushing evokes in others – it has been found, for example, that people who do something wrong and who then blush are treated much more leniently than those who make the same error but who don't blush.[19]

Blushing is an integral part of embarrassment, and it's often accompanied by other signs of embarrassment, like speech disturbances and half-hearted smiles, as well as looking down at the ground, touching the face or flicking out the tongue. In this respect blushing operates like a form of appeasement, showing other people our discomfort and regret. However, unlike other forms of appeasement, blushing is entirely outside our control – we can't redden our face deliberately and we can't switch off a blush once it's started. That's what makes it such a painful experience for the person who's blushing, and a significant *tell* for everyone else.

Tongue Tells

When children or adults are involved in a task they often push their tongue out between their lips. The 'tongue show', as it's called, is associated with effort and concentration. It has been proposed that it also functions as an unconsciously motivated signal of rejection – in other words, people stick out the tip of their tongue to show others that they don't want to be approached.[20] There is in fact some experimental support for this theory because it has been found that individuals are more hesitant about approaching someone who is busy and showing the tip of their tongue than they are about approaching someone who is equally busy but whose tongue is concealed.[21] There may of course be nothing mysterious about all of this; it may simply be that we are slow to approach individuals who have their tongues out because we don't like disturbing people who are clearly preoccupied.

However, there is evidence that the tongue show is used in other situations to keep people at arm's length. In a detailed analysis of some film of a young couple kissing on a park bench, Adam Kendon found that the girl controlled the intimacy of the encounter by occasionally withdrawing, and that as she did so she would occasionally expose the tip of her tongue.[22] Presenting her tongue was a way of showing her boyfriend that she was temporarily inaccessible. In most cases of the tongue show people aren't aware that the tongue is sending a signal. The young girl on the park bench probably didn't know that she exposed her tongue, let alone that she was using it to control her boyfriend's enthusiasm. Although he responded to her tongue shows, it's very unlikely that he was fully aware what was happening.

When people are embarrassed they often produce a brief 'tongue flick'. This is quite different from the tongue show, because while the tongue show can be sustained for several minutes, a tongue flick usually lasts no longer than a second – the tongue simply darts out of the mouth and then flicks back again. While the tongue show is associated with mental concentration and with inaccessibility, the tongue flick is a *tell* of embarrassment. When someone is being teased or they feel that they've been caught out, it's not uncommon to see them flick out their tongue, sometimes while they're smiling. It's quite possible that this brief exposure of the tongue is also designed to keep other people at arm's length.

Grooming Tells

In the world of apes and monkeys individuals who occupy similar positions in the social hierarchy normally take turns to groom each other by removing insects, lice and dead skin from each other's hair. This type of grooming is reciprocal: it's an expression of friendship and solidarity between equals. As such, it's quite different from what takes place when a subordinate individual grooms a dominant individual. In this situation the grooming is about the ratification of power. That's why it's all one-way, directed from the subordinate towards the superior, never the other way round.

When we compare this with human touching, we find that it's the same between friends, but quite different between people of unequal status. Friends, for example, frequently reassure and show their affection by touching each other. However, where power differences are concerned, human patterns of touch are the opposite way round to what they are with apes and monkeys – because while dominant people reserve the right to touch their subordinates, subordinates need to ensure that they don't touch their superiors. With humans, therefore, status grooming has largely been shifted to speech – when we want to curry favour with our boss, we resort to 'grooming talk'. In other words, instead of using our hands to stroke his body, we use our words to stroke his ego.

Grooming talk is designed to help people appear like-able and unthreatening to others. The desire to be liked by other people is very deep-seated – in fact it's essential to a social species like ours – and it's especially important when the people we're hoping to impress happen to be more powerful than us. There are two basic strategies that individuals can use in this kind of situation. The first is 'self-deprecation' – saying negative things about oneself – and the second is 'other-promotion' – saying positive things about someone else. Self-deprecation can be achieved by minimizing one's own achievements, con-cealing one's talents, or by denying any responsibility for one's achievements or those of other people. Submissive people often use these techniques when they're talking to dominant individuals. This makes them appear un-threatening and it makes the dominant person feel more self-important.

Powerful people sometimes use self-deprecation strategies with their subordinates, but their intention then is usually to invite contradiction. When the boss turns to one of his subordinates, after he's made a presentation to a client, and says, 'You know, I don't think I did very well', the boss isn't asking his subordinate to agree with him, he's laying a 'flattery trap' by discreetly inviting the sub-ordinate to say something complimentary like, 'That's not true, boss, you were brilliant!' Flattery traps are also used by subordinates and by equals. For example, when a couple are returning from a dinner party and the wife says, 'The other women there tonight were gorgeous', she's not inviting her husband to agree with her – she's hoping that he'll say something like, 'Nonsense, darling, they weren't a patch on you!'

The beauty of the flattery trap is that one can hear positive things about oneself without having to say them oneself. By luring people into making compliments one can get them to say things that they cannot disown later on, and which are likely to influence how they think about one in the future. Years ago, psychologists discovered that if people can be persuaded to publicly endorse opinions that aren't their own, they are likely to agree with them later on.[23] The same applies with the flattery trap. If you can entice someone to say positive things about you, they're more likely to be impressed by you in the future.

There are several ways that people can ingratiate themselves to others. One is by agreeing with everything they say; another is by doing them favours. The third, and by far the most popular strategy, is by complimenting and flattering them.[24] When we compliment someone we're aware of what we're doing, but very seldom aware of our motives or the way that they unconsciously shape what we're trying to achieve. Most of us would be horrified to discover just how much we alter our behaviour in the presence of powerful and attractive people, in the hope that they'll like us and find us interesting. And yet we're constantly doing it – agreeing with what they say, concealing our real opinions, telling them how clever they are, and generally behaving in a way that makes us more acceptable.

Ingratiation is a pervasive part of our social lives; it's also the essential lubricant in business. It oils the wheels of the organization, reducing the friction between people at different levels and smoothing their ascent up the corporate ladder. Research reveals the sad truth that individuals who make a business of ingratiating themselves with their superiors enjoy more career success than those who concentrate on getting the job done properly.[25]

Ingratiation has obvious benefits for corporate employees because it allows them to curry favour with their boss, at very little cost to themselves. However, it always carries the risk that it will be recognized for what it is, and that the motives of the ingratiator will be called into question. When the ingratiator is of lower status than his or her target, there's a much greater danger that the target will decide that the ingratiator is not being sincere, simply because he or she has so much to gain. There are several tricks that people use to make their ingratiation less transparent:

◆ **DOWNGRADING.** To disguise their motives people often choose a less potent version of ingratiation – for example, complimenting someone rather than doing them a favour. Because favours involve more time and effort than compliments they're much more likely to be noticed and to raise suspicions.

◆ **DILUTING.** Another trick is using a 'diluted' rather than a 'concentrated' form of ingratiation – for example, complimenting the boss on a particular phrase in his speech rather than on the whole speech.

◆ **SIMPLIFYING**. Strategies that combine different types of ingratiation are much more obvious than those that consist of just one kind. That's why the most effective forms of ingratiation are those that consist of a single type.

◆ **CAMOUFLAGING**. To work properly, ingratiation needs to be conducted in the right context and it should be consistent with the relationship that the ingratiator has with the target. No suspicion is raised, for example, when a junior member of the board compliments the CEO on his speech to the investors. However, when the same person makes a flattering remark about the CEO's new hairstyle it's likely to set alarm bells ringing. The CEO's secretary, on the other hand, could comfortably comment on his new hairstyle because it's part of her role to make sure that he looks smart.

◆ **SELECTING**. Research shows that people who have high self-esteem like to be flattered, but that those with low self-esteem don't. It also shows that people regard compliments that are consistent with how they see themselves as being genuine, and those that are at odds with how they see themselves as being phoney.[26] For example, a chess master who considers himself to be brilliant but unattractive would regard a compliment about his intelligence to be genuine, but a compliment about his looks to be false. To be successful, an ingratiator needs to know not only who to flatter, but what to flatter them about.

◆ **COVERING**. We are much more likely to take a

compliment at face value when it's directed at us than when we hear it being targeted at someone else. Maybe that's because our critical faculties become weaker when we're being flattered, or because we're more objective when someone else is being flattered. Either way, the people who are least impressed by flattery are those who observe it happening. They're also the ones who are most likely to undermine the efforts of ingratiators by calling their motives into question. Seasoned ingratiators who know this try to ensure that other people aren't present to witness their attempts at ingratiation, or if they are that they feel obliged to support the ingratiator's opinions.

People use these strategies to enhance their ingratiation and to reduce the chances of being found out. It may not be necessary, however, to go to all these lengths, because most people are suckers for flattery. As the Earl of Chesterfield remarked in a letter to his son in 1752, 'Every woman is infallibly to be gained by every sort of flattery, and every man by one sort or another'.

4. Conversation Tells

The most obvious thing about conversations is that people take turns. It's unusual for more than one person to be speaking at a time, and when it does happen for any length of time it's because the conversation has temporarily broken down. The reason why we take turns is because of the limitations of our brains: we cannot talk and listen to someone else at the same time. Psychologists who study conversation have found that people are remarkably skilled at taking turns. They have discovered that the time that elapses between one person completing their turn and the next person starting to talk can be so brief as to be almost non-existent – in some instances it's less than 50 thousandths of a second! These are called 'smooth transitions', because the switch between one speaker and the next is so seamless.[1]

The universal rule of conversations is 'one person at a time', and although most conversations follow this rule, there are times when people speak at the same time and don't listen to each other. Some cases of 'overlap talk' arise because the listener is trying to interrupt in order to take over the speaker role. However, as we shall see later on, other cases of overlap talk arise, not through competition, but purely because the listener wants to encourage the speaker.

In order to take turns in a conversation it's necessary for the speaker and the listener to show each other whether or not they want the floor. In principle this could be achieved by each person declaring what he or she wants, but this method would be very clumsy and inefficient. Instead, turn-taking is organized through a set of conventionalized signals that people produce while they are talking or listening.[2] Any conversation therefore operates at two levels – an 'official' dialogue, where people exchange ideas and opinions, and an 'unofficial' dialogue where they exchange signals about turn-taking and demonstrate how committed they are to the conversation. By using turn-taking signals the listener can indicate whether he or she wants to 'avoid' the speaker role or to 'take' it, and the speaker can signal whether he or she wants to 'hold' the floor or 'yield' the floor to the listener.

Turn-avoiding Tells

There are several ways that a listener can demonstrate that he or she doesn't want to take over the role of speaker and is happy to remain in the listener role. One is by producing 'back-channel' signals.[3] These consist of verbal responses like 'uh-huh', 'yes' and 'yeah', repetition of the speaker's words, nods and brief smiles, which are designed to show that the listener agrees with the speaker or understands what the speaker is saying.

As we saw in the last chapter, the meaning of nodding depends on its tempo, with slow nodding conveying agreement, and rapid nodding signalling either enthusiastic agreement or impatience and a desire to take over the role of speaker. Head-shaking also conveys different messages, depending on how rapidly the head is moved from side to side. When the head is shaken rapidly it shows that the listener disagrees with the speaker and would like to take over the speaker role. When the head is shaken slowly it can convey an entirely different meaning. If, for example, the listener has just told an incredible story and the listener responds by shaking his head slowly, it demonstrates that the listener shares the speaker's incredulity, and implies that the listener doesn't want to assume the speaker role.

There are three other ways that the listener can show that he or she does not want the floor. The first is by producing an 'attentiveness display'. By remaining silent, orienting towards the speaker, and gazing intently at the speaker, the listener can show that he or she is interested in what the speaker has to say and therefore has no desire to take over the speaker role. The second is by producing an 'unintention display'. Unintention displays are the opposite of 'intention displays'. For example, if you're listening to someone and you want to say something you can usually request the floor by producing an intention display, like leaning forward, lifting a finger or opening your mouth slightly. These movements get the message across because they are preparatory to speaking. Unintention displays, on the other hand, consist of actions that hinder your ability to speak, like folding your arms, pressing your lips together or placing a hand or a finger over your mouth – in other words performing actions that are the opposite of preparatory movements to speak.

The third way that listeners demonstrate that they don't want the floor is by asking questions. These can take the form of queries which stand on their own, like 'Do you come here often?', or they can take the form of tag questions like 'isn't it?' or 'don't you think?' which are tagged on the end of statements. Asking questions invites the other person to assume the speaker role or to continue occupying it. Women often use this ploy when they meet a man for the first time; they produce lots of back-channel signals and ask lots of questions, which make them look attentive. A man who is treated in this way by a woman tends to assume that she is genuinely interested in what he has to say, and this encourages him to keep talking – sometimes to the point of taking up permanent residence in the speaker role. Because the man is so caught up in what he's saying, he often forgets to ask the woman about herself. Women often start out facilitating men's conversations, and then end up regretting it.

Turn-taking Tells

When you are in the listener role there are several ways you can show the speaker that you want the floor. One is by producing 'alerting signals' – for example, raising your hand or widening your eyes slightly to show the other person that you want to speak. Another way is by opening your mouth and breathing in audibly – in other words, producing slightly exaggerated versions of the 'preparatory movements' that you would normally perform just before you started talking. The third way is by producing 'negative back-channel'. Instead of supporting the speaker with 'back-channel signals', you can try to persuade the speaker to give up the floor by sighing, looking away, or impatiently nodding your head – in other words, doing things that are designed to discourage the speaker from continuing. Finally, you can always try to take the floor by interrupting the speaker. Interruptions occur when two people are talking at the same time, but not all cases of simultaneous talk count as interruptions. There are three kinds of overlap talk:

◆ **SUPPORTING**. This occurs when the listener makes a positive remark while the other person is talking. For example, while the other person is talking the listener might say, 'I completely agree with you'. Although this interjection overlaps with the speaker's talk it doesn't count as an interruption because it's not designed to transfer the speaker role to the listener – it's intended to keep the speaker and the listener in their present roles.

◆ **SNIPING**. This occurs when one person is talking and the listener says something like 'Rubbish!' or 'I don't agree'. Again, although there is overlap talk, these interjections are not necessarily cases of interruption because the listener may have no intention of usurping the speaker's role – the listener may simply want to express a point of view, and possibly unsettle the speaker in the process.

◆ **INTERRUPTING**. Interruptions occur when the overlap talk is a product of competing desires for the floor – for example, when one person is speaking and the other person talks across that person in an attempt to secure the floor for him- or herself. Successful interruptions occur when the speaker relinquishes the floor to the interrupter, and unsuccessful interruptions occur when the speaker manages to see off the challenge and hold on to the floor.

Interrupters use several tricks to ensure success. One is to raise their volume – it's been discovered that interrupters who talk louder than the other person are more likely to acquire the floor.[4] Another trick is to appear resolute. Interrupters who talk without hesitation, and who remain unaffected by the fact that the other person is also talking, are more likely to succeed. So are interrupters who continue to talk beyond the point where most interrupters give up the challenge.

There are two critical points in overlap talk. One is the 'accident point' and the other is the 'challenge point'. For example, when the listener thinks that the speaker is about to give up the floor and starts to talk, both of them are likely to end up talking at the same time. Because the interrupter has no intention of grabbing the floor from the speaker, he or she is likely to stop talking at the 'accident point', which is about one second into the overlap talk. By stopping at this point, rather than later, the interrupter can show the speaker that the overlapping talk was accidental. He can also get this message across by stopping the interruption in mid-sentence rather than at the end of the utterance. The other critical point in overlap talk is the 'challenge point'. This is the point where interrupters normally give up the challenge, and it occurs about two to three seconds after the beginning of overlap talk. Interrupters who are serious about taking the floor may need to go beyond this point, and in the process they lay themselves open to the accusation that they are interrupting. Half-hearted interruptions tend to peter out before they get to this stage.

Interruptions are affected by a variety of factors, including status, gender, familiarity and culture. When there's a status difference, the high-status person is more likely to interrupt the low-status person.[5] On balance men are more likely to interrupt women than vice versa. In this context interruption is often used as a means of exercising control over the conversation and therefore over the other person. That's why men are more likely to interrupt women during the early stages of acquaintance – when they're treating them as women rather than individuals and trying to assert themselves. People have very different attitudes to interruption, and so do different cultures. In Mediterranean societies interruption between close friends is often the norm, and it's not unusual to find situations where several people are speaking at once. This is also true of some Jewish families, where interruption is used as a way of showing solidarity and enthusiasm.[6] To categorize these interruptions as battles for control of the floor is to misunderstand them – they're just a way of getting involved and voicing one's opinions.

Turn-yielding Tells

So far we've looked at what happens when the listener wants to continue in his or her role, as well as the various strategies listeners can use in order to usurp the speaker's role. But what about the speaker? How do speakers hold on to the floor, and which signals do they use when they want to relinquish the floor?

When speakers want to give up the floor they send 'turn-yielding signals' to the listener. As we've already seen, some of these signals are transmitted before the end of the turn, making it possible for listeners to make a 'smooth transition', where the beginning of their turn coincides with the end of the previous speaker's turn. One of the ways that speakers signal the end of their turn is by altering their pattern of gaze – if the speaker is looking elsewhere, he or she may signal that the turn is coming to an end by looking at the listener.[7] This is crucial when there's a group of people – in this situation the person whom the speaker looks at last is most likely to become the next speaker.[8]

The end of a sentence usually marks the 'completion point' of a turn, but because each turn contains so many completed sentences this in itself is not enough to show when the speaker is about to end their turn. Additional signals are required. One of these is a drop in vocal pitch. Hand gestures can also serve as signals that the turn is coming to an end. Occasionally the end of a turn is marked by a particular phrase – one example is the habit that some people have of completing their turn with the expression, 'I don't know' or 'I don't know, really'. Some people shrug their shoulders, which conveys a very similar message at the end of their turn. Starkey Duncan, who has made a detailed study of turn-taking signals, has pointed out that people sometimes produce turn-holding signals at the same time as turn-yielding signals, and that when this happens the presence of a single holding signal is enough to eliminate the effects of any number of yielding signals.[9]

Turn-holding Tells

In order to hold on to the floor the speaker needs to give the impression that he or she has lots more to say. This can be done in several ways. It often involves the eyes. In a two-person conversation the listener usually looks more intently at the speaker than the speaker does at the listener. One reason why speakers are less visually attentive than listeners is because they need to marshal their thoughts while they're talking, and they find it more difficult to do this when they're faced with the distracting sight of the listener. The other reason is that looking serves as a turn-yielding cue. So for the speaker who wants to continue talking it's better not to look at the listener too much – it might give the false impression that the speaker is about to give up the floor.

From the speaker's point of view, the end of each sentence represents a potential 'completion point' which the listener may construe as the end of their turn. To continue talking, the speaker needs to produce additional signals to show that the end of the sentence doesn't mean the end of the turn. The Dutch psychologist, Johanneke Caspers, has discovered that speakers use speech melody to indicate that they want to continue talking. To signal this intention the speaker raises the pitch on the final stressed syllable and maintains the pitch at this level until the next pause.[10]

The speaker can reinforce the impression that he intends to continue talking by producing narratives in the form of stories or jokes. Another way is by enumerating a series of points. For example, in a discussion about religion the speaker is less likely to be interrupted if he tells his female companion that there are five proofs for the existence of God, and then starts to go through them one at a time. She's unlikely to interrupt him while he's talking about, say, the third proof of God, because she knows that there are still two more proofs to come. A similar floor-holding technique is found in the use of expressions like 'and', 'also', 'moreover' and 'in addition' – all these speech 'connectives' inform the listener that the speaker has more to say.

The hands are sometimes used for the same purpose. As we'll see in the chapter on *foreign tells*, it's not unusual for Italians to hold the floor by counting with their fingers. Having indicated that he's going to produce a list of points, the speaker either raises or clasps each finger in turn to show where he is in the list of things he's talking about, and therefore how many points he still intends to cover. The advantage of this manual method of enumeration is that the number of issues to be covered is not left behind in something the speaker said earlier – it's crystallized in what the speaker is doing with his hands at that very moment, so it's difficult to ignore. Using the hands in this way also gives the speaker an excuse to keep his hands moving, which is a sure sign that he intends to keep talking.

Speakers also hold the floor by discouraging interruptions and by not succumbing to them when they do occur. They can discourage interruptions by being emphatic, by looking away from the listener, by keeping the hands in motion, by producing lists, and by talking in a way that minimizes the opportunities for listeners to start talking. Speakers who hold strong opinions use a range of 'attempt-suppressing' strategies to prevent listeners taking over from them. One of Margaret Thatcher's favourite emphatic gestures is the 'eye-flash', which she uses to emphasize what she's saying and to demonstrate that she's somebody to be reckoned with.[11] Mick Jagger also uses the eye-flash gesture to underline what he's saying.

When speakers are interrupted, there are several things they can do to hold or retrieve the floor. Talking louder is one option. Another strategy is to use what Albert Scheflen called a 'transfix'.[12] If you watch people in conversation you'll notice that when speakers are interrupted they sometimes continue to hold the posture they were in when they were interrupted. A speaker who had his hand raised at the time will freeze it in mid-air, just as if he were playing a game of 'statues', and will continue to hold that position until he can regain the floor. By keeping his hand in this fixed position, he shows that he has not completed his turn and that he intends to stay that way until the speaking role returns to him. When he realizes that he's not going to get the turn back immediately, he's likely to lower his hand. In that way he can signal that he's abandoning his claim to the speaker role.

Alternatively, speakers can hold the floor by relegating the other person to the listener role and making sure they stay there. We have already seen that one of the things that listeners do spontaneously is produce back-channel. This can take the form of supportive nods, 'uh-huhs' and various remarks that are intended to encourage the speaker while demonstrating that the listener has no desire to take over the role. People who like to hold on to the speaker role instinctively know that the best way to keep the other person in the listener role is to encourage them to produce back-channel. This can be done in two ways. One is by using expressions like 'you see', 'don't you think', 'right?', 'OK' and Frank Bruno's trademark, 'know what I mean?'.[13] These expressions are examples of 'back-calling' because they call on the listener to provide back-channel and therefore push the other person deeper into the role of listener. The other way to elicit back-channel is by rewarding the listener whenever she produces back-channel. If the speaker smiles or looks affectionately at the listener every time she says 'uh-huh', it shouldn't be long before the listener is producing more back-channel, and in the process excluding herself from taking over the role of speaker.

An expression like 'you know what I mean' can serve as an instance of back-calling, especially when it has a rising, interrogative contour. But the same expression can also serve as a 'comprehension marker' or an 'agreement marker' – in other words, as a declarative statement that summarizes the presumed understanding or agreement between the speaker and listener. When the speaker says, 'you know what I mean', he isn't necessarily asking the listener to provide back-channel; he may simply be trying to get the listener to accept his point of view.

Some speakers try to do all the talking and to ensure that they have the listener's undivided attention. When speakers defend their role aggressively, listeners are inclined to respond by orienting their body away, averting their gaze and generally looking for an opportunity to escape. This is an inversion of the normal state of affairs, where the listener pays more attention to the speaker than the speaker does to the listener. A listener who's retreating in this way does not represent a threat to the talkative speaker because she's not after the speaker role. However, in order to secure his occupancy of the speaker role, the speaker sometimes needs to make sure that the listener remains in hers. Sometimes this can be done physically. For example, during the nineteenth century, the conversational practice of 'button-holding' (or 'button-holing') was widespread – the speaker would grab hold of a button on the listener's coat in order to get his attention and stop him getting away. The English essayist, Charles Lamb, provides a slightly exaggerated description of the practice:

I was going from my house in Enfield to the India-house one morning, and was hurrying, for I was late, when I met Coleridge, on his way to pay me a visit; he was brimful of some new idea and, in spite of my assuring him that time was precious, he drew me within the door of an unoccupied garden by the road-side, and there, sheltered from observation by a hedge of evergreens, he took me by the button of my coat, and closing his eyes commenced an eloquent discourse, waving his right hand gently, as the musical words flowed in an unbroken stream from his lips. I listened entranced; but the striking of the church recalled me to a sense of duty. I saw it was of no use to attempt to break away so, taking advantage of his absorbtion in his subject, I, with my penknife, quietly severed the button from my coat and decamped. Five hours afterwards, in passing the same garden, on my way home, I heard Coleridge's voice, and on looking in, there he was, with eyes closed, – the button in his fingers, – and his right hand gracefully waving, just as when I left him. He had never missed me.[14]

Talk Tells

When we're talking to people, we tend to focus on what they say, rather than how they say it or the precise expressions they use. Careful attention to the actual words that people use can often provide a unique insight into what they are thinking.[15]

◆ **PRONOUNS**. People who frequently use the word 'I' tend to be concerned with themselves, although it does depend on the context in which the word is used. Those who prefer to use 'we' are often trying to avoid making any reference to themselves as individuals. Use of 'we' can also denote an inclusive frame of mind – for example, one man might go on holiday with his wife and then talk about the experience using the word 'I', while another might use the word 'we' to give the impression that he'd been on holiday with his wife, even though he hadn't. Then there's the use of the royal 'we'. A famous and rather revealing example of this occurred after the birth of Margaret Thatcher's grandchild, when she announced to the press, 'We are a grandmother'.

◆ **ATTRACTORS**. People differ widely in terms of how comfortable they are with being the centre of attention. Individuals who like to be in the limelight tend to talk about themselves. They also show a preference for 'dropping', which can take the form of 'name-dropping', 'place-dropping' or 'experience-dropping'. Of these three, name-dropping is the most effective means of increasing one's social status because it exploits the need that all of us have to keep our opinions consistent. For example, if you like person A and you know that person A likes person B, then you are more likely to like B, because it keeps your opinions in line with each other. If you were to decide that you didn't like B your opinions would be unbalanced. The same principle applies with name-dropping. When your work colleague comes over to you and tells you about a famous person whom he's just met, he's not simply passing on a bit of news – he's actually encouraging you to like him more because someone whom you admire appears to like him.

◆ **DEFLECTORS**. People who are shy or who want to avoid the attention of others often resort to linguistic 'deflectors'. In conversation they frequently ask the other person questions about themselves, or they steer the conversation towards topics that are closer to the other person's interests. This automatically shifts the spotlight away from them and reduces the chances that they will have to reveal something about themself. The other deflecting strategy that shy or insecure people use is to talk about impersonal matters. This deflects attention from themselves and the other person, and shifts it towards less threatening topics like architecture or the weather.

◆ **CONTRASTORS**. Words like 'but', 'however' and 'nevertheless' are used to set up a contrast. They're favoured by people who like to point out that things aren't always what they seem, or who want to put forward another point of view. People often set up contrasts by describing one set of affairs, only to negate part of it later on. For example, your friend might tell you that her husband is very loving, but that he does like to have his privacy. By setting up this contrast, your friend is doing several things – she's showing you that she doesn't have a one-dimensional view of her husband, and that she doesn't approve of his desire for privacy.

◆ **SOFTENERS**. People often say things that are designed to soften the impact of what they are going to say next. If you're going to criticize someone, you might say something like, 'I don't want you to take this the wrong way', before you tell them what you think about their table manners, the company they keep, or their inability to arrive on time. Softeners like 'I hope you don't think I'm being rude' and 'I don't want to be critical' are usually two-faced because they provide a cloak under which people can be rude and critical while denying that it's their intention to do so. The sociologist Eugene Weinstein called these linguistic devices 'pre-interpretations', or 'printerps' for short.[16] The potency of the printerp lies in its ability to defuse other people's negative reactions – by telling someone that you don't want them to take your next remark the wrong way you are in effect ruling out their normal response. You're also providing yourself with a linguistic bunker – somewhere you can hide if the other person does take offence and brings out the big guns. Of course it doesn't follow that the person who is offered a printerp automatically accepts it. For example, you might say to your friend, 'I don't want you to take this amiss'.

Before you've had a chance to say anything else, your friend might jump in and say 'But!' This is your friend's way of rejecting the softener, showing that your efforts to prepare the ground for what follows simply haven't worked. Weinstein pointed out that interpretations can also be offered afterwards. A remark like 'That's not what I meant' is a 'post-interpretation', or what he calls a 'posterp' – it's designed to rule out certain interpretations retrospectively. The 'pre-apology', or 'prepalog', also tries to mitigate the effects of what is about to follow. When people say things like 'I hate to tell you this, but . . .' or 'I've never done this before', they are trying to get the other person to lower the standard against which their next remark or next action is likely to be judged. Prepalogs play an important role in requests because they protect the 'face' of everyone concerned. Saying something like 'I don't want to be a nuisance, but . . .' warns the other person that a request is about to be made and that it's not based on any presumption. Because it's polite and submissive, it puts the other person in an awkward position where a refusal is likely to make him or her appear unreasonable.

◆ **HEDGES**. Everyday speech is full of expressions like 'well', 'sort of', 'kind of', 'like' and 'you know'. These conversational fillers are sometimes called 'hedges'.[17] There has been a lot of debate about why people use hedges, and about who uses them most. For example, people often use hedges like 'kind of' (or 'kinda') and 'sort of' (or 'sorta') when they say things such as 'It's kind of cold today'. These hedges indicate imprecision; they show that the speaker should not be held to account for the inaccuracy of the statement, and they suggest that there's something peculiar about whatever they're describing. In the United States most educated people prefer 'kind of' and 'sort of' to 'rather', although 'rather' is often favoured by upper-class people in the north-east – presumably because of its exclusive, English associations. 'Kind of' is generally preferred to 'sort of', but 'sort of' enjoys a lot of popularity in the southern states.[18]

For a long time it was held that the expression 'you know' is a sign of powerlessness, and that is why women use it more often than men. There is now some doubt whether women do use the expression more frequently. It's also becoming clear that 'you know' performs several different functions, depending on where it appears in an utterance, whether it's preceded by a pause, and whether it's spoken with a rising, falling or level intonation. Janet Holmes, who has made a special study of 'you know' in everyday speech, has discovered that women don't use the expression more frequently, but that men and women often use it for quite different purposes – while women use 'you know' to underline their confidence in what they're saying, men use it to express uncertainty and to show that they're being imprecise.[19] 'You know' can be used as a form of 'back-calling' – in other words, as a means of eliciting back-channel and support from the listener, and enabling the speaker to continue. When it's used as a 'verbal filler' it can perform the same task as expressions like 'sort of', 'you see' and 'I mean', which speakers use to keep speaking and to discourage other people from trying to take the floor. When it appears at the end of an utterance, 'you know' can be used to show that the speaker is prepared to relinquish the floor. Equally, the expression can take on a 'search function', helping the speaker to remember the next word or phrase. This is often what's happening when 'you know' is preceded by a pause.

Posture Tells

The way people use their bodies often provides clues to their commitment to a conversation. When two people are talking to each other, they spend some of the time looking at each other and the rest looking elsewhere. People who spend a lot of time looking away give the impression that they are not interested in the other person. Knowing this to be the case, even when we find someone extremely boring we try not to look away too much, for fear that we will reveal our feelings. Instead, we watch the other person politely, creating the false impression that we find them interesting.

The three main sources of information provided by the body are the eyes, the torso and the legs. People are generally aware of what they're doing with their eyes, so gaze doesn't always prove to be a very reliable source of information about individuals' feelings towards each other. Because people are far less aware of where their torso is facing, it's often a much better indicator of their feelings. However, when it comes to gauging someone's commitment to a conversation, the best place to look is at their legs and feet.

There are two reasons for this. One is that people are often quite unaware of these parts of the body. In fact, if we produced a scale of body awareness, we'd find that people are more aware of their front than their back, and most aware of their head and face, followed by their arms, hands and torso, and least aware of their legs and feet. The second reason why the legs are especially informative is that they are associated with primitive impulses of flight. When people feel threatened they react either by defending themselves or by trying to escape. In the process of preparing to escape they often produce intention movements that give rise to various postures.[20] Because these are outside conscious control they reveal people's true feelings about the person they're talking to.

◆ **THE PARALLEL STANCE**. Here the legs are straight and parallel, so that the feet are planted close together and the weight of the body is evenly distributed between them. People who adopt the parallel stance are usually being non-committal – they're neither showing that they intend to go nor that they wish to stay.

◆

THE STRADDLE STANCE. Again the legs are straight, but this time the feet are spread apart. As we saw earlier, the straddle stance is typically a posture of dominance because it widens the body, takes up more space and surreptitiously presents the genitals. But because the feet are set apart, the straddle stance is also a posture of immovability – it shows that the person does not intend to go. If you watch a group of young men standing in a circle – say, in a sports club after a match – you'll often find them adopting the straddle stance. This posture is an expression of their solidarity. By standing with their legs apart they're showing that they're macho *and* that they have no intention of leaving.

◆　**THE SCISSORS STANCE**. In the scissors stance the legs are crossed, just as if they were the blades of a pair of scissors. This posture can be performed with both legs straight (the 'scissors stance') or with one leg bent across or behind the other (the 'bent blade stance'). The scissors stance is the classic posture of immobility. It's a perfect example of an 'unintention display' because it shows that the person is committed to the conversation and has no intention of leaving. Because it is completely devoid of any suggestion of impatience, the scissor stance also comes across as a gesture of submissiveness.

◆ **THE BUTTRESS STANCE.** In the buttress stance most of the body's weight is on the 'support' leg, while the other leg acts as a buttress – rather like a flying buttress on a cathedral. In this posture the support leg is straight and the buttress leg is either straight or bent – typically it's bent at the knee and the foot is positioned so that it's pointing away. This standing posture enjoyed enormous popularity as a form of male display from the Middle Ages until the middle of the nineteenth century – in fact from the appearance of men's hose until the disappearance of tight breeches. It enabled men to 'show the leg' and to assume a posture that distinguished them from the common classes.[21] Nowadays the buttress stance pretends to be a convenient way of resting one leg while the other supports the body. What it really shows, however, is that the person wants to leave. That's because of its close similarity to the act of walking. When someone starts to walk away they automatically transfer the weight of their body on to one leg so that the other leg is free to make a step. That's very similar to what happens in the buttress stance, where most of the body weight is supported by one leg. Although the other leg doesn't actually take a step, the fact that it could do so shows that the buttress stance is really a disguised intention movement to depart. This is especially true when someone repeatedly shifts his or her weight from one foot to the other. When you see someone with the buttress stance it's worth looking at where the toe of their buttress foot is pointing because it often shows what they're thinking. Sometimes the foot is pointing at someone who the person is secretly thinking about; most of the time, however, you'll find that it's pointing in the direction where they're hoping to make their escape.

One of the lessons we learn from watching conversations is how skilled people are at synchronizing their turns and timing their interjections and interruptions down to a few milliseconds. In spite of our remarkable talent for co-ordinating conversations and knowing what to say to each other, we have very little conscious awareness of the principles on which our expertise is based. Next time you get a chance, ask someone whose conversation you've just witnessed what they've been doing, and see what they say. You might find that they can offer you a fairly detailed account of who said what to whom. But they won't be able to tell you how they oriented towards the other person, how they used their hands and eyes to hold the floor, or how they managed to ward off several attempted interruptions. Most of us are like this. In spite of our enormous talent as conversationalists, we're remarkably ignorant of the *tells* that we produce and those that we respond to. Listening to other people's conversations and watching them more closely won't necessarily make us more interesting conversationalists. But it will give us a much better understanding of the way that people try to control the floor and attempt to influence each other.

5. Political Tells

Politics is all about appearances – it's as important for politicians to convince other people that they have certain principles as it is to conceal the fact that they are prepared to abandon these principles in favour of power, money or fame. In public polls about the integrity of different professions, politicians regularly appear near the bottom of the league table, usually just above second-hand car salesmen. This reflects the widespread public distrust of politicians, and the recognition that what they pretend to do and what they actually do, are very different things. Politicians have long recognized this two-faced feature of politics. In many cases it seems to be what attracted them to the profession in the first place.

Health Tells

Although politicians come in all shapes and sizes, some aspects of appearance are more conducive to success than others. Height seems to be a significant factor – especially when you consider that only three of the past US presidents were shorter than the national average for their period. Abraham Lincoln, for example, was a big person in more ways than one, measuring in at 6 feet 4 inches. Of course there have been more diminutive, and no less effective, heads of state – like Mussolini and Haile Selassie – but they made up for their lack of height in other ways, and where possible concealed it. Mussolini made himself look taller by standing on a box when he addressed the crowds from his balcony. Whenever Haile Selassie sat on the imperial throne a pile of cushions would be placed under his feet so he could avoid the indignity of having his feet dangling in mid-air. It's widely assumed that Napoleon was also short – we sometimes refer to someone who's short and overbearing as having a 'Napoleonic complex' – but there's no evidence to support this notion. In fact Napoleon was about 5 feet 6 inches, which was the average height of a Frenchman in his day. It's possible that he simply looked short beside the grenadiers of his Imperial Guard, who were specially selected for their height, and that's why we still think of him as unusually short.

It's essential for political leaders to look fit because people unconsciously associate the health of the body politic with the health of their head of state. That's why President Franklin D. Roosevelt, who'd had polio, tried to hide both his physical disability and the fact that he spent so much time in a wheelchair. It's why George W. Bush goes jogging in public, why Bill Clinton did the same when he was in office, why George Bush Sr played tennis, why Ronald Reagan made it known that he pressed weights, and why Richard Nixon squeezed all the publicity he could out of his early days as a football player. There are even photographs of the young Nixon playing American football without a helmet – a practice which, his critics reckoned, explained some of his peculiar political decisions in later life. John F. Kennedy and Bobby Kennedy were brought up in a family that believed in the virtues of team games, although JFK found it difficult to take part after he'd injured his back during the Second World War. Once, when he was addressing a group of sports coaches, Bobby Kennedy announced that, 'Except for war, there is nothing in American life – nothing – which trains a boy better for life than football.'

Symbolically, the fitness of the US President is very important. One need only think of the time when President Jimmy Carter went jogging with his aides and collapsed from exhaustion. The famous photograph of Carter, with his legs buckled underneath him and a vacant look on his face, sent a reverberating shudder round the country. It was this revelation of his vulnerability, coupled with the failed attempt to rescue the US hostages in Iran, which led to the freefall in Carter's popularity, and to his eventual defeat by Ronald Reagan. Photographs, and their ability to engrave an image on people's minds, play a critical role in the public image of politicians. For example, when George W. Bush nearly choked on a pretzel it was fairly easy to dismiss the incident as a joke. However, had a photographer been present to record the event, we might have been exposed to a very undignified spectacle (definitely not what one expects from the leader of the western world!) and Bush's reputation could have been irreparably damaged.

Hair Tells

One of the features that helps to create an impression of youthful vigour in a politician is a full head of hair. A few years ago, Neil Kinnock, the former leader of the Labour Party, who has hardly any hair, wrote a teasing letter to William Hague, the then leader of the Conservative Party, to warn him that his lack of hair was likely to disqualify him from ever becoming Prime Minister. Several months later the Conservative Party was defeated at the polls and Hague was forced to resign, only to be replaced by Iain Duncan Smith, a man with even less hair than Hague. If 'Kinnock's Curse' works, the Conservatives are likely to remain the party of opposition until they elect a leader with a full head of hair.

Because babies often don't have any hair on their head and people lose their hair as they get older, baldness can be a sign of extreme youth as well as age. In Hague's case the lack of hair, coupled with his baby-like features, made him look too young. It gave the impression that he was unprepared for a life in politics. All things being equal – which of course they never are in politics – it's an advantage for politicians to have a full head of hair and to look youthful and vigorous. Because they are associated with age and maturity, beards don't offer politicians any special advantage, unless – as in the case of Fidel Castro – the beard is being used to support an image of the politician as a revolutionary. When the CIA was thinking of ways of removing Castro during the 1960s, they came up with the idea of developing a depilatory lotion which, when applied to Castro's chin, would completely remove his beard and expose the unknown face beneath.

Although they never pursued the idea, they realized, quite correctly, that without his beard Castro would have been unrecognizable.

Walking Tells

Politicians also try to create an impression of youthful vigour through their postures and movements. Interestingly, posture provides less opportunity to convey an image of strength, largely because it's easier to fake. That's why politicians put so much effort into the way they move their head, arms and hands, and the way they walk.

The way an animal moves provides a very clear picture of its strength, agility and determination, and it's the same with politicians. John F. Kennedy was the first President of the television age, and he used it to full advantage. During the famous Kennedy–Nixon debates in 1960, people who had listened to the first debate on radio put Nixon ahead. However, those who had watched the debate on television put Kennedy ahead of Nixon, and as things worked out, actually offered a more accurate prediction of the final result. It is television's capacity to capture those rather primitive aspects of demeanour – to put appearances on a par with substance – that helped Kennedy to get elected, and which has made or broken politicians ever since.

How politicians walk sends very strong messages about what they're like – or rather, how they want to be seen by others. These messages are sometimes conveyed by walking speed – for example, whenever Prime Minister Harold Wilson boarded an aeroplane he made a habit of running up the stairs so that everyone thought he was fit. But it was Ronald Reagan who managed to transform walking into a form of art. If you ever watched him closely you'll have noticed that he moved in a way that conveyed an impression of weighty momentum – and, by suggestion, of political substance as well. This was partly achieved by his resolute stride – making it look as though his aides were struggling to keep up with him – and partly by the vigorous way in which he moved his arms.

When people walk, their arms swing through an arc in the sagittal plane (i.e. the plane that's in line with the movement of their body through space). The full extent of the arc, forward and back, provides an index of vigour, because young people tend to swing their arms higher at the front and further up at the back, partly because they move faster than older people. Swinging the arms *across* the body also helps to create an impression of masculine strength.

There are two factors at work here – one being the difference between men and women, and the other being the exaggerated effect of body-building on gait style. When men and women stand upright, there's a tendency for men's arms to rotate slightly inwards (what physiologists call 'pronation') and for women's arms to rotate slightly outwards (what physiologists call 'supination'). This sex difference is partly due to the fact that women can bend their arms further back at the elbow than men. This is called the 'carrying angle' and it's been explained as resulting from the fact that women have wider hips than men and spend more time carrying babies.

Because women have a greater carrying angle than men, their arms swing further on the back-swing than men's. In order to distinguish themselves from women, and to emphasize their masculinity, men use more upswing than back-swing. The other reason why men show more pronation in their arms is that the *latissimus dorsi* muscles under their arms are more developed. This has the effect of moving their shoulders forward and rotating the arms inwards. This effect is very noticeable in body-builders. Because body-builders have over-developed *latissimus dorsi* and deltoid muscles, their arms are pronated more than most, and the gap between their arms and chest is accentuated, giving them a more simian, ape-like appearance. Also, because their thighs are over-developed, body-builders tend to have a more rolling gait, swinging their legs outwards as they move forward.

It's often said that a picture is worth a thousand words. It's also true that, in politics, a moving image is worth a thousand pictures – especially when it comes to walking style. News footage of Ronald Reagan striding through the White House or across the lawn gave the impression of a happy, energetic young man who was totally in control. Reagan created this impression by subtly incorporating features of the body-builder's gait into his walking style, by swinging his arms across his body and by rotating his hands to the point where they almost faced backwards. At the same time, by keeping his hands open and relaxed he increased their apparent size, eliminated any suggestion of latent anxiety, and created a subliminal image of someone who was ready to reach for his gun.

While Reagan was a consummate political performer – possibly the best that American politics has ever seen – there's no evidence that he was interested in what other people's behaviour revealed about their personality or their motives. He was a great believer, however, in the art of divination with jellybeans. He once famously remarked that 'you can tell a lot about a fellow's character by his way of eating jellybeans' – for example, does someone show himself to be a creature of habit by picking out just one colour, or does he reveal his impulsiveness and lack of self-consciousness by grabbing a whole handful. In more ways than one, Reagan's presidency was a 'jellybean presidency'. A large jar of jellybeans always presided over the important meetings that he held in the White House, and at the inaugural gala in 1981 it's reported that some 40 million jellybeans were consumed!

In a recent survey in America Ronald Reagan was voted the third-greatest US President of all time, behind George Washington and Abraham Lincoln.[1] The result of this poll surprised many political pundits because Reagan didn't produce any impressive legislation or particularly in-spiring speeches, and he'd been involved in the Contra scandal. However, pundits often overlook the fact that politicians are judged by their demeanour as much as by their policies.[2] Little things, like the way politicians walk or smile, can have a far greater impact on how they are remembered than all their political achievements and failures. In the end, Reagan's blunders, his political gaffes, his ignorance and his somnolent attitude to the office of President – all these things were forgiven because he was able to produce the right *tells*.

During his presidency Clinton also adopted a macho walking style, and George W. Bush has followed in his footsteps. Indeed, George W. Bush is probably the fittest US American President there's ever been. He runs a seven-minute mile, which puts him in the first or second percentile in the fitness rankings for men of his age. You can see that Bush is fit from his build and from the way he walks, although there's a strong suggestion of artifice in his gait because he doesn't have the muscles to warrant the body-builder's lope that he's cultivated. Nevertheless, Bush's walking style sends a very clear signal of masculinity to the electorate. It can also unnerve people who meet him. This happened when Prime Minister Tony Blair met President Bush at Camp David in 2002. The television news footage showed the two leaders walking together, Bush casually dressed in a leather bomber jacket, and Blair in an open-necked shirt. Bush is striding presidentially, with his arms pronated and extended away from his body, and his hands relaxed and facing backwards – just like a body-builder. Not to be outdone, but not wanting to mimic his host, Blair strolls along with his hands casually tucked into his trouser pockets – something he never does in public! Here Bush has clearly upped the ante in the masculinity stakes and Blair has tried to match him. By tucking his hands into his pockets Blair is trying to show that he's also tough and relaxed, but that he's not prepared to play Tonto to Bush's Lone Ranger.

Defensive Tells

In *The Prince* (1532), his famous treatise on politics, Machiavelli observed that 'men rise from one ambition to another; first they secure themselves from attack, and then they attack others'. The threat to politicians can come from other political parties, the electorate or the media. It can also come from their own party; politicians may therefore find it necessary to attack their allies more vigorously than their foes. In order to survive, politicians need to be constantly on their guard against attack. If you watch politicians making political speeches you'll notice that they often gesticulate with their hands while they're talking. Closer inspection of their hand movements shows that when politicians are feeling insecure they often produce hand postures that are symbolically defensive – their hands may, for example, cross their body, or the palms of their hands may be pushed forwards as if they are about to parry an imaginary blow.

The facial expressions of politicians can also be revealing. One of Bill Clinton's trademark *tells* is the 'oxbow mouth', where the lower lip is pushed upwards, shaping the mouth into an inverted 'U'. Bill Clinton uses this expression when he wants to show that he's determined. George W. Bush and Tony Blair use the gesture for the same purpose. While the oxbow mouth provides a display of resolution, the fact that it also involves a tensing of the muscles over the chin shows that it is essentially a defensive gesture – it's how people react when they think someone is about to punch them on the chin, and it's how politicians give themselves away when they're feeling vulnerable. That's why Richard Nixon was photographed so often with an oxbow mouth during the Watergate scandal, and why Bill Clinton produced the same facial expression so often during the Monica Lewinsky affair.

There are five other ways that politicians can defend themselves against attack: (1) by adopting a friendly demeanour; (2) by modulating their voice so that they sound more attractive and less threatening; (3) by producing appeasing signals; (4) by kissing babies; and (5) by creating the impression that they're popular and adorable.

Friendly Tells

Politicians often attempt to ward off aggression by presenting themselves as amiable individuals – in other words, as the kind of people whom nobody would ever have any reason to attack. Ronald Reagan had this down to a T. It was crystallized in his famous remark, during the presidential debate, when he turned to Jimmy Carter and said, 'There you go again' – making it appear that Carter was somehow being unfair by trying to expose him. Reagan's smiles were usually broad and generous. Unlike those of many other politicians, which are restricted to the mouth region, Reagan's smiles frequently extended to the eyes, showing that his feelings of friendship and enjoyment were genuine. The key thing about a genuine smile is that it's much more likely to elicit reciprocated smiling from other people, and this in turn is likely to make them feel more positively disposed to the person who smiled in the first place. Genuine smiles are like magnets – they act at a distance, realigning people's feelings and making them point in the same direction. That's what makes them so effective as a defensive weapon in politics.

Reagan frequently employed an upgraded version of the smile – the 'drop-jaw smile'. It's no accident that Bill Clinton, who was equally concerned with outward appearances, also made a habit of using the drop-jaw smile – possibly even more than Reagan. But what distinguishes the drop-jaw smile from other smiles and makes it so special?

Smiles can include various degrees of mouth opening. At one extreme are cases where the mouth is hardly opened at all. This can produce a 'sealed smile', where the lips remain together during the smile, a 'top-teeth smile', where just the top teeth are seen, or a 'full-teeth smile', where the top and bottom teeth are exposed. On the other hand, in a 'drop-jaw smile' the mouth is opened wide and either the top teeth or both sets of teeth are exposed. The distinctive feature of the drop-jaw smile is that it looks almost exactly like the chimpanzee 'play-face', which is the evolutionary precursor of human laughter. Because they are more dramatic, drop-jaw smiles can be seen at a greater distance. But what really sets drop-jaw smiles apart from other smiles, and recommends them to politicians, is the fact that they *look* like laughter. This affects other people in three ways. Firstly drop-jaw smiles convey a primitive message of playfulness. Secondly, they don't contain any suggestion of appeasement, like other smiles do. Thirdly, because laughter is much more contagious than smiling, drop-jaw smiles are likely to induce the same feelings in other people. A drop-jaw smile therefore makes a politician look playful and unthreatening, and makes other people feel playful and unthreatened.

There are other ways that politicians create an impression of friendliness. One of Reagan's *signature tells* was his 'head-twist' – a wry half-smile accompanied by a cock of the head, which he would use whenever he wanted to appear folksy and familiar. In fact, in terms of both its movement and its message, Reagan's head-twist was very similar to a wink. Like a wink, it was confined to one side of the face. Its message, like that of the wink, was one of complicity – it was a way of making other people feel included. But Reagan's head-twist also had a juvenile, almost rascally, quality to it. It made him look like Huckleberry Finn, or one of those naughty, freckled-faced kids in the matinée movies. The gesture worked because it made Reagan look vulnerable and endearing.

Vocal Tells

Reagan had other endearing tricks up his sleeve. One was his deep voice; another was his breathy way of speaking. Deep voices are associated with dominance, masculinity and concern – all qualities that Reagan managed to project with his voice. 'Breathy' voices are often contrasted with 'tense' voices. In a breathy voice there's a high rate of airflow over the vocal cords, while in a tense voice the rate of airflow is low. As a result, tense voices tend to sound metallic, whereas breathy voices sound relaxed and airy – in fact it's often said that a breathy voice sounds like 'voice mixed with air'. People with breathy voices sound warm, while those with tense voices tend to sound cold.[3] However, breathy voices are acoustically inefficient because they require a lot of effort and because they're more difficult to understand. On the whole, women tend to have more breathy voices than men, which is one of the reasons why they sound more warm and sexy. Women with particularly breathy voices include the Hollywood actress Audrey Hepburn and the British actress Joanna Lumley.

Male politicians who speak with a breathy register don't

necessarily sound more feminine – they just sound warmer. In Reagan's case, however, the story doesn't end there, because he often spoke in a whisper, especially when he was on television. In recent years whispered voices have become very popular, particularly among male movie stars. Whispered speech is, by definition, breathy speech at a lower volume. The attraction of quiet, low-volume speech is that it creates an illusion of physical closeness and psychological intimacy. When Reagan used to deliver his cosy, fireside chats on television all these vocal qualities combined – the depth of his voice making him sound masculine, his breathiness making him sound warm, and the whispered delivery making him appear intimate and friendly.

It's no wonder that other politicians have taken a leaf out of Reagan's book and modified their voice in order to make them sound more attractive. Reagan's old pal Margaret Thatcher, for example, was advised to lower her voice a few octaves so that she would sound softer and more concerned. Similar shifts in vocal register can be heard in other British politicians, some of whom have been coached to lower their voices in order to make them sound less agitated and more human.

Evidence of the advantages offered by a deep voice may be found in a study conducted by Stanford Gregory and Timothy Gallagher, in which they compared the voices of US presidential candidates in eight of the national elections since 1960 (this did not include the last election).[4] The authors examined 19 debates. Using spectral analysis, they measured what's called the 'fundamental frequency' of each candidate's voice, paying special attention to the spectrum below .5 kHz. When they compared each pair of candidates they discovered that in every one of the eight elections the candidate with the deeper voice also got the highest percentage of popular votes! This provides clear proof, if proof is needed, that politics isn't just about principles. Crucially, it's about possessing a voice that sounds convincing and presidential.

Appeasement Tells

One way for politicians to avoid being attacked is to signal that they have no intention of attacking others.[5] Another way is to produce an appeasement display that 'cuts off' other people's aggression. The first strategy can sometimes be seen during Question Time in the House of Commons, when the government of the day and the opposition parties face each other across the large table on which are situated the two dispatch boxes. In the front rows, right in the middle of their party, but on opposite sides of the house, sit the Prime Minister and the Leader of the Opposition – looking for all the world like oriental potentates at the head of their armies, ready to do battle. At Question Time the standard practice is for the Leader of the Opposition to rise to his or her feet, to approach the dispatch box, ask a question, and then sit down. Next, the Prime Minister rises and approaches the dispatch box. He then answers the question (or doesn't answer the question) and sits down. The rules of the house entitle the Leader of the Opposition to ask three questions altogether.

The way that the Prime Minister and the Leader of the Opposition position themselves at the dispatch boxes reflects the temperature of their political exchange. When the exchange is reassuringly polite, each tends to face the other directly while standing at their dispatch box. However, when the debate gets heated, there's a marked tendency for the Prime Minister and the Leader of the Opposition to orient their bodies away from each other. This is 'flanking', and it's found throughout the animal world. As we've seen, when dogs meet in the park for the first time, they usually approach each other side-on, presenting their vulnerable flanks to each other in order to signal that they don't intend to attack. It's exactly the same in the House of Commons. By orienting their bodies away from each other, the Prime Minister and the Leader of the Opposition may appear to be directing their remarks towards their supporters who are located behind them. In fact they are instinctively exposing the undefended sides of their body in order to show that they have no intention of getting into a physical fight – just as dogs behave when they meet in the park.

Baby-kissing Tells

Elections are a time for politicians to run around kissing babies. Sometimes it seems like 'open season' – wherever you look politicians are lifting babies up, hugging them and planting their lips on their poor unsuspecting cheeks. It's generally assumed that politicians kiss babies because they want people to think that they're healthy, nurturing, loving individuals. In fact, baby-kissing is nothing of the sort – it's merely a way for politicians to defend themselves against attack. For example, when a dominant baboon is chasing a subordinate baboon it's not uncommon for the retreating baboon to pick up an infant baboon and to use it as a shield. This has the immediate effect of 'cutting off' the dominant baboon's aggression. It works because baboons, like humans, are programmed not to hurt babies. So when a male politician picks up a baby and holds it aloft, he's not showing how much he loves babies – he's actually using the baby to 'cut off' the aggression that he unconsciously feels the electorate harbours towards him.[6] In other words, he's not saying, 'Look how much I love babies; aren't I a nice guy?' Instead he's saying, 'Look, I'm holding a baby. Don't try to hit me! You might accidentally injure the baby!'

There are some politicians who don't kiss babies, presumably because they don't feel threatened or because they don't feel the need to enlist the kind of protection that a baby affords. Margaret Thatcher was one of these – in fact it's very difficult to find a photograph of her kissing a baby. There was a famous occasion, however, when she was visiting a farm and chose to lift up a baby cow. History does not recall whether she actually kissed the calf, or if she did, where she planted the kiss. President Lyndon B. Johnson, it seems, also preferred to pick up animals rather than babies. On one occasion he grabbed his pet beagle by the ears and lifted the poor dog off the ground. The dog didn't seem terribly concerned, but animal lovers everywhere were incensed. Instead of making LBJ look endearing, it had the opposite effect, and it wasn't long after this event that his popularity started to decline.

Adulation Tells

Another way that politicians can deflect aggression is by making themselves appear popular and adorable. This works on the simple psychological principle that we are more likely to feel positively disposed towards someone if they're popular. Their true qualities aren't that important – what actually shapes our feelings and makes us want to associate with someone is the fact that other people like or admire that person. It's exactly the same with politicians – the more we see them being applauded or adored, the higher they rise in our estimation. Politicians understand this process, and that's one of the reasons why they go to such lengths to surround themselves with admirers.

Basically politicians have three types of admirer – the general public, the party faithful, and the adoring spouse. The most convincing demonstrations of public adulation occur when a politician moves through a crowd of the party faithful who are clamouring to touch him or her. The more dramatically people reach out, the faster the politician moves through the crowd and the more he or she appears to enjoy the experience, the more irresistible, even god-like, the politician appears to be. This kind of adulation is essential to politicians and it can be achieved in several ways. As the sociologist Max Atkinson points out in *Our Masters' Voices*, politicians use a fascinating range of strategies to elicit applause from an audience.[7] One trick is to use 'contrasting pairs', where an undesirable option, for example, is compared to a highly favourable outcome. Another is the 'three-part list', which conveniently provides the audience with clues about when to start applauding. The way that politicians control applause is also critical. For example, a politician who tags a remark on to the end of a punch line once the applause has begun is likely to kill off the applause. On the other hand, politicians who choose their moment carefully, and who use their hands to dampen the applause, are likely to give the impression that they're both modest *and* in control. Ideally, of course, a politician should only attempt to discourage applause when it already shows signs of ending.

In the US it's traditionally been assumed that the task of the First Lady is to stand by her man. For example, Bess Truman, the wife of President Truman, believed that her role in life was to 'sit beside her husband, be silent, and be sure that his hat is straight'. In fact the main responsibility of the First Lady is to elevate the President in the eyes of other people by appearing attentive and impressed. Nancy Reagan played the 'adoring wife' role to perfection. When Ronald spoke in public, she always watched him intently, giving him a doe-eyed, Bambi look, as if she were in the grips of a teenage infatuation. While Nancy's adoration of her husband tended to be almost entirely ocular, as well as rather frozen, Hillary Clinton's support for Bill Clinton was more tactile and affectionate. Cherie Blair also produces a very convincing performance of the adoring wife. By gazing attentively at Tony whenever he speaks, or when he's being applauded at the party conference, and by clutching his hand whenever she gets a chance, she manages to elevate him in our eyes. After all, if she adores Tony Blair so completely, shouldn't we?

There are occasions when the tables are turned, and presidents or prime ministers show how much they adore their wives. However, these occasions are rare, and they're often ironic. When John F. Kennedy and the First Lady

The *Adoring Wife Role*. By hugging her husband in public, Cherie Blair unwittingly makes the Prime Minister appear more appealing and lovable to other people.

made a state visit to France in 1961, Jackie was at the height of her popularity. At a state banquet JFK jokingly remarked that he would be remembered as the man who accompanied Jackie Kennedy to Paris. Psychologists have found that men who are associated with attractive women gain an enormous amount of admiration from other men. By drawing attention to Jackie, and being ironic, JFK was only doing himself a favour.

Most of the adulation aimed at politicians comes from people who can be seen or heard. There are, however, cases where adoring members of the public remain out of sight. If you watched Ronald Reagan or Bill Clinton when they were in office you'll have noticed that they often waved knowingly at individuals in the crowd. Reagan, for example, would sometimes nudge Nancy, point to some-one out of view, wave and give them a huge smile. Some of these people, one suspects, did not actually exist – they were 'phantom friends' whom Reagan would pretend to wave at in order to make himself look amiable and popular. This suspicion is reinforced by the fact that Reagan had very bad eyesight, which made it difficult for him to pick out individuals at a distance.

Offensive Tells

When politicians are not defending themselves against attack, they're usually attacking other people. Their aggressive motives are sometimes concealed in their iconic hand gestures or made explicit in their verbal insults. There are five aggressive activities that politicians mimic when they're feeling aggressive, and each is

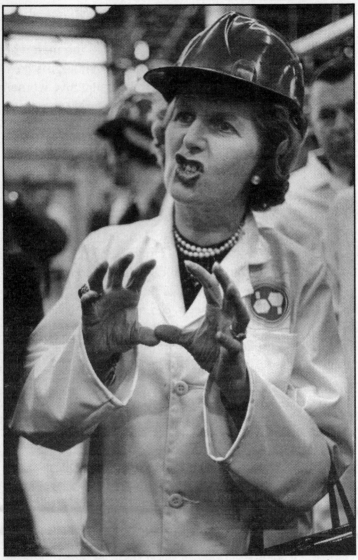

Iconic Hand Gestures. Politicians' intentions towards other people are often revealed in their unconscious movements and gestures – perfectly demonstrated here by Margaret Thatcher.

associated with a different group of hand postures:

◆ **PUNCHING**. When politicians want to make an emphatic point they frequently form their hand into a fist and use it like a club to beat time to what they're saying. Sometimes the closed fist is raised in the air as a salute, at other times it may be slammed down on the lectern as a way of emphasizing a key point, or out of anger or frustration. In its role as a club, the aggressive implications of the fist are obvious – it is being used, symbolically, to crush whatever the speaker feels needs to be destroyed. There are occasions when the hands are used to grab an object which could serve as a symbolic weapon. For example, when Nikita Khrushchev addressed the United Nations in 1960, he got so cross that he took off his shoe and banged it on the lectern!

◆ **PRODDING**. Politicians often use an extended forefinger to make their point or to issue a warning. Sometimes the finger is raised in the air, didactically. At other times it may be used like a dagger or a sword, thrusting downwards or in the direction of the audience or an imaginary adversary.

◆ **GRIPPING**. In order to harm someone it's sometimes necessary to grab hold of them first. When they are making political speeches, politicians often reveal their aggressive feelings towards others by grabbing hold of imaginary people or issues and then shaking or squeezing them.

◆ **SCRATCHING**. The fingernails provide a primitive means

of tearing into other people's flesh. Women sometimes threaten other people, either seriously or playfully, by baring their fingernails. There's a very fine divide between grabbing an imaginary friend and threatening an imaginary friend with one's fingernails – it all comes down to a slight inward curl of the fingers which lines the fingernails up for attack.

◆ **CHOPPING**. As the martial arts have shown, the outer edge of the hand can be used to chop and injure other people. Politicians who want to cut through an issue often use a downward chopping motion of the hand. The Labour politician Tony Benn often does this. John Major also used this gesture when he was Prime Minister: when talking on a sensitive issue he would bring his hand down and to the side in a cutting motion to show that he wished to sweep issues and problems away. Major has always been a keen cricketer – it's possible therefore that what appears to be a dismissive, sweeping action of the hand is really a symbolic cricketing stroke which he uses to knock other people's ideas all the way to the boundary.

Although Major was a consummate politician, he disliked the rough-and-tumble of parliamentary Question Time, especially when he was Prime Minister. This was evident from the 'flight reflex' that he exhibited at the dispatch box. Whenever he rose to answer a question, he would place his notebook on the dispatch box, and then address the house. But a fraction of a second before he'd completed his statement, he would begin to make tiny preparatory movements, like moving his feet or re-arranging his notebook. Sometimes, as he was finishing his statement, he would give the dispatch box a tiny push to propel himself backward. His barely concealed eagerness to return to his seat showed that he was never entirely comfortable with the cut-and-thrust of Question Time. I'm sure he would much rather have been at Lord's, watching the cricket.

Insulting Tells

Party politics is very much like primitive warfare. A set-piece battle between two tribes in New Guinea, for example, often begins with the two warring parties taking up positions on nearby hills, making sure that they're far enough apart to avoid each other's missiles but close enough to be heard by the other side. From their secure positions the warriors then shout boasts and insults at each other. After a while, they descend into the valley, a skirmish takes place, someone is wounded, and the two armies return to their villages to lick their wounds and to talk endlessly about their courageous exploits during the campaign.

Talk, it turns out, is the most important part of primitive warfare. The same is true of politics. In both cases the opposing factions spend a lot of time boasting about themselves and their glorious achievements, and slagging off the other side. Boasts and insults are essential to politics because they provide parties and politicians with a means of enhancing their own reputation and self-esteem, while devastating that of the opposition. Apart from undermining people, insults also serve other valuable psychological functions. One is to enrage the person who's under attack to the point where they engage in a hasty and ill-considered response that makes them look even more stupid. Another function is to increase one's own reputation as the originator of well-aimed, amusing and destructive remarks about other people.

Political insults fall into several categories:

◆ **PARTY INSULTS**. This category of insults is aimed at the opposition, rather than at individual politicians who represent the opposition. Typically they draw attention to the incompetence of the other party, like Winston Churchill's famous remark about the Labour Party: 'They are not fit to manage a whelk stall.' Harold Macmillan's damning dismissal of the Liberal Party also falls into this category: 'As usual the Liberals offer a mixture of sound and original ideas. Unfortunately none of the sound ideas are original and none of the original ideas are sound.'

◆ **COLD INSULTS**. The purpose of these insults is to make someone appear cold and unemotional. Referring to Robert Peel, Benjamin Disraeli said, 'The Right Honourable gentleman is reminiscent of a poker. The only difference is that a poker gives off the occasional signs of warmth.'

◆ **EMASCULATING INSULTS**. These, of course, are designed to undermine someone's masculinity. Prime Minister Lloyd George, for example, once said of Herbert Samuel, the Liberal politician, 'When they circumcised Herbert Samuel they threw away the wrong bit.'

◆ **UNQUALIFIED INSULTS**. These insults create the impression that the person does not have the necessary qualifications to do the job. Winston Churchill, for example, once described Clement Attlee as 'A modest man who has much to be modest about'.

◆ **ANTHROPOMORPHIC INSULTS**. Here the person being insulted is compared to an animal so as to make him or her appear beastly or ineffectual. Picking on him once again, Churchill described Clement Attlee as 'A sheep in sheep's clothing'. On the same ovine theme, Denis Healey once said of Sir Geoffrey Howe: 'Being attacked by him is like being savaged by a dead sheep.'

◆ **UNPRINCIPLED INSULTS**. Here the object of the insult is represented as someone who pretends to have principles but in fact doesn't have any at all. Adlai Stevenson, for example, described Richard Nixon as 'the kind of politician who would cut down a redwood tree and then mount the stump to make a speech for conservation.'

◆ **PHONEY INSULTS**. These insults draw attention to the deceitful and phoney aspects of someone's character. Gerald Ford, for example, once said, 'Ronald Reagan doesn't dye his hair; he's just prematurely orange.'

◆ **STUPIDITY INSULTS**. Here the person is represented as unintelligent. Lyndon Baines Johnson's famous remark about Gerald Ford is a good example: 'He is so dumb he can't fart and chew gum at the same time.'

Insults are the Exocets of political weapons. If the target is right and they're carefully aimed, they can have a devastating effect on how a politician is perceived. In some cases the damage can be permanent. The British now find it extremely difficult to talk about Geoffrey Howe without thinking of a dead sheep, while in America it's almost impossible to have a conversation about Gerald Ford without someone mentioning chewing gum or farting.

Interview Tells

There are several ways that political interviews are supposed to differ from ordinary conversations. Typically the interviewer should make the first move, set the agenda, ask the questions, and have the last word. The politician, on the other hand, is expected to follow the interviewer's lead, to answer the questions without waffling, and not to ask the interviewer questions unless clarification is needed. This is the way political interviews are supposed to be conducted. In practice, however, they often turn out to be quite different.

Interviewers ask politicians two types of question – 'closed questions', which require a 'yes' or 'no' answer, and 'open questions', which allow the politician to give an answer without saying 'yes' or 'no'. Regardless of which type of question they pose, interviewers are always trying to get politicians to give 'direct' answers – that is, responses that address the question, rather than 'indirect' answers which don't address the question. In the early 1990s, Sandra Harris studied political interviews in Britain and discovered that 'direct' answers featured in only 40 per cent of politicians' responses.[8] In other words, 60 per cent of their responses did not address the interviewers' questions.

This tendency to dodge the question was most marked with closed questions, which are by far the most common type of question that interviewers put to politicians. Here she found that only 20 per cent of closed questions elicited either a 'yes' or 'no' answer. When she compared political interviews with other types of interview she found that the percentages of indirect answers were much lower in other types of interview, ranging from 4 per cent for medical interviews to 15 per cent for magistrates' interviews – compared with 60 per cent for politicians! The fact that politicians don't provide straight answers to straight questions is a major reason why the public regards them as evasive. They're also seen as underhand and slimy because of the way they answer questions, or don't answer them. Research by Peter Bull and his colleagues at York University shows that there are several ways that politicians dodge the question.[9] They include the following:

◆   **MAKING A POLITICAL POINT**. In the vast majority of cases where politicians fail to answer the question, it's because they're using the opportunity to make a political point that is not directly relevant to the question. This suggests that politicians and interviewers see political interviews quite differently – while the interviewer is trying to get the politician to answer the question, the politician is using the question as a soapbox from which to make his or her views known to the public. It also shows how politicians work to their own agenda, deciding in advance what they're going to say in an interview, regardless of what questions they're asked.

◆ **GOING ON THE ATTACK**. This is the next most common response. Politicians often dislike the questions they're asked. Sometimes it's because they feel the question is biased or intended to make them look silly; at other times it's because they think the question is factually incorrect or just plain objectionable. Faced with a nasty question, politicians can either play by the rules and provide something that looks like an answer, or else they can attack the question and say what they dislike about it. Attacking the question is actually a fairly common response and it offers two clear advantages – it puts the spotlight back on the interviewer and helps to unnerve the interviewer and discourage him or her from asking difficult questions later on. It's even more intimidating when the politician attacks the interviewer by suggesting that he or she is uninformed, biased or unreasonable. Politicians differ in their preferences for these two strategies. For example, when she was Prime Minister, Margaret Thatcher was more likely to attack the interviewer, whereas Neil Kinnock, the Leader of the Opposition, was more likely to attack the question.

◆ **GIVING HALF AN ANSWER**. The next most common way of dodging a question is to offer an incomplete answer. This happens when a politician responds to a question that has several parts, or deals with only part of a question, or starts to answer the question but gets distracted and fails to provide a full answer.

◆ **REFUSING TO ANSWER**. Politicians often refuse to answer questions when it's clearly legitimate for them not to give an answer – for example, when they're asked to divulge confidential information or to make predictions. In these cases they can get away by appealing to a higher principle, such as the need to keep a secret or be discreet.

◆ **IGNORING THE QUESTION**. This often happens when the interviewer interrupts the politician to ask another question. Instead of answering the new question, the politician simply continues to answer the original question, behaving as if the new question had never been asked.

◆ **REPEATING THE ANSWER**. Politicians may refuse to answer a question, insisting that they have already answered it. This also conveys other messages – it suggests, for example, that the politician is fully aware of what's happening, and that he or she is not prepared to play along with the interviewer. There are, however, cases where the politician will use the same form of words in response to apparently different questions. This is intended to make the politician look confident, and the interviewer incompetent.

There are several reasons why politicians' answers are equivocal and vague. For a start, using imprecise language allows politicians to give answers that don't offend anybody. When the electorate is divided on a controversial issue it's obviously not in the politician's interests to give an answer that's likely to alienate large numbers of people

– it's far better to say nothing on the subject, while appearing to voice an opinion, or to answer a different question altogether.

Another reason why politicians equivocate so much is that they don't like being constrained or bossed about by interviewers. When she was Prime Minister, Margaret Thatcher was extremely evasive in her answers during political interviews – much more so, in fact, than Neil Kinnock, the Leader of the Opposition. A big motive for her equivocation, one suspects, was the desire to show that she was her own man, and that she was quite capable of setting the agenda for the interview. However, when it came to closed questions – that is, questions that require a 'yes' or 'no' answer – she gave many more direct answers than Neil Kinnock. Far from being inconsistent, these two findings show how much Margaret Thatcher liked to play the dominant role – on open questions she would equivocate in order to show who was boss, while on closed questions she would give direct answers to show that she was supremely confident and wasn't worried about alienating people who disagreed with her.[10]

In TV interviews the spotlight is very much on the politician. After all, it's the politician who does most of the talking and who's on the screen most of the time. Because interviewers play a supporting role, it's natural to assume that they have less responsibility for what happens during the interview, or that the interplay between interviewer and politician isn't important. However, this interplay *is* extremely important. It was very evident in the interviews that took place when Margaret Thatcher was in power. It was not unusual, for example, for interviewers to interrupt Margaret Thatcher – in fact she was interrupted more often than any of the other political leaders at the time. At first it was assumed that this might have had something to do with the fact that she was a woman, while all the interviewers and other political leaders were men. This would have been consistent with the general finding that men interrupt women more often than they do other men, and more often than women interrupt men or other women. It was even suggested that Margaret Thatcher was being interrupted more often because she was inadvertently giving off more 'turn-yielding' signals, which misled interviewers into thinking that she was about to stop talking.[11]

The fact that Margaret Thatcher tended to give long, rambling answers may also explain why she was interrupted so often; as she began to drift away from the question, interviewers would ask another question in order to try and bring her back to their agenda. What's interesting about these cases of interruption is that Margaret Thatcher hardly ever gave up the floor – when she was interrupted by the interviewer she simply kept on talking as though nothing had happened. This reinforced her image as a tough politician and exasperated the interviewers who had to deal with her.

In the early days of television, political interviews were modelled on the cosy exchanges that took place in gentlemen's clubs. In 1951, for example, when Leslie Mitchell interviewed the Prime Minister, Anthony Eden, he began by saying, 'Well now, Mr Eden, with your very considerable experience in foreign affairs, it's quite obvious that I should start by asking you something about the international situation today – or perhaps you would prefer to talk about home? Which is it to be?' On that occasion Eden chose to talk about home affairs.

Political interviews in Britain remained obsequious until the arrival of Reginald Bosanquet, who is credited with producing the first aggressive interruption of a British politician, although by today's standards it was a model of reticence. It happened in 1957 when Bosanquet interviewed Harold Macmillan. 'Sir', he interjected, 'as time is short could we question you on a domestic matter which I think is uppermost in our minds at the moment?' 'If you must', replied Macmillan.

Gone are the days when interviewers apologized for interrupting, or allowed politicians to set the agenda for the interview. Nowadays interviewers have much more power and they are prepared to be combative. Politicians are now understandably nervous about interviewers, especially when, like the BBC's Jeremy Paxman, they are reputed to eat politicians for breakfast. Paxman is best remembered for a television interview in which he asked Michael Howard, the then Home Secretary, whether he had threatened to overrule the director of the Prison Service. The Home Secretary gave an evasive answer, so Paxman kept repeating the same question until he got a satisfactory answer. Indeed, he asked the same question a total of fourteen times!

For a combative interview to take place it's necessary for both parties to play by the rules. There are occasions when both parties get hot under the collar – the altercation in 1988 between Vice President George Bush and Dan Rather, the CBS anchor, over the Iran–Contra affair is one example – and there are times when the interviewee decides that enough is enough and leaves.[12] This has happened several times with politicians. In 1982, when Robin Day was interviewing John Nott, the Defence Secretary, he referred to him as a 'here-today-gone-tomorrow politician'. Nott stood up and left the room. Henry Kissinger also walked out on Jeremy Paxman when Paxman asked him, quite rightly, whether he felt like a fraud accepting the Nobel Peace Prize.

Because interviewers now potentially wield more power than politicians, politicians need to find ways of ensuring that interviewers don't give them a tough time. One way to do this is for politicians to stamp their authority on the interview by showing that they are not prepared to be interrupted. Another is to be emphatic about their opinions. George W. Bush, for example, frequently uses the expression, 'make no mistake about it', to press home his point of view. One of his *signature tells* is a 'micro-nod', a barely perceptible dip of the head, which he tags on to the end of a statement, like a corporeal full stop – as if to say, 'There you are, I've told you now. There's nothing more to be said on the subject!' One of Margaret Thatcher's *signature tells* is the 'eye-flash'. Whenever she wants to emphasize a statement and make it appear incontrovertible, she momentarily enlarges her eyes, using them at the end of her utterance to create a pair of ocular exclamation marks. This is quite different from what happens in the 'eye-puff', where the eyes are opened wide in order to create an impression of childish attentiveness.

Another option available to politicians is to intimidate the interviewer. This can be done by undermining the interviewer, attacking the question, and suggesting that the interviewer is misinformed or biased – in short, by breaking the interviewer's rhythm and undermining his or her confidence. One way to do this is by producing lots of 'negative back-channel signals'. These are the discouraging signals that people use when they're in the listener role – things like puzzled expressions, gaze aversion, and preparatory speech movements. Listeners use these signals to indicate that the speaker isn't making sense, that they don't agree, and that they'd like to take over the speaker role as soon as possible. They are the opposite of 'back-channel signals'. Back-channel signals are the encouraging signals – such as nods and 'uh-huh' sounds – that listeners produce when they want to show the speaker that they understand and agree with what he or she is saying, and that they have no intention of taking over the speaker role in the conversation. When George W. Bush is being asked awkward questions, he often resorts to 'negative back-channel' in order to throw the interviewer off balance. He does this by looking around, by smiling artificially, and by giving the impression that he's about to start speaking. Negative back-channel can certainly help politicians to keep difficult interviewers at bay. After all, it's what interviewers use when they want to give politicians a tough time.

Because politics relies so heavily on appearances it appeals to people who are fascinated by human behaviour. So does its reliance on subterfuge and pretence. Because politicians spend so much time pretending to be something they're not, there's a much greater chance that they will inadvertently reveal their true feelings, or their real intentions, in what they do. The high drama of politics, the way that politicians abandon their colleagues, cut secret deals, switch allegiances, create smokescreens, cover their backsides, deflect blame and take credit where it's not due – all these things make the appearance of *tells* all the more likely.

6. Greeting Tells

Greetings perform several important tasks. First of all they provide people with an opportunity to acknowledge each other and to enter into conversation. Secondly they give people a chance to demonstrate that they can be relied upon to abide by the wider conventions of society, and thirdly they allow them to reaffirm or work out what kind of relationship they're going to have with each other. Greeting rituals differ enormously from one culture to the next. However, within a community they tend to follow a fairly stereotyped pattern – that way the participants know what's expected of them and what the other person is likely to do next. In spite of this, there is always enough variation between greetings to allow inferences to be drawn about the participants. In fact, by watching how people greet each other it's often possible to see what kind of people they are and what their attitudes are to each other.

Transition Tells

Most greetings consist of three phases – a 'recognition phase', where the participants notice each other and signal their mutual recognition, an 'approach phase', where they move towards each other, and a 'meeting phase', where they shake hands, embrace, or whatever.[1] When a large distance separates people to begin with, and there are others around, it can take quite a while for them to get through all these phases. On the other hand, when they start off close to each other, there's a tendency for the approach phase to disappear and for the other phases to be compressed into one.

The way that people behave during each phase can be very revealing. In western society, the recognition phase can take several forms, depending on how well the participants know each other and the level of intimacy they are trying to achieve. Basically there are two clusters of distance signals. One consists of 'polite' signals, like raising the eyebrows, smiling with the lips together, presenting the palm of the hand, and nodding or dipping the head. The other cluster consists of 'enthusiastic' signals, like waving one or both arms, open-mouthed smiles, laughter, and loud calls to the other person. In order to underline their feelings of exhilaration, people often widen their eyes and drop their jaw, simulating the facial expression of surprise. As a rule, people who are acquainted tend to exchange polite recognition signals, whereas people who know each other well are more likely to exchange enthusiastic recognition signals, especially when they haven't seen each other for some time. However, because recognition signals imply equality, they are seldom used between people of different status.

Similar distinctions are noticeable during the approach phase. Polite distance signals, for example, are often followed by a detached approach, with one or both parties walking slowly towards the other. This detachment can often be seen in the way that people avert their gaze, cross their arms over their body, or engage in forms of displacement activity, like touching their hair or rearranging their clothes, as they walk towards each other. Enthusiastic distance displays, on the other hand, are usually followed by a hurried approach, where the attention of both parties remains fixed on the other person, and where there are preparatory signals which indicate whether the parties are lining up to embrace or kiss each other or shake hands.

Normally there's no doubt about what's going to happen when two people reach each other, simply because of the situation, the nature of their relationship, or the amount of time they've been apart. But there are occasions when it's not entirely clear how people are going to greet each other. Most of the time, however, people use the approach phase to show whether they intend to hug, kiss or shake hands. You only need to stand in the arrivals lounge of an international airport to see how differently people behave, depending on how they're about to greet each other – the approach phase that precedes a hug or a kiss is usually quite different from one that occurs before a handshake. When people do have a problem deciding what to do, it's usually about whether they should shake hands or greet the other person verbally.

Greeting rituals can be divided into two types – greetings of respect, which are designed to emphasize differences in power, and greetings of solidarity, which convey messages of friendship and equality. In medieval times, men and women would pay homage to their over-lord by kneeling on one knee. Later on the bow was introduced for men. This was done by drawing back the right leg so that both knees were bent, and by leaning forward. Removing or doffing the hat was also part of the greeting ritual and this was done either before or during the act of bowing. The corresponding salutation for women at the time was the curtsy, which involved genuflecting both knees and lowering the body.[2] All these greetings of respect involved body lowering. They were also distinguished by asymmetry, which meant that the subordinate person greeted the superior while the superior effectively did nothing.

Greetings of solidarity, on the other hand, were symmetrical – they consisted of a mutual kiss, and some-times an embrace. Kissing was used as a gesture of affection as well as a sign of goodwill between men and women, and between members of the same sex. Although the handshake was around at the time it was not used as a greeting. Instead it was employed to seal agreements. Writing during the seventeenth century John Bulwer described how the handshake was used to secure financial agreements and how the language of the handshake differed from one London market to another. The 'fish dialect of Billingsgate', he tells us, was very different from the 'Horse Rhetorique of Smithfield'.[3] It was only much later, towards the end of the Victorian era, that the handshake was employed as a greeting of solidarity.

Handshake Tells

Do handshakes make a difference? The answer is yes, they do. This is illustrated by a rather clever experiment conducted by Allen Konopacki in the US, where a 25-cent coin was left in a public telephone booth.[4] Most of the strangers who used the booth immediately afterwards picked the coin up and put it in their pocket. As they were emerging from the booth a student would approach these people and ask them whether they had seen his quarter. Over 50 per cent lied and said that they hadn't seen the coin. In the second half of the experiment the student greeted each person emerging from the booth, introduced himself, shook their hand, and then asked whether they had seen the quarter. Now, only 24 per cent of the people who had pocketed the coin lied. In this situation shaking people's hands clearly made a difference because it created a bond of solidarity that made it much more difficult for people to lie.

One of the things that recommends the handshake as a greeting of solidarity is its symmetry – the fact that both people perform the same action. However, when we look more closely at how people actually shake hands, we find that they often perform slightly different actions, and that these serve as an important source of information about the kinds of people they are and how they feel about each other.[5] These *handshake tells* aren't always apparent to people who aren't involved in the handshake. In some cases they're not even evident to the other person who's involved in the handshake.

Handshakes can vary according to who initiates them, how the hand is presented, how many pumps they include, who controls the handshake, whether they are accompanied by a smile, what people say when they greet each other, and so on. The grip itself can vary according to how tightly or limply the hand is held, the temperature of the hand, how dry or damp it feels, its position in relation to the other person's hand, and what the rest of the body is doing. Basically, there are eight types of handshake:

◆ **THE BONECRUSHER**. One of the cardinal rules of handshaking is that the grip should be neither too tight nor too limp, and that each person should adjust the pressure of their grip to that of the other person. There are people who violate these requirements by squeezing the other person's hand. Sometimes this is done unwittingly. Most of the time, however, it's done as a show of strength or a way of putting the other person in their place. People who want to show others that they are not as weak and ineffectual as they look often use the bonecrusher as a form of compensation.

◆ **THE LIMP HANDSHAKE**. A limp handshake occurs when someone offers a hand that is totally relaxed. It doesn't exert any pressure on the other person's hand, and it doesn't contribute to the mutual production of the handshake. A person who offers a limp handshake is someone who, in more senses than one, doesn't connect with the other person. Like their hand, they remain passive and detached – they're simply not focused on the person they're greeting. This often happens with people who are self-important or who have to shake hands with lots of people. Chairman Mao, for example, is reputed to have had a very limp, non-committal handshake.

Sometimes a weak handshake is a cultural convention – in West Africa handshakes tend to be very soft.[6] However, other motives are sometimes at work. Women who want to cultivate an impression of languid femininity often present a rather limp hand to the person they're greeting. Strong people often do the same, but in their case it's to emphasize their strength. It's said that Mike Tyson offers a relaxed, almost tender hand when he greets people outside the boxing ring – the complete opposite to what happens inside the ring.

◆ **THE FIRM HANDSHAKE**. A firm handshake occurs when the fingers are wrapped round the other person's hand and the grip is neither too tight nor too loose. William Chaplin and his students at the University of Alabama conducted a detailed investigation of the relationship between handshake style and personality.[7] They discovered that people who are extroverted and emotionally expressive tend to use a firm handshake, whereas people who are neurotic and shy don't. They also found that people who have an open attitude to new experiences use a firm handshake, but that this only applies to women. Men who have an open attitude to new experiences are no more likely to use a firm handshake than a limp handshake.

◆ **THE LIMPET HANDSHAKE**. There are some people who won't let go when they get hold of someone's hand – they hang on like a limpet. There are several motives behind the limpet handshake, but they all come down to the issue of control. By holding on to someone's hand after a handshake someone can set the agenda and engage the other person for much longer than he or she would otherwise have wished. We have all encountered people like this, or else we have seen them in action. They are so desperate to make sure someone doesn't leave, or that they don't take over the conversation or change the subject, that they clamp their hands on them and won't let go. It's interesting that people who are trapped in this way seldom have the nerve to pull their hand away. They usually remain stuck to the person until they can think of an excuse to extricate themselves, or until someone else comes to their rescue.

◆ **THE CLAMMY HANDSHAKE**. People who have sweaty hands often try to disguise this fact by wiping their hand on their clothes before they shake hands with someone. A quick wipe may remove the surface sweat, but it doesn't always remove the clammy signs of anxiety. Another trick that people with sweaty hands use is to cup their palm slightly so as to reduce the surface area of their hand that comes into contact with the other person's hand during the handshake. Not every clammy hand, however, is a sign of nervousness. It is estimated that 5 per cent of the population has hyperhidrosis, a chronic sweating condition, which is due to genetic factors rather than anxiety.

◆ **THE REINFORCED HANDSHAKE**. When people want to make their handshake more enthusiastic or intimate they sometimes clasp the other person's right hand in both their hands. This is just one of several versions of the reinforced handshake – in other versions the left hand may be placed on the other person's shoulder, upper arm or forearm. People who produce reinforced handshakes automatically put themselves in control of the greeting by increasing the amount of physical contact, and therefore their commitment to the other person. Single-handed handshakes can sometimes be indifferent, but a reinforced handshake cannot.

◆ **THE RELOCATED HANDSHAKE**. In a symmetrical handshake the participants' hands should meet midway between them – in other words in the middle of no man's land. There are two ways that the handclasp can be relocated so that it takes place in one person's space. The first is the 'huddled handshake', where one person pulls the other person into his personal space, thereby creating a handshake that's on his own terms. The second is the 'invasion handshake', where someone fully extends her arm, so that the handclasp is forced to take place in the other person's space, rather than her own. To the outside observer the culmination of these two types of handshake may look rather similar, but to the participants they feel quite different, because they are aware who is pushing or pulling whom, and who ends up deciding where the handshake should take place.

◆ **THE UPPER HANDSHAKE**. Another way that people can make a handshake asymmetrical and impose themselves on the other person is by rotating their forearm so that their own hand ends up on top, and the other person's below. Even though they may not be consciously aware of what's happening, the person who manages to get his or her hand on top – in the prone position – automatically gains an advantage over the person whose hand is below, in the supine position. That's because prone positions are associated with dominance and control, while supine positions are connected with submission and passivity. Even if they are completely unaware of the position of their hands, the person whose hand is on top will feel more dominant, and the person whose hand is below will feel more submissive.

Although we tend to think of handshakes as unimportant, they can reveal a great deal about the way people resolve issues of dominance. For a handshake to work it is essential that the participants co-operate so that their hands actually meet. By watching how people position their hands it's possible to see if both have their hands in the same position, or if one person is trying to gain the upper hand. What one person stands to gain by having their hand on top, the other stands to lose, not only by having their hand below, but also by having to accept that position in order to make the handshake work.

Power Tells

The way politicians shake hands tells us a lot about the silent expression of power. Like most men who occupy positions of power, President Harry Truman was used to having his own way, and this showed in the way he shook people's hands. When he met General Douglas MacArthur at Wake Island in 1950, the two of them were photographed shaking hands, with Truman's hand above and MacArthur's hand below. Consistent with this, Truman is

The *Upper Handshake*. A display of dominance is often revealed by literally taking the upper hand when shaking hands. Following their televised debate, JFK, who not only won the debate but went on to win the 1960 US presidential election, has his hand on top, while the loser, Nixon, has his underneath.

talking and smiling, while MacArthur is looking quite unhappy. The two men were not seeing eye to eye at the time, and it wasn't long afterwards that Truman took the drastic measure of relieving MacArthur of his command of the UN forces in Korea. There is also a photograph of President Harry Truman in 1953, just before he stepped down, greeting President-elect Dwight Eisenhower. Once again Truman has his hand on top and Eisenhower has his below – exactly what you'd expect from the imperious President and the much more easygoing President-elect.

When John F. Kennedy met Richard Nixon for their famous televised debate in 1960, the two men were photographed shaking hands. There's no indication in the face of either of them as to who was feeling more confident at the time – both are smiling and looking very composed. However, their handshake does contain a crucial *tell* – Kennedy has his hand on top, while Nixon has his below. This is a perfect example of a *foretell* because it appears to prophesy Kennedy's victory over Nixon. Of course *foretells* aren't really prophetic. They just look that way because both the *tell* and the event are caused by other factors – in this case, possibly Kennedy's popularity and Nixon's unconscious realization that he wasn't going to win the election.

When heads of state meet in front of the cameras, it's essential that they both appear in a positive light and that neither overshadows the other. When two statesmen are standing side by side, there's nothing to favour one over the other. However, when they're shaking hands, the leader on the left of the picture has a natural advantage because his or her arm is showing, while that of the other leader remains hidden. This is the 'left-side advantage'.

News coverage of George W. Bush and Tony Blair often shows them standing close together, shaking hands. Bush is usually on the left of the picture and Blair on the right. When viewers look at these images they simply see two heads of state greeting each other. They seldom notice the asymmetry of the picture, and the way it affects their perception of the two leaders. Because more of Bush's arm is in view, he appears, subliminally, to be more in control and therefore the more powerful of the two. This effect is more pronounced when the two leaders are standing close to each other, engaged in a 'huddled handshake', because in these circumstances one hardly sees the arm of the person on the right at all. Some politicians seem to know this instinctively, and they sometimes take steps to try and minimize the disadvantages of appearing on the right of a picture. There are two ways of doing this:

◆ **RELOCATING THE HANDSHAKE**. By extending their arm early and forcing the handshake to take place in the other person's space, a politician can ensure that more of their right arm appears in the photograph. This is exactly what Nikita Khrushchev did when he met President Kennedy in Vienna in 1961. At the time Kennedy was feeling distracted because his back was giving him a lot of trouble. Khrushchev, on the other hand, felt that he could run rings around Kennedy, whom he regarded as a political lightweight. This is apparent in the way that he took the initiative during the handshake. As they approached each other, Khrushchev, who was on the right, reached forward so that the handshake took place in Kennedy's body zone rather than his own. With his arm extended, Khrushchev looked confident and friendly. Kennedy, whose arm was bent, looked cautious and tense. By a simple ruse, Khrushchev had managed to turn the meeting to his own advantage. A very similar event took place when President Nixon met Chairman Mao in Peking in 1972. In the famous photograph of their meeting, Nixon appears on the left, but Mao appears to dominate the encounter because he has his arm fully extended and it looks as if he is shaking Nixon's hand, rather than the reverse.

◆ **OPENING THE HANDSHAKE**. When two politicians are shaking hands and facing each other directly, the politician on the left has the 'left-side advantage'. However, when the two politicians are oriented more towards the camera, the left-side advantage starts to disappear because the arm of the person on the right comes into view. There is a famous photograph of Richard Nixon shaking hands with Elvis Presley, in which Presley appears on the right of the picture. Because both men are oriented towards the camera, Presley's entire right arm is visible, and he therefore appears to be just as important as the President.

Politicians who discover that they are about to end up on the right side of the picture don't need to resign themselves to looking passive when they shake hands with someone. By extending their arm towards the other person or by angling their body towards the camera they can effectively eliminate the disadvantages of appearing on the right.

The symbolic importance of handshakes cannot be overestimated, especially in the political sphere. The relationship between the US and Cuba, for example, has been very tense since Castro came to power. Although there have been high-level contacts, they have not been made public for fear of upsetting the exiled Cuban community in the US. However, when Bill Clinton attended a meeting of world leaders at the United Nations in 2000, he happened to bump into Fidel Castro. On the spur of the moment the two leaders shook hands, exchanged a few pleasantries and then went their separate ways. When a White House spokesman was asked if Clinton had shaken hands with Castro, he denied that anything of the sort had happened. Later on, when the White House realized that too many people had witnessed the handshake to allow a cover-up, it relented and admitted that a brief, impromptu exchange had indeed taken place and that the two men had shaken hands. The fact that it was considered necessary to deny that a handshake had taken place illustrates how powerful the handshake can be as a symbol of acceptance. In politics a handshake is never neutral.

Nowhere was the power of the handshake more evident than in the historic meeting that took place between Yitzhak Rabin and Yasser Arafat on the White House lawn in 1993, orchestrated and overseen by Bill Clinton. Before the meeting took place there was a lot of nervousness because nobody knew how Rabin and Arafat would behave when the moment came for them to shake hands. The White House Press Secretary, George Stephanopoulos, remembered the preparations in great detail:

On Saturday morning we practised the handshake. This was just a dry run; four guys in jeans around my desk, trying to figure out how to make this diplomatic tango flow. First came the signatures, with multiple copies of the treaty, all needing multiple signatures. Then the President would turn to his left, shake Arafat's hand; turn to his right, shake Rabin's hand; take a half-step back, with his arms slightly lifted from his sides, and hope that Arafat and Rabin would reach across his belt for the picture of the decade . . . The last thing I said to Clinton was 'think about your face'. He knew enough not to have a big grin at the big moment; but if he over-compensated, it might look glum . . . We practised a closed mouth smile.

When the big day came, everything worked according to plan:

The ceremony floated past like a dream. Rabin still looked fretful; Arafat was ecstatic; and at the climactic moment Clinton seemed more presidential than ever – calm, confident and fully in control as he took his half-step back with his half-smile in place, and gently cleared a path. The crowd took a collective breath. Then Arafat and Rabin grasped each other's hands, pumped them up and down, and the entire lawn exploded.[8]

The famous photograph of Rabin and Arafat shaking hands is full of fascinating *tells*. Clinton completely dominates the occasion – not only is he in the centre of the picture, unobstructed by the others, but he stands a good head above Rabin and Arafat, reinforcing the message that the US is bigger, stronger and more benevolent than any other country. The most interesting feature of the photograph is the way that Clinton's arms are stretched out, with the hands open, extending beyond and including the other two protagonists. With this posture Clinton takes on a quasi-religious role. Not only does he seem to be solely responsible for the *rapprochement* between Israel and the Palestinians, but he also appears, rather like the famous statue of Christ the Redeemer above Rio de Janeiro, to be offering a benediction on the newly formed relationship.

Hugging Tells

Before the Berlin Wall came down, hugs were an integral part of politics in Eastern Europe. In those days a manly bear hug was the standard greeting between communist leaders, with possibly a kiss or two on the cheek thrown in for good measure. Nowadays the political bear hug has all but disappeared, largely because of its association with a defunct political ideology. Today's politicians in Eastern Europe are much more likely to shake hands.

Outside the political arena, the embrace serves as a greeting ritual for people who are very close, who haven't seen each other for a long time, or who feel the need to comfort and console each other.[9] In some respects the embrace is more intimate than the social kiss, because while one wouldn't think twice about giving one's host or hostess a kiss on the cheek as one leaves their house, one wouldn't dream of hugging them unless one knew them very well. There are several types of hug and each contains important *tells*.

◆	**SIDE-ON HUGS**. A side-on hug occurs when two people are standing side by side and one or both of them puts an arm round the other and gives a squeeze. This type of hug is often used by people who are worried that their affectionate actions might be misinterpreted – a man, for example, might hug his male friend in this way because he doesn't want anyone to think he's gay, or the boss might give his female secretary a side-on hug because he doesn't want anyone to think he's making a sexual advance.

◆ **FULL-FRONTAL HUGS**. This is the real thing – a hug where the bodies of the two people completely overlap. People who want to express their affection for each other, and who aren't concerned about what others think about them, prefer this type of hug.

◆ **HALF-MOON HUGS**. A half-moon hug is produced when two people face each other while they hug, but their bodies only partially overlap. It's used by people who are worried about the sexual inferences that might be drawn from a full-frontal hug.

◆ **STRAIGHT-UP HUGS**. How comfortable people are with a hug can often be seen in what they do with their pelvis and where they place their feet. Those who are committed to a hug, and who are not trying to exploit it for other purposes, usually stand up straight, so that their body just makes contact, or almost makes contact, with that of the other person.

◆ **CONCAVE HUGS**. People who are reluctant to hug someone tend to reveal their feelings by placing their feet further away. This reduces the chances of their body coming into contact with that of the other person. Pelvis position is another critical *tell*, because people who are uncomfortable about hugging tend to pull their bottom away from the other person.

◆ **CONVEX HUGS.** When someone wants to show that they are attracted to the person they are hugging they usually position their feet close, and push their pelvis towards the other person. Because most of the 'official business' of social interaction takes place above the waist, what individuals do with their feet and hips during a hug may be noticed by the person who's being hugged, but it's seldom spotted by the other people who happen to be nearby. For the student of *tells*, however, they are a rich source of information about what is happening between people 'unofficially'.

◆ **PATTED HUGS.** Where people place their hands and what they do with them during a hug is also highly informative. Most people grasp or envelop the other person in their arms. The more intense their feelings for the person, the tighter they hug them and the longer they sustain the embrace. Watching people hugging each other it's noticeable how many hugs include multiple pats on the back – usually by one person rather than both people. Patting is very revealing because it looks like a form of reassurance, and that's how we all tend to think of it. However, the real purpose of patting during a hug is to act as a release signal – it's a 'release pat'. Watch two people who are about to embrace each other and you'll soon spot the critical role that patting plays in bringing the hug to a close. You'll see a man walk over to a woman he knows and wrap his arms around her. She responds by placing her arms around him. A few seconds later she pats him on the back. The man immediately releases his hold and they both disengage. What the man doesn't realize is that he's unconsciously acting on instructions from the woman – by patting him on the back she's telling him that the hug is over. The woman is equally oblivious to what's happening – obviously, she knows that she's patting the man on the back, but she doesn't realize that she's using the pat as a 'termination signal'. In the context of the embrace, patting therefore serves as a *stealth tell* – it pretends to be something it's not. It may look like a gesture of affection, but its real purpose is to draw the hug to a close, and to do so without causing any offence.

Kissing Tells

Some societies have strict rules about how individuals should greet each other, based on their gender, age and social rank. There are also unwritten rules in our society, but these tend to be more fluid and ill defined. There are situations, for example, where it's not entirely clear whether we should kiss someone on the cheek or shake their hand, even though the choice that we make could have far-reaching consequences. During the presidential election Al Gore and George W. Bush appeared, separately, on the *Oprah Winfrey Show*. Gore had acquired a reputation as something of a kisser before he appeared on the show – he'd given his wife, Tipper, an enormous kiss at the Convention the previous month.

However, when Gore appeared on Oprah's show he politely shook her hand. Bush, in complete contrast, kissed Oprah on the cheek. The way that the two candidates greeted Oprah reinforced the public's perception of Gore as cold and stiff, and of George W. Bush as open and friendly. Little things, like the way someone greets other people, can often have an enormous impact on how they are seen.

Broadly speaking, there are two types of kiss:

◆ **CHEEK KISSES**. These tend to be social kisses and they are used for greetings and farewells.

◆ **MOUTH KISSES**. They are usually part of sex and romance. However, there are cases where mouth kisses appear as part of the greeting ritual.

The English are widely regarded as rather cold and undemonstrative. It therefore comes as something of a surprise to discover that there was a time when the English were the undisputed kissing champions of Europe. During the fifteenth century it was common practice for men and women to exchange kisses of friendship, even when they were strangers.[10] When the Dutch scholar, Desiderius Erasmus, visited England in 1499 the custom had reached epidemic proportions. He wrote a letter to a friend, telling him: 'Whenever you come you are received with a kiss by all; when you take your leave, you are dismissed with kisses; you return, kisses are repeated. They come to visit you, kisses again; they leave you, you kiss them all around. Should you meet anywhere, kisses in abundance, wherever you move, there is nothing but kisses.'[11] These kisses were not the customary pecks on the cheek that one finds today – they were kisses on the lips! Most Europeans at the time considered this practice highly improper, and even the French (whom we now regard as a nation of great kissers) were scandalized by the English social habit of kissing on the lips.

The English kissing custom started to decline during the sixteenth century, but it lasted up to the Restoration in 1660, when it was abandoned. At that point the English joined the league of non-kissing nations. However, over the past few decades things have started to change and social kissing is now making a serious comeback.

The way that people kiss each other socially tells us a lot about what kind of people they are, their attitudes to each other, and how they feel about kissing.

◆　**HAND KISSES**. Up until the last world war it was common for men in Europe to greet women by kissing their hand. This practice has disappeared among young people, but there are still some elderly men who have retained the custom of kissing women's hands when they meet them.

◆　**HEAD KISSES**. Kissing someone on the forehead or the top of the head is another one-sided way of kissing people – it's how parents kiss their young children and it's also used as a form of benediction. If someone kisses you on the head it shows that they have a protective attitude towards you.

◆　**CHEEK KISSES**. Social kisses typically consist of kisses on the cheek. In countries where the convention is established, everybody knows which side to start and how many kisses to exchange. In countries like the US, the UK and Australia, where kissing customs are still evolving, people are often unsure about which cheek to kiss first, and how many times they should kiss the other person.

◆ **VACUUM KISSES**. When people ostensibly kiss each other on the cheek they sometimes miss the target altogether and end up kissing the air instead. These 'vacuum kisses' fall into two types – 'missed kisses', where the parties' cheeks touch but their lips don't connect with the other person's cheek, and 'air kisses', where they go through the motions without making any physical contact at all. Air kisses appear when people are uncomfortable about physical contact, and both types of vacuum kiss are common among women who don't want to disturb their make-up or leave traces of lipstick on the other person.

◆ **FEIGNED KISSES**. If you watch people kissing socially, you'll notice that there are some people who press their cheek against the other person's without even pursing their lips, let alone kissing the air. These 'feigned kisses' pretend to be real kisses but they don't offer anything more than the cheek. They tend to be produced by people who are passive by nature, and who would rather be kissed by somebody than have to kiss them. The interesting thing about a feigned kiss is that the other person doesn't usually notice it – it's only people nearby who see what's really happening.

◆ **VOCALIZED KISSES**. Some kisses on the cheek are silent, while others include an audible smack of the lips. Other kisses are accompanied by loud vocalizations like 'mwah!' Sometimes these sound like signs of appreciation, and on other occasions they come across as something of a joke. But, in spite of the exaggeration and the laughter that accompanies them, these sounds are actually signs of discomfort being made by people who want to distance themselves from the kiss by mocking it. People who are totally at ease with social kissing – like the Italians or the French – don't accompany their kisses with vocalizations. It's only those who are self-conscious about social kissing – like the British – who find it necessary to exaggerate and accompany their kisses with loud noises. It's their way of drawing attention to the kiss so that they can disown it.

Name Tells

When people meet for the first time they usually introduce themselves or someone else introduces them. Self-introductions are fairly straightforward – they can occur at the beginning of an encounter or some time after people have struck up a conversation. An introduction performed by someone else tends to be a bit more complicated because the introducer has to orchestrate the meeting, name the people being introduced (the introducees), and possibly say something about them.

When introducers describe or 'package' introducees, they need to perform three tasks – firstly, they need to legitimize the introduction, secondly they need to say something favourable about each person, and thirdly they need to provide a basis on which the introducees can construct a conversation. The ideal 'package' does all three things. However, some introducers are so eager to legitimize the introduction that they end up exaggerating the achievements of the introducees (e.g. 'This is Susan – she's the most brilliant pianist in the country!'), while others are so concerned about offering an authentic description that they fail to offer the introducees anything to talk about (e.g. 'Can I introduce you to Charles – he's working on a revision of Fermat's theorem!').

The essential part of an introducer's role is to name the introducees (e.g. 'Susan, I'd like you to meet Charles. Charles, this is Susan'). While this requirement seems simple enough, it is fraught with all kinds of problems, not least being the prospect that the introducer will forget someone's name. Because introducers are under a lot of pressure to perform, it's very easy for them to botch this crucial part of the introduction. It's often quite difficult to introduce people whom one doesn't know well. But knowing somebody well doesn't necessarily make things any easier, because it's quite common for the introducer to draw a blank when he or she tries to remember the name of a close friend. Fortunately there are several strategies that introducers can use to save their own face, and that of the person whose name they are struggling to remember.

One strategy is for the introducer to ask the person what their name is at the start of the introduction. 'I'm sorry,' the introducer might say to one of the introducees, 'but I can't remember your name'. When the introducee says, 'Margaret Smith', the introducer comes back with, 'Yes, I know it's Margaret; I just wasn't sure about your surname!'

Another strategy is for the introducer to create an audible space where the name is normally offered, in the hope that the person will quickly provide his or her own name. In this situation introducees are usually very obliging. When the introducer, for example, says, 'And this is . . .', and leaves enough space to indicate that he is about to offer the name, the introducee will usually come to the rescue. '. . . Margaret Smith', she'll say, before anyone notices that the introducer has forgotten her name. Another strategy is to package each person so that the omission of their name isn't obvious. Yet another is to hurriedly excuse oneself at the critical point where names are normally provided – for example, 'May I introduce you to each other . . . Oh no! My mother-in-law has just arrived! I have to go! . . . Could you please introduce yourselves to each other?'

Some people make a point of remembering someone's name when they're introduced to them. For example, when he's introducing Bill to Tom, the host says, 'Bill, may I introduce you to Tom.' As they are shaking hands, Bill says, 'Hello, Tom', and Tom says 'Hi, Bill'. Repeating someone's name in this fashion provides a very convenient way of remembering their name, as well as showing the other person that you've taken the trouble to remember it. In the US and Canada, where this practice is fairly widespread, it is judged very favourably. People who repeat names are liked more than those who don't, unless the person who's doing it has something to gain by being pleasant, in which case name repetition is seen as a form of ingratiation.

There are several reasons why people forget the names of people whom they've just met. One is that they're not paying attention. Another is that there are too many distractions. The third is that there are too many names to remember, and the fourth is that they're so anxious that they can't file the information away. The people who are best at remembering names are highly motivated. Many use a mnemonic to help them. The British Prime Minister Benjamin Disraeli is reputed to have had a remarkable memory for names, but it wasn't infallible. Asked what he did when he couldn't remember someone's name, he confessed that he always resorted to the same strategy – he'd turn to the person and say, 'How is the old complaint?' Disraeli claimed that it always worked.

Parting Tells

Memory is governed by 'primacy' and 'recency' – the things we remember best are those that we heard first or heard last. It's the same with social encounters. What shapes our opinions more than anything else is what happens when we first meet someone, and what happens when we leave that person. That's why we invest so much effort in greeting and parting rituals – we instinctively know that the way we appear to others depends on how we say hello and goodbye.

In some respects parting rituals are rather similar to greeting rituals. Like greeting rituals, they are concerned with transition.[12] They also have a rather similar, but reversed, temporal structure to greetings – while greetings consist of a 'recognition phase', an 'approach phase' and a 'meeting phase', partings are made up of a 'separation phase', a 'withdrawal phase' and a 'farewell phase'.

Imagine that two young people, a man and a woman, are having a drink in a bar after work. At some point the woman realizes that it's time for her to leave, so she quickly steals a glance at her watch. This is the first 'advance cue' that she intends to leave, and it marks the beginning of the 'separation phase'. This phase provides the young man and woman with an opportunity to co-ordinate their expectations so that they are both on the same 'departure schedule', and nobody gets left behind. This is achieved through a complicated exchange of signals. For example, after the woman has glanced at her watch, the man might absentmindedly touch his briefcase. They continue talking for a while. She then orients her body towards the door, unconsciously signalling where she's aiming, and he immediately responds by finishing his drink. At each stage in this choreographed sequence, each person is signalling their intention to leave and the other is providing clearance – one person's actions are saying, 'I'm planning to leave; what do you think?' and the other person's responses are saying, 'That's fine by me. I'm quite happy to draw this to a close.'

The signals exchanged by people who don't know each other very well are usually very tentative. The signals exchanged by close friends are also quite subtle. But even when the signals between friends are bold and explicit, they're usually accompanied by mitigating assurances that are designed to make sure that the other person doesn't feel abandoned. If, for example, the young woman in the bar had suddenly got to her feet and announced, 'I'm off now', she would probably have tried to reassure the man that it wasn't her choice, and that her imminent departure had no bearing on their friendship whatsoever.

When people part company they need to do two things – they need to bring the encounter to a successful close, and they need to show that the relationship they enjoy with the other person won't be affected by their departure. To get the first part of this message across, the participants need to send out 'closure signals'; to convey the second part of the message they need to provide each other with 'relationship signals'.

There is an enormous range of closure signals that people can use. Some are linguistic, others non-verbal. One of the ways that people draw a conversation to a close is by reducing the amount of time they spend looking at the other person, and the amount of 'back-channel signals' they produce while the other person is speaking. As we've seen, 'back-channel signals' consist of nods and 'uh-huh' sounds that are designed to encourage the other person and to show that one doesn't want to take over the speaker role. Reducing these signals usually sends a clear message to the other person that the conversation is starting to wind down. The head, arms and legs are also used to get this message across. Rapid nodding of the head, shifting the weight from one leg to another, placing the hands on the armrest of the chair – all these 'intention displays' are used to show that one is preparing to leave. Some closure signals are bold and clear. Most, however, are very subtle. But even when they are barely visible, most closure signals manage to reach their target.

Relationship signals are designed to reassure the other person that the end of the encounter does not signal the end of the relationship. This message is conveyed by several kinds of talk:

◆ **JUSTIFICATION TALK**. People who are about to leave often announce that they're going because they have to, not because they want to leave. During a party, for example, a guest might turn to the hostess and say, 'I'm sorry we have to leave so early, but we promised the babysitter we'd be home by eleven o'clock.'

◆ **CONTINUITY TALK**. People try to reassure each other by projecting their relationship into the future. When they say goodbye to someone they say things like, 'See you soon', 'Let's keep in touch' or 'I'll call you next week.'

◆ **EVALUATION TALK**. People try to protect their relationship by expressing their gratitude to the person they're leaving. When they leave a social gathering, for example, they tell the host and hostess how much they enjoyed the evening. Similarly, when they bump into an old schoolfriend and are saying goodbye, they often express their pleasure with remarks like, 'It's good to see you again.'

There's often a lot of pressure on departing guests to exaggerate their appreciation, especially when they've heard other guests telling the host and hostess how much they enjoyed the evening. They feel (a) that they should not be outdone by the previous guests, and (b) that they should say something original. This can very rapidly give rise to a form of 'gratitude escalation', where each departing guest feels compelled to produce a more florid expression of thanks than his or her predecessor. Mark Knapp captures the situation thus:

Take, for example, the final moments of a cocktail party. Several guests are lined up ahead of you saying goodbye to the hostess; you hear each guest preceding you say something like: 'Cynthia, we've had a great time. It was so much fun. Thanks a lot . . .' Now it's your turn. Because of the attending farewells preceding you, you may be forced to add emphasis which you may not feel, but which is demanded lest you be seen as unoriginal and un-appreciative. Hence you boom out with: 'Cynthia . . . just fantastic! I can't remember when I had a better time. You and Zeke must come over to our house sometime.' Later, as your wife questions the wisdom of your spontaneous invitation, you discover that you yourself aren't sure why you extended the invitation in the first place.[13]

During a parting ritual people often move away from each other and then back again. If you watch people saying goodbye, you'll notice how one of them takes a step back, or several paces away from the other person, and then returns to their former position, sometimes repeating this process a number of times. This is the 'yo-yo phenomenon'. It's very common in spaces that encourage this kind of movement, and where the participants aren't under any pressure to leave in a hurry. If you watch people chatting on the street you'll often see one or both of them moving away and then back again as a prelude to leaving altogether.

Some years ago, when I was watching people in the centre of Oxford, I recorded one couple that made a total of seventeen moves away from each other before they finally separated! On the surface the 'yo-yo phenomenon' looks like a bad case of indecision – or a theatrical *fausse sortie*, where an actor pretends to exit and then returns immediately to the stage. But it's neither; it's the con-sequence of closure signals and relationship signals competing with each other. When people start to close a conversation, one of the things they do is move away. Similarly, to show that the relationship is still important, they move towards the other person. In order to signal that they want to bring the encounter to a close *and* that their relationship is still intact, people frequently end up moving back and forth. It's the alternation of these two types of signal that gives rise to the yo-yo phenomenon.

Before people physically separate, they may hug, kiss or shake hands – the decision often depends on what they did when they greeted each other. However, this doesn't necessarily mean the end of the separation phase, because they will often recycle some of the earlier elements of the ritual, sometimes repeating the entire sequence before they actually move away from each other. The 'withdrawal phase' of the parting is often fairly straightforward – one or both people simply turn on their heel and walk away. But even at this late stage in the proceedings there are *tells* that reveal what people are thinking.

When people are approaching each other they usually focus on the front of their body – adjusting their tie, buttoning up their jacket or rearranging the front of their hair. However, when people move away from each other they usually focus their attention on the back of their body because they know that this is most likely to be noticed by the other person. The way that people adjust the back of their body is often a giveaway. For example, when some-one smooths the back of their hair just as they are about to withdraw, it shows that they recognize – even un-consciously – that they may be observed from behind as they walk away.

The habit of attending to the back of one's body prior to

leaving is very much the prerogative of women, simply because women are more likely to be judged or admired from behind than men. Women will sometimes put their hand behind them and pull their jersey down over their bottom as they're about to walk away. This is the *hind-hide tell*, and it shows that the woman in question is worried about the size of her bottom. Women who are proud of their backside, or who wish to draw attention to it, are more likely to flatten out their dress or to position their hands close to their bottom before they walk away.

While people are moving away, they sometimes enter a 'farewell phase', where they throw a glance over their shoulder, or turn around and wave, before continuing on their way. When the parting is inconsequential people don't turn around. But when the parting has an emotional significance they often experience a strong temptation to turn around and have a final look at the other person before going on their way. One of the reasons why people turn round is that they regret the parting and don't want the separation to take place. Another motive is to check whether the other person is still watching them – when you've just left someone it's always reassuring to discover that they haven't broken off yet, and that they're watching you until you finally disappear from view. Partings, like greetings, are all about ratifying relationships and providing the other person with reassurances. The fact that these goals are regularly achieved by the exchange of brief utterances and fleeting gestures shows what a crucial role *tells* play in our lives.

7. Royal Tells

On a state visit to Brazil, the Duke of Edinburgh is reputed to have asked a Brazilian admiral whether the glittering display of medals on his chest was won on the artificial lake outside the capital, Brasilia. 'Yes, sir', replied the admiral, 'not by marriage'. Royalty is of course not based on achievement – it's based on parentage and marriage. Like celebrities, the royals are constantly in the limelight, but while celebrities need to work hard to stay there, the royals remain famous regardless of what they do.

People who want to retain a position of dominance need constantly to remind others how important they are – they need to adopt a dominant demeanour, insist on their point of view, and see off anyone who might try to challenge their position. That's not the case with royalty. Because their position derives from who they are rather than what they do, they don't need to behave dominantly. Because they're secure in their position, and because people are always deferring to them, they can actually afford to send out affiliative and friendly signals. In some cases they may even try to endear themselves to other people by behaving submissively.

Friendly Tells

People often feel awkward and self-conscious when they meet royalty – they get flustered, tongue-tied and don't know what to say. Even powerful individuals who run large corporations can be reduced to gibbering, inarticulate idiots when they meet members of the royal family. To counter this effect, and to put people at their ease, the royals make a habit of producing friendly signals – they smile, make jokes, and are attentive to what people have to say. This is the modern face of royalty. However, if you watch some of the early film footage of the British royal family you won't find much smiling. Although George V, for example, is reputed to have had a good sense of humour, he didn't show it in public. Most of the images we have of him are rather severe. When this was pointed out to him he replied, 'We sailors never smile on duty.' His first son, Edward, Prince of Wales, was renowned as a practical joker, although this side of his character became less evident after he succeeded to the throne as Edward VIII, and it seemed to disappear altogether after his abdication. George VI, who succeeded his brother Edward, projected an image of someone who was serious and unfunny. He seldom smiled in public, preferring to adopt the dutiful demeanour of his father, George V.

The person who is largely responsible for the shift to a more engaging style of royal behaviour is Queen

Elizabeth, the Queen Mother. During the blitz in late 1940 she made several visits to the East End of London, where she met people and talked to them about the hardships they were experiencing. Those who met her were struck by her friendly informality, and by the way she focused on what they were saying. In his diaries, Harold Nicolson describes the effect she had on people at the time:

> . . . when the car stops, the Queen nips out into the snow and goes straight into the middle of the crowd and starts talking to them. For a moment or two they just gaze and gape in amazement. But then they all start talking at once. 'Hi! Your Majesty! Look here!' She has that quality of making everybody feel that they and they alone are being spoken to. It is, I think, because she has very large eyes which she opens very wide and turns straight upon one.[1]

The accessibility of the monarchy was given a further boost in 1970 when the present Queen, who was on an official visit to Australia, performed the first royal 'walk-about' by strolling along a cordoned crowd and meeting people who had come to wave at her as she drove by. In those days the walkabout offered people an opportunity to shake hands with the Queen and, very occasionally, a chance to exchange a few words with her. Nowadays the royal walkabout is even more informal, and the Queen and the Duke of Edinburgh make a point of engaging people in conversation. When Charles, Anne, Andrew and Edward move down a line of well-wishers, there's even more joking, smiling and laughter.

Humour plays a major role, both in the public's perception of the monarchy and the monarchy's perception of itself. Robert Lacey relates an incident when the Queen and Prince Philip were driving down a muddy lane near Sandringham, and the vehicle splashed mud all over a woman walking down the lane.[2] The woman shouted something, and the Queen called back to her, 'I quite agree with you, madam.' 'Hmmm,' said Philip, 'what did she say, darling?' The Queen replied, 'She said, "Bastards!"' When he was younger the Duke of Edinburgh was known for his pranks, and the Queen, like her mother before her, has a reputation for being a gifted mimic. Anne has a bluff, irreverent sense of humour, while Charles does a good line in wry self-effacement. Humour also lubricates the royal family's relationship with the public. For example, if you watch Prince Charles shaking hands with members of the public you'll notice that the exchanges are often interspersed with laughter, some of it provoked by his amusing remarks, some of it in response to what other people are saying.

These good-humoured exchanges carry important messages because they show that Charles doesn't always stand on ceremony, and that he possesses the quality that the British value more than any other – a sense of humour. Robert Provine from the University of Maryland has discovered that laughter often functions as a submissive signal – in other words, that subordinate individuals use laughter to appease dominant individuals, while dominant individuals try to get people to laugh so that they can retain the upper hand.[3] This is evident when Charles is moving through a crowd, cracking the occasional joke, ostensibly to make everyone feel relaxed but really so that he can elicit appeasing peals of laughter. Sometimes one of the crowd will make a wisecrack that gets Charles laughing. The fact that this happens doesn't undermine the idea that laughter is about appeasement – it just shows that Charles is sometimes happy to be submissive.

One of Prince Charles's signature *tells* is his habit of raising his eyebrows. He uses this gesture in conversation, usually when he's talking to someone he doesn't know well, and when he wants to show that he's being attentive. Charles's eyebrow-lift is invariably accompanied by a very slight widening of the eyes, which shows that he's interested in what the other person is saying. The degree of eye-widening is critical, because if he raised his eyebrows without opening his eyes it would suggest that he was being haughty. Equally, if he were to open them wide it would give the impression that he didn't believe what the other person was saying. As a rule dominant individuals don't raise their eyebrows; if anything, they lower them in order to appear more threatening. By raising his eyebrows, Charles is therefore producing a submissive display. He's trying to appear attentive, but in the process he's un-intentionally producing an appeasement signal. This doesn't necessarily mean that Charles comes across as being submissive – because his identity depends on his royal status he can afford to produce the occasional appeasement display without appearing submissive.

Distance Tells

The pomp and circumstance surrounding the monarchy is designed to give it a sense of mystery and detachment, and to underline the fact that members of the royal family are very different from the rest of us. Gravity and formality are essential features of royalty because they separate the monarchy from its subjects. The problem, of course, is that formality comes into conflict with accessibility, making it difficult for a sovereign to inspire both respect and affection. The competing demands on monarchs have been recognized for a long time. In *The Book of the Courtier*, published in 1528, Baldassare Castiglione wrote about the difficulty that the ruler encounters when he tries to combine mildness and fierceness.[4] Writing in 1641, Sir Robert Naunton described how Queen Elizabeth I had 'the stile to winne the hearts of the people'. She did this by 'coupling mildnesse with majesty' – the first she had inherited from her mother, the second from her father.[5] Nowadays royalty still has to contend with the competing demands of appearing regal and affable. One without the other doesn't work. It's essential that royals appear elevated but not out of reach, and that they come across as friendly without being overly familiar.

One way that the monarchy retains its distance is through its demeanour. Members of the royal family usually remain physically inaccessible and contact with them tends therefore to be on their own terms. During walkabouts it's the members of the royal family who decide who they're going to greet. They're also the ones who initiate the greetings by extending their hand and who bring the exchange to an end, often again with a handshake. Symbolic distance is also reflected by physical distance, with the Queen standing within arm's range, but not too close to the other person.

The journalist Simon Hoggart has suggested that the Queen has three basic expressions, 'a dour glare, verging on a scowl, delight, and lively interest . . . It is the last one she uses at garden parties'.[6] On ceremonial occasions the

Queen usually adopts a rather grave expression, but there are times – for example, when her horse does well in the Derby – when her spontaneous emotions come to the fore. The Queen is at her best on formal social occasions and when she's being completely relaxed. It's situations that are neither one thing nor the other that she seems to find most difficult.

Symbolic distance is sometimes conveyed by language – for example, the way that members of the royal family might refer to 'we' or 'one' when they mean 'I' or 'me'. The use of 'we' by monarchs has a long tradition – it derives from the notion of the ruler as more than a single individual, which is said to go back to the time when the Roman Empire was split in two, with one Emperor in Rome and another in Constantinople. Queen Victoria is reputed to have said, 'We are not amused' to show that she, herself, was not impressed. This is misleading on two counts. Firstly, there is no record that she ever used this expression. Secondly, there is lots of evidence that Queen Victoria was frequently amused – her journals repeatedly include the phrase, 'I was very much amused', and it's known that she was given to uncontrollable attacks of the giggles.[7] But royal use of the term 'we' isn't always straightforward. Edward VIII, for example, often used the term in correspondence with his beloved Wallis Simpson. In one letter he wrote, 'not anybody or anything can separate WE ... God bless WE'.[8] The reference here was not to himself, but to both of them, where 'WE' was obtained by combining the first letters of Wallis and Edward.

Members of the royal family are more likely to use the pronoun 'one' when referring to themselves. When he was asked about the prospect of being King, Charles once replied, 'I didn't wake up in my pram one day and say "Yippee . . ." you know. But I think it just dawns on you, slowly, that people are interested in one.' The use of 'one' often replaces the first person with the third person singular, making it sound as if the speaker is talking about someone else instead of himself. This draws attention away from the speaker and shifts it towards their role. When someone refers to him- or herself as 'one' it reduces their individuality. But most crucial of all, it creates a distance between the speaker and the person who's being addressed because it treats the speaker as if he or she isn't present.

Hand Tells

Symbolic distance is also conveyed by posture. If you watch members of the royal family, you'll notice that they have distinctive ways of holding their hands:

◆ **THE HANDCLASP**. The Queen uses several hand postures, but her favourite appears to be the 'handclasp', where the palm of one hand is placed in that of the other – in her case the left hand usually rests on top of the right. The Queen also employs a related posture, where several of the fingers of one hand clasp one of the fingers of the other hand. In both of these postures the hands are linked in front of the body, and in most cases they're positioned demurely on the lap. Both postures are essentially defensive; because the hands are occupied they also appear to be unthreatening.

◆ **THE HANDBAG**. Like many women of her generation, the Queen often walks around with her handbag suspended from her arm. But unlike that of other women, hers is largely decorative. It isn't stuffed full of make-up, parking tickets and money, because someone else carries things for her. The Queen does occasionally use her handbag to send cryptic signals – it's known, for example, that when she reaches for her handbag it's a signal to her assistants that she's about to move on to something else.

◆ **THE CRANE POSTURE**. The Duke of Edinburgh has a habit of walking around with his hands clasped behind his back. This is the 'crane posture', and it's widely recognized as one of the Duke's trademark *tells*. He also performs the 'half crane' by placing his left hand behind his back when he's shaking hands. The act of placing the hands behind one's back is a dominant gesture, because it exposes the body and leaves it unprotected from frontal attack. It's the body's way of saying, 'Look at me. I'm so confident that nobody will attack me that I am prepared to keep my hands behind my back, where they're not in a position to defend me.' As far as we can tell, the Duke of Edinburgh only adopted the crane posture after the coronation; prior to that he preferred to clasp his hands in front of him. One of the things that attracted the Duke to this posture is the fact that it makes him look confident. The other is that it makes him look very different from the Queen – while her hands are neatly folded on her lap, his are tucked away behind him. So strong is the Duke of Edinburgh's need to distinguish himself, that if the crane posture hadn't existed, he would have needed to invent it.

◆ **THE POUCH POSTURE.** In order to ensure that he isn't confused with his parents, Charles has avoided the hand-clasp and the crane. Instead of clasping his hands in front or behind him, he's developed a habit of slipping his right hand into his jacket pocket. This is the 'pouch posture', and in Charles's case it consists of several discrete elements. First of all there's the act of turning up the flap, so that the hand can be placed in the jacket pocket; then there's the business of placing the hand in the pocket; finally there's the abbreviated sequence where he fiddles with the flap without placing his hand in the pocket. The pouch posture is clearly motivated by an unconscious desire to conceal the hand – not both hands, mind you, just the hand that's the stronger of the two. When people conceal their hands it shows that they either want to hide their feelings or that they need to restrain their impulses. When Charles puts his hand in his pocket he sometimes uses his thumb as a 'stop', so that while his fingers remain hidden his thumb is still exposed. This, in itself, is interesting because actions that give prominence to the thumbs are 'macho' gestures – it's what tough guys do when they tuck their thumbs into their belt or push their hands into their trouser pockets and leave their thumbs outside.

Touching Tells

Touch is often used as a marker of status. The social psychologist, Nancy Henley, has pointed out that while high-status individuals reserve the right to touch their sub-ordinates, they in turn aren't entitled to touch their

THE BOOK OF TELLS

superiors. Touch, she suggests, acts as a 'status reminder' – the idea being that by observing patterns of touching in a group of people it's possible to work out who has control over whom.[9] We can see this very clearly with royalty. When members of the royal family are doing a walkabout, it's they who initiate the handshake and who therefore grant people permission to touch them. Because of the association between power and touch, there are strict rules against people unilaterally touching the monarch. Apart from shaking her hand, nobody is allowed to touch the person of the Queen. When this rule is violated, as it was when the Australian Prime Minister put his arm around the Queen in 1992, it almost caused an international incident.

This tactile attitude of Australians towards royalty goes back a long way. When Edward, the Prince of Wales, visited Australia in 1920, it seemed as though everyone was trying to make contact with him. He recorded the spectacle in his journal:

> The 'touching mania', one of the most remarkable phenomena connected with my travels, took the form of a mass impulse to prod some part of the Prince of Wales. Whenever I entered a crowd, it closed around me like an octopus. I can still hear the shrill, excited cry, 'I touched him!' If I were out of reach, then a blow on my head with a folded newspaper appeared to satisfy the impulse.[10]

There was a time, during the Middle Ages, when it was widely believed that people who suffered from scrofula, a glandular disease which was called 'the King's evil', could be cured by being touched by their monarch. This belief in the 'royal touch', as it was called, lasted from the time of Edward the Confessor right up to 1714, when Queen Anne performed the last royal touch by an English monarch.[11] Although people no longer believe in the curative power of the royal touch, there is something very primitive about the desire to touch and be touched by royalty. That's why so many people reach out to shake their hand. In these situations, touch becomes a medium of assimilation – by touching a member of the royal family people feel that they are incorporating some of the royal magic into themselves and connecting themselves to something that's timeless.

The way people touch each other sometimes exposes things about their relationship that they would rather keep hidden. A dramatic case of this occurred in 1953. At the time Princess Margaret was having a secret love affair with Group Captain Peter Townsend, who had been equerry to her father, the King. The secrecy was necessitated by the fact that Margaret was only twenty-two, while Townsend was thirty-eight. To complicate matters further, he was divorced. The romance became public knowledge during the coronation. Before the ceremony began, Princess Margaret was waiting in Westminster Great Hall. Townsend was standing nearby. She turned towards him and absentmindedly brushed a piece of fluff from his lapel. It was this tiny gesture – this *tell* of intimacy – that revealed to the world that Princess Margaret was in love with Peter Townsend.

One of the things that made Princess Margaret's gesture so noticeable was the fact that she belonged to a family that was not given to public displays of affection. Even to this day, the royal family rarely touch other people, except to shake hands, and there's very little physical contact between the family members in public. In fact, if it were a foreign country, psychologists would probably refer to the royal family as a 'non-contact culture' – that is, a society where touch is reduced to the bare minimum. For example, when the Queen and the Duke of Edinburgh went on a round-the-world tour of the Commonwealth in 1953, they left Charles, who was five years old at the time, in the care of his nanny. When they returned six months later, Charles was taken to the airport to greet his parents. When his parents appeared, they didn't lift Charles up and give him a big hug or a kiss; instead they greeted him with a handshake – in other words, they resorted to a greeting that most people would reserve for strangers and acquaintances, even in those days, but not for children, and certainly not for their own child whom they hadn't seen for half a year!

The low frequency of touch within the royal family is partly due to the fact that its members need to project an image of inaccessibility, even among themselves. It also arises from the heavy schedule of duties that the Queen and the Duke of Edinburgh have always had to fulfil, and the reduced opportunities they have had to be with their children. When Charles was young he would usually only see his mother twice a day – for half an hour in the morning and half an hour in the early evening. The rest of the time he was cared for by nannies.[12]

If there were a scale for measuring royal touch, the Queen and Prince Philip would definitely be at one end and Princess Diana would have been at the other. The tactile side of Diana's personality was evident, both in the way that she brought up her children – she was constantly cuddling and touching William and Harry – and the way she related to members of the public. While the established members of the royal family were busy cultivating an image of regal detachment, Diana's instinct was to make contact with individuals. When people were waiting to meet her she would often rush over to greet them. Instead of keeping her distance, she would move into their physical space, creating the impression that she was meeting them on their terms rather than hers. Diana's style in public was one of 'immediacy'.[13] By getting close to people, being open and receptive, and giving them her undivided attention, she created an atmosphere of informality and warmth that made an indelible impression on those who met her – one that, in many respects, was similar to the feelings that the Queen Mother had aroused during the Second World War.

People who met Diana felt touched by her – all of them figuratively, and some of them literally. When Diana opened a purpose-built AIDS clinic at the Middlesex Hospital in 1987, she was photographed holding hands with a young man who was suffering from AIDS. This image had an enormous impact on people's perceptions of the disease. At the time there was a great deal of prejudice towards AIDS sufferers. By sitting down beside an AIDS patient and holding his hand, Diana completely rejected such prejudice. With no more than a touch, she demonstrated that people with AIDS are no different from any other patients suffering from life-threatening diseases.

It's often said that Diana was adored because of her charity work, because she was vulnerable and because she was so beautiful. All these factors undoubtedly played a part, but the thing that endeared her to the public more than any other was the way she physically touched people. Touch is the most primitive expression of love and friendship. By reaching out to individuals, Diana touched a very deep chord in people.[14] She also showed her feelings – something that the royal family seldom do. While Diana was alive, Charles seemed content to accept the restrictions on outward displays of emotion dictated by royal convention. Diana, on the other hand, vaulted over these restrictions to get to people, and they loved her for it. Since Diana's death, Charles has become much more tactile in his relationship with William and Harry. He's been seen hugging and even kissing them – doing things that Diana did with the boys, but which he himself wasn't exposed to when he was a child.

Charles Tells

When they were together it was always assumed that Diana was the shy one and that Charles was rather composed. It's true that Diana was a shy person. But it's also the case that Charles is given to spells of self-consciousness. This is evident from the range of 'displacement activities' that he produces when he's in the public eye.

◆　　**THE CUFF-LINK FIDDLE**. Several of Charles's habits consist of *threshold tells* – that is, they occur as he's crossing an invisible boundary from one situation to another. Watch him emerge from a chauffeured car at a gala performance and you'll see how he characteristically draws his hand across his body and reaches for the opposite

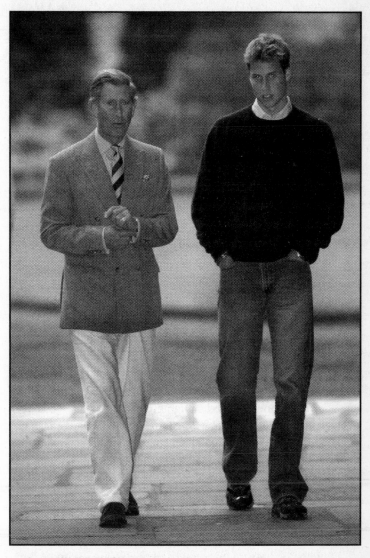

The *Cufflink Fiddle*. A sure sign of anxiety or self-consciousness is revealed in this small but highly significant gesture – as demonstrated here by Prince Charles.

cuff. This is Charles's 'cuff-link fiddle' – he resorts to it whenever he's on display and in transition. Although Charles has made the cuff-link fiddle his own, it's very similar to the *anxiety tells* that other people display when they're approaching someone – like crossing their arms over their body, rearranging their clothes or touching their hair. Most people have access to a range of *anxiety tells*, dropping one in favour of another. But Charles has remained faithful to the cuff-link fiddle since he first discovered it as a young man. His cuff-links have become emotional lightning conductors, a means of dispelling his anxieties and providing him with a sense of security – very similar, in fact, to what psychoanalysts call a 'transitional object'. Charles has also, it seems, passed this habit on to other people, because Tony Blair has become a cuff-link fiddler too.

◆ **THE TIE TUCK**. Charles's habit of straightening out his tie is another one of his *threshold tells*. He usually does this by tucking his tie into his jacket. In fact the action is now so ingrained in him that he will straighten out his tie even when it doesn't need straightening, or when it isn't even there! When he's wearing black tie he frequently slips his hand under the lapel of his jacket, just as if he were wearing a tie and wanted to straighten it out.

◆ **THE NASAL FOLD WIPE**. Charles also has a habit of wiping his index finger down the fold between his nose and cheek. He tends to do this on public occasions, when he's aware that crowds of people are watching him.

◆ **THE EARLOBE RUB**. Another of Charles's *tells* is the

'earlobe rub', which involves grabbing his earlobe and surreptitiously giving it a quick rub. He does this when he's feeling mildly self-conscious.

◆ **THE ASIDE.** Charles has a very distinctive way of talking out of the side of his mouth, which he does when he wants to put brackets around what he's saying – it's his way of showing that he's changing, for example, to a more jocular mood. Actors sometimes produce an 'aside' as a way of showing that they're dealing with a parenthetical issue or that they're colluding with the audience. That is what Charles is essentially doing when he talks out of the side of his mouth – he's stepping out of his normal role and into a more intimate role that he hopes to share with his audience.

The fact that he exhibits any displacement activity at all is quite revealing. After decades of royal duties we would expect Charles to be fairly immune to the unsettling presence of large crowds. Evidently he isn't, because whenever he's confronted by lots of people his hand reaches for the security of his tie or his cuff-links or both. Although Charles is very much a man of the world, these little forms of displacement reveal a sensitive and potentially vulnerable side of his character.

Diana Tells

Diana had several quite distinctive mannerisms, most of them associated with shyness. She had a habit, for example, of looking down at the ground when she was talking to people, and she was also given to bouts of blushing. These outward signs began to disappear with age, but her feeling of awkwardness was never far from the surface. There were six facial expressions that Diana made her own:

◆ **THE EYE-PUFF**. Diana had very large eyes, which she accentuated by adopting an 'open-eyes' expression. One of the things that people find irresistible about very young babies is the size of their eyes relative to the rest of their face – their huge eyes act as 'innate releasers', making people feel protective and nurturing. Grown women can appear more vulnerable and elicit similar responses by expanding their eyes. This is what Diana did – she widened her eyes and made people feel that they needed to look after her.

◆ **THE SPENCER SMILE**. Diana was renowned for her radiant smile. This wasn't an artificial smile – it was the genuine article, the heartfelt smile with all the features of authenticity, like symmetry and activation of the muscles round the eyes.

◆ **THE PURSED SMILE**. Diana had an unusual habit of pursing her lips and pulling them to one side while she was smiling. This was in fact a restrained smile, and she used it when she was feeling shy or embarrassed. By restraining her smile in this way she showed that she was amused, but that she felt it was inappropriate to show her amusement.

◆ **THE DIPPED SMILE**. The dipped smile is performed by

smiling while the head is lowered and the eyes are looking up. This reproduces the look that the young child
gives to grown-ups, where the eyes are looking up at the
adult. When Diana adopted this expression it made her
appear younger and more vulnerable. As we shall see in
the discussion of *sexual tells*, the dipped smile is also a
'come-on', and that's why Diana appeared so seductive
when she used this smile.

◆ **THE HEAD-CANT SMILE**. Occasionally Diana would tilt
her head to one side while she was smiling. As we saw
earlier, head-canting also gives the impression of vulnerability and submissiveness. By tilting her head to one side
Diana made herself appear completely unthreatening.

◆ **THE TURN-AWAY SMILE**. This occurred when Diana's
head was turned away from the other person while looking at them and smiling. This produces what Charles
Darwin called a 'hybrid expression', made up of actions
which convey two opposing messages – smiling, which
signals approach, and turning away, which signals avoidance.[15] The tension between these two messages gives
the hybrid expression its irresistible appeal – like a metal
alloy, it's stronger than its constituent elements.

When people talk about Diana's smile it's the turn-away
smile that they usually remember. In many ways this was
Diana's *signature tell* because it encapsulated both her
openness and her shyness, and it highlighted her indecision. The turn-away smile is neither one thing nor the
other – it's neither an attempt to turn away nor a whole-
hearted smile. In this respect it's rather like Diana herself

– someone who was like everyone else and who shared their sentiments, but someone who also happened to be a member of the royal family.

William Tells

One of the things that Prince William has inherited from his mother is his height. At 6 feet 3 inches he's very tall for a member of the royal family – in fact, when he ascends to the throne he'll be the tallest British monarch ever, taller even than Henry VIII. For a long time William had a habit of stooping. It was an adolescent way of making himself look less conspicuous. In his case it was also a way of hiding from the unwanted attention of the press and people who treat him as if he's something special. The stooping habit has now largely disappeared, but William can still be socially withdrawn – just like Diana was on occasions. In fact, several of William's *tells* can be traced to his mother. There are also some *tells* that he owes to his father.

◆ **THE HEAD DIP**. Like his mother, William is naturally reticent. That's one of the reasons he likes to ride around on his motorbike with his helmet on – it allows him to travel incognito. William doesn't like to be treated differently and he has a strong dislike of the press, because of the paparazzi, whom he sees as responsible for his mother's death. When he's on display or feeling pursued, his natural instinct is to lower his head and look down. It's his camouflage, his way of pretending that the people who are bothering him aren't there. Like Diana, William also has a habit of lowering his eyes when he's talking to people. This isn't another escape attempt – it's simply an expression of his shyness. William's maternal grandfather, Lord Spencer, was a rather shy person too. In his youth he was also very good looking. William is unusually handsome for a member of the royal family, and lots of young girls find him irresistible. The other thing that girls like about him is his reserve – it allows them to imagine that they're doing the chasing. This is borne out by the fact that, in 1998, he received more than a thousand Valentine cards. It was illustrated even more dramatically that year when William travelled with Charles and Harry to Canada. There he was repeatedly mobbed by hundreds of screaming girls – just as if he were a pop star!

◆ **THE SPENCER SMILE**. Like Diana, William has an infectious smile, which we're seeing more and more. The smile is broad and generous, and it usually shows signs of genuine pleasure. This is particularly noticeable when his guard is down and he's feeling unthreatened. When William is under pressure to appear jovial his smiles are usually more artificial – they're briefer, his gaze is averted, and they don't enlist the muscles round the eyes. William also uses the pursed smile that was so characteristic of his mother. Like her, he compresses his lips and pulls them to one side.

◆ **THE TIE TIDY**. One of William's *threshold tells* is the 'tie tidy'. For example, when he gets out of a car wearing a tie and jacket and he walks towards a building, he often straightens out his tie. Like other *threshold tells* this

action occurs when he's in transition – it's a way of marking the change, preparing for what's about to happen,
and displacing anxiety. Although William's 'tie tidy' and
Charles's 'tie tuck' both involve ties, they're guided by
quite different motivations. When Charles tucks the end
of his tie away he's making sure – functionally and
metaphorically – that there aren't any loose ends around
and that what's superfluous is put out of view. When
William tidies his tie he's not trying to conceal anything
– he's just smartening up what's already visible.

At the moment William still has the mannerisms of a
youngster. If you watch him standing beside Charles,
you'll see a middle-aged gentleman with his hand in his
jacket pocket, and a young man, with his pelvis pushed
forward and his legs on display, assuming the pose of an
athlete. Over the next few years William is going to
change, and so will his mannerisms. Some of his habits
may become ingrained, while others are abandoned in
favour of new ways of behaving. One issue that still needs
to be resolved is what he does with his hands – will he
follow the Duke of Edinburgh and keep his hands behind
his back, or will he model himself on his father and tuck
one of them in his pocket? Or is he more likely to develop
his own distinctive style of behaviour?

8. Anxiety Tells

People become anxious when they feel threatened. This is a normal, self-protective response to a perceived danger, and it often precedes actions that are designed to deal with the threat. How anxious someone feels is likely to depend on their personality and how threatened and helpless they feel. Most people only feel threatened and anxious occasionally. Some people, however, don't appear to experience any anxiety at all, while at the opposite extreme there are people who seem to be in a permanent state of nerves.

Psychologists distinguish between two types of anxiety – 'trait anxiety' and 'state anxiety'. As the term implies, trait anxiety refers to anxiety that is a trait, in other words, part of someone's personality. A person with trait anxiety tends to feel anxious, regardless of the situation. State anxiety, on the other hand, is a response to a particular situation. This is the natural way to respond – to feel anxious when circumstances are threatening, and to feel relaxed when the situation isn't threatening. Of course the whole notion of threat is highly subjective – people who have high levels of trait anxiety, for example, tend to see most situations as threatening.

When humans or animals are under attack there are several strategies at their disposal – they can fight, flee or freeze.[1] Each of these responses involves very different actions – attacking or defending oneself against the assailant, running away or keeping perfectly still. Although they differ superficially, these strategies are all associated with heightened physiological arousal, which involves increased heart rate, breathing and palmar sweating. These processes are automatic and involuntary – in other words, people don't have any control over them – so they provide a very reliable indication of emotions. One of the distinguishing features of heart rate is that people don't always notice small increases but they do notice it when their heart starts pounding. In the case of sweating, people are often painfully aware that their anxiety is apparent to other people, and that is why they go to such lengths to cover it up. Heart rate and sweating are united by the fact that they're almost impossible to fake; breathing is different because people can pretend to breathe faster or slower than normal.

As a rule, we don't want others to notice our symptoms of anxiety, because it shows that we aren't fully in control. It also undermines our confidence and puts other people at an advantage. Although we can't always control our anxiety, we can take steps to ensure that other people don't notice it. In fact it's often our attempts to conceal our anxiety that reveal what we are really feeling.

Sweating Tells

Sweating is central to thermoregulation – when we get hot our sweat glands produce more sweat, which evaporates and cools the surface of the skin. But sweating also occurs in response to highly charged emotional events, like giving a speech in front of a crowd of strangers, sitting in the dentist's chair, or preparing to jump out of a plane with a parachute. Research on sweating shows that while thermoregulatory sweating occurs all over the body, but less noticeably on the palms, emotional sweating is concentrated on the face and the palms of the hands, where the sweat glands are most densely packed.

Emotional sweating often catches people unawares, especially when they're inclined to be self-conscious. I've often watched people who appear to be completely composed stand up to give a speech, only to see perspiration pouring down their forehead a few minutes later. It's also happened to me on several occasions – one minute you're feeling confident and in control, and the next you're sweating profusely. Sometimes all it takes is a stray idea, a moment of self-doubt, to initiate the sweating. Once you start to perspire it's very difficult to stop. That's partly because sweating, like blushing, is very labile, but it's also because sweating feeds on itself – when you realize that other people can see you sweating this makes you more anxious, which in turn encourages you to continue sweating, and so the vicious cycle continues. But sweating need not disqualify people from public speaking. The British Prime Minister, Tony Blair, is a good example of someone who often sweats profusely when he's speaking in public, but who has not allowed it to hinder him in any way.

People can detect increases in their heart rate and sweating. They recognize, however, that while an increase in their heart rate isn't evident to others, an increase in their perspiration is. The way people react to their own sweating is often very revealing, and so are the little tricks that they use to cover it up. If you watch people who are about to shake hands with someone important, you'll see that they sometimes wipe their right hand discreetly before extending it for the handshake. This is usually done on the pretext of performing a completely different task, like putting their hand in their pocket or straightening out their jacket. For good measure, it's usually done when other people's attention is elsewhere. One way to reduce the chances of sweating is to remove some of one's clothing. You often see male politicians take their jacket off when they walk on to the stage to make a speech. This is partly done to create an impression of informality and resolution – to show the audience that the politician is prepared to get his hands dirty – but it's also done to help the politician keep cool, calm and collected.

Breathing Tells

When people are breathing normally they breathe about once every five seconds, each time taking in about 600 cubic centimetres of air. Breathing is largely performed by two sets of muscles – the muscles of the chest, and the muscles of the abdomen. In normal breathing the abdominal muscles do more work than the chest muscles. The chest muscles, however, are more involved in deep breathing, and there's a tendency for women in the west to use their chest muscles more than men.[2] The reason for this difference between the sexes is not entirely clear, but it may have something to do with the cultural premium that is placed on women having a flat stomach and large breasts.

When someone feels threatened and anxious their breathing rate increases, they breathe more with their chest, and their breathing becomes shallower. As the psychologist William James put it, 'When a fearful object is before us we pant and cannot deeply inspire'.[3] This is a natural defensive reaction, and it serves the purpose of preparing the individual for 'fight or flight'. However, there are cases where people continually hyperventilate in the absence of any immediate threat by breathing too fast and by taking in too much air. Someone who is hyperventilating is likely to increase their breathing rate from once every five seconds to once every three seconds, and to increase their air intake by 50 per cent. Although hyperventilation draws more oxygen into the lungs, it has the adverse effect of reducing the amount of carbon dioxide in the body, which in turn makes the person feel disoriented, dizzy and anxious.

People who breathe normally – that is, slowly and with large tidal volume – tend to be confident and emotionally stable. In contrast, people who breathe fast and with shallow breaths tend to be worried, shy and unsure of themselves. Habitual hyperventilators pay a high price, because they're prone to chronic anxiety, panic attacks and even heart problems.[4] It is still not known what causes what – whether unusual breathing patterns are responsible for disabling psychological effects, or whether people develop unusual breathing patterns because they feel anxious and despondent. However, it is possible to alleviate people's feelings of anxiety by getting them to breathe properly. This supports the idea that our moods are influenced by the way we breathe, rather than vice versa.

Breathing is one of those things that we do without thinking – although we can deliberately alter our breathing pattern, we never have to think about breathing because our autonomic nervous system does the job for us. Maybe it's because we don't think about breathing, or because we take it for granted, that we pay so little attention to it. When we're with other people we're seldom aware of how fast they're breathing, or whether they're breathing more with their chest than their stomach. If we were more attentive to how people breathe we'd know a lot more about what they are feeling.

Posture Tells

The three options that are available to an animal under attack – fight, flight or freeze – are reflected in the way that anxious people use their bodies to defend themselves, to escape symbolically, and to appear inert and unthreatening.

The 'fight' response is reflected in the rigid postures that anxious people adopt, where the muscles are tense and the body creates a defence against the outside world. Wilhelm Reich referred to this as 'body armour', and Alexander Lowen called it 'psychosomatic armoury'.[5] Lowen noticed that people who are anxious and who therefore feel the need to protect themselves from others, often show hypertonicity of the chest wall – the region that is most likely to be subjected to a frontal attack. He also made the point that the arms and hands are potential weapons, which can be used for attack or for counter-attack. When people rely on their hands and arms, there's no need for any other form of defence. However, when aggression isn't an option they often transform their body into a protective shield. Lowen suggested that 'psychologically the armour is the expression of the attitude of stiffening to meet an attack rather than striking back. Dynamically the tension in the front is produced by pulling back the shoulders and pelvis, thus putting all the frontal muscles on the stretch at the same time that they are contracted. When the front and the back of the body are thus encased in a rigid sheath of tight muscles, we can say that the organism is armoured.'[6]

The 'flight' response is found in the way that anxious people move their bodies. While the movements of confident people tend to be smooth, those of anxious people are often jerky and uneven. This can be seen in their breathing pattern, which sometimes consists of a series of 'stepped' inhalations rather than a single, smooth inhalation of air. Anxious people are often restless, producing lots of sudden hand movements close to the body, as opposed to infrequent movements which are smooth and away from the body. The constant shifts of posture produced by anxious people look like an overflow of excess energy, which in one sense they are. But these agitated movements are best understood as disguised and regressed attempts to escape from what is perceived as a threatening situation. When an anxious person taps his foot impatiently it means that he is preparing his feet for a getaway, and when he plays with his hands or fiddles with his keys it shows that he wants to get down on his hands and knees and crawl away as fast as possible. Most of the time he doesn't notice what he's doing, let alone recognize the significance of his actions. Other people are often oblivious too – even if they do notice his agitated movements, they don't necessarily recognize them as an expression of his desire to escape.

The 'freeze' response is revealed in people's postures. Anxious people tend to adopt rigid postures and to sit or stand in ways that maximize auto-contact. When they're standing, they're inclined to select postures like the 'scissors stance', where the legs are straight and crossed, either at the knee or at the calf. When anxious people are sitting they often cross their legs, usually at the thigh, but sometimes at the calf or the ankle. When their legs aren't crossed, they tend to be close together, often with the feet tucked under the chair. As we saw earlier, these are essentially submissive postures, but they also help people to feel less anxious. Crossing the legs, for example, gives people the feeling that their genital region is protected, and this makes them feel more secure.

Postures that bring the thighs together also increase the amount of contact that people have with themselves, and therefore the degree of comfort that they feel. Ideally, most people prefer to be comforted by others. But if others aren't available or willing to provide it, people often resort to comforting themselves. One way they achieve this is by pressing their thighs together. An extreme version of a self-comforting posture is 'the pretzel'. Here the legs are crossed at the thigh and the foot that belongs to the leg on top is curled round the ankle of the other leg, making the person look as if they've been tied up by a mad contortionist. As we saw earlier, leg-cross postures serve as 'unintention displays' – they show other people that the person has no intention of moving. In this respect they're examples of the 'freeze' response – it's what animals do when they're in danger of being spotted by a predator.

Anxiety also produces other forms of inactivity. For example, when people feel anxious they often feel the need to urinate, although when other people are nearby the impulse is usually reduced. Even when they're not feeling anxious, men find it difficult to urinate with someone standing beside them. This extended 'micturition latency', as psychologists have labelled it, is most evident in public toilets, where men are often flanked by complete strangers.[7]

Hand Tells

Anxiety is often evident in the way that people use their hands. When people are feeling anxious they often manipulate objects – you'll see them playing with their keys, twisting the ring on their finger or tugging at their clothes. Anxious people also touch themselves as a means of gaining comfort. They may rub their hands together – this was one of George Bernard Shaw's *trademark tells* – or they may tug their earlobe, stroke their chin or run their fingers through their hair. Where people touch themselves is often very revealing. For example, a man who tugs at the skin under his chin reveals that he's worried that he's putting on weight.

Zoologists have discovered that when animals have conflicting motives they often engage in 'displacement activities' which are quite unrelated to their immediate goals.[8] This also happens with humans. When people experience conflicting motives – as they do when they feel anxious – they often produce 'self-directed behaviours' which draw off some of the excess energy and give them a temporary feeling of comfort. These actions are sometimes called 'adaptors', because they help people to adapt to their internal conflicts. The main focus of self-directed behaviours like adaptors is the head and the face.[9] If you go into a hospital waiting room or an area where people are lining up for benefits, you'll notice that people frequently touch themselves on the face – one person might support her chin in her hands, while another is scratching the side of his face or smoothing down his hair. These self-comforting gestures are often unconscious; they are designed to alleviate the anxiety that people feel when they find themselves in awkward situations.

It's noticeable that when individuals perform self-directed actions, they don't make contact with just any part of their body – instead they touch themselves where other people might caress or stroke them if they were available to do so.[10] Anxious people spend so much time stroking their hair because this is how their mothers comforted them when they were babies. Self-comforting adaptors are therefore regressive – they take people back to a time when their parents alleviated their distress by touching and caressing them. As adults we don't usually have our parents around to provide us with a sense of security. So instead, we do to ourselves what our parents once did for us.

When people feel anxious they often externalize their anxiety by fidgeting or by manipulating objects that are close at hand. One thing they do is play with their glasses. How they manipulate them can be very revealing. For example, people who chew or suck the ends of their glasses are actually engaging in a very primitive form of self-comforting. They are like the baby who sucks its thumb or chews its blanket – they're taking comfort from having something in their mouth. Then there are people who hold their glasses in their hands, opening and closing them but making sure that they look symmetrical. These people tend to be neat and compulsive and they have a strong need to be in control. People who are constantly removing their glasses tend to be indecisive and evasive – they can never decide whether they should have their glasses on or off. In some cases it's done to confound other people, so that they don't know what's going to happen next. Then there are people who constantly breathe on their glasses and polish the lenses. They too need to be in control and to know what's happening – they like a clear view of the world.

The purpose of some adaptors is to offer protection rather than comfort. There are five main 'protective' adaptors. These include the 'eye-cover', where a hand is placed over the eyes, the 'mouth-cover', where a hand is placed over the mouth, and the 'face-cover', where the palms of both hands are used to cover the whole face. People often use these covering gestures when they've received bad news or when they've just witnessed some- thing distressing. All three actions can be seen after the results of a political election have been announced – victorious candidates can usually be seen smiling, laugh- ing and raising their hands, while the defeated candidates are covering their eyes or mouth, or even their whole face.

By covering their eyes, people are preventing themselves from seeing the thing that is distressing them, and by covering their mouth they are simultaneously concealing their distress and preventing themselves from saying something they might later regret. These covering gestures are essentially symbolic. For example, when you hear about an air crash on the radio, you are as likely to cover your eyes as your ears – by covering your eyes you are behaving as if you had actually seen the accident, not just heard about it.

The other two 'protective' adaptors are the 'head-clasp' and the 'cradle'. The best place to see these gestures is at a sporting event like a football match, especially when there's a lot at stake for both sides. When a player shoots at goal and narrowly misses, you often see the supporters clasp their head in despair – the hands rise up and cover the top of the head, creating a manual crash helmet. This is a natural, unlearned response, and it's found all round the world. It works metaphorically because it's designed to shield the head, not against physical blows, but from the psychological damage of witnessing some terrible spectacle.

In 1996 the England football team played Germany in the semi-finals of the European Championship in Turin. At the end of the full period the score was 1–1, so the match had to be decided on a penalty shoot-out, where six players from each side have to take turns at getting the ball past the other team's goalkeeper. The teams were level at five points apiece, when Gareth Southgate, the England midfielder, stepped up to the line to take his shot at goal. This was a crucial point: if he missed and the next German player got the ball in the net, Germany would win and go on to the final, and England would be out of the competition. When Southgate placed the ball, walked back and started his run he knew how important it was to get the ball into the net. Maybe it was the weight of responsibility resting on his shoulders, or maybe he had a momentary loss of concentration – but, instead of striking the ball cleanly, he tapped it softly, and the German goalkeeper had no problem stopping it before it got near the goal mouth. As Southgate turned and began his lonely walk back across the pitch, he realized the grave consequences of his missed penalty. While he was walking back towards his team mates, with his eyes downcast, Southgate did what so many football players do when they're in the depth of despair – he 'cradled' the back of his head in his hands.

There isn't much that a football player can do to console himself in this kind of situation – he can't talk to himself or pat himself on the back or give himself a hug. However he can comfort himself by performing the 'cradle'. Although he doesn't realize it, by placing his hands round the back of his head he is repeating the action that his mother used to support his head when he was a helpless baby. The sense of security that he felt then is intimately connected in his mind with the sensation of having the back of his head supported. By clasping the back of his head in his own hands, the player is therefore substituting himself for his mother.

The 'cradle posture' isn't only seen on the football pitch – it can be found wherever people feel insecure and need to protect themselves from threats, either real or imagined. If you watch a heated boardroom meeting you're likely to witness a few examples of the 'cradle'. In fact there are

The *Eye-cover, Cradle* and *Head-clasp*. Clear demonstrations of disbelief and disappointment are evident in these gestures when the Liverpool football team narrowly fails to score against Manchester United.

two postures you are likely to see, which look very similar but their functions are quite different. One is the 'cradle'; the other is the 'catapult'. In both gestures the hands are clasped round the back of the neck, but while the elbows are pulled back and the chest is expanded in the case of the 'catapult', the emphasis in the 'cradle' is on supporting the head. The 'catapult' is in fact a disguised gesture of aggression. By pulling his elbows back and expanding his chest, a man increases his apparent breadth and makes himself look threatening. While his hands appear to be taking refuge behind his head, they are actually waiting to ambush anyone who strays too close. As we have seen, the purpose of the 'cradle' is completely different. Here the hands perform a purely supportive role – there is no sense in which they are being pulled back in preparation for attack. Both the 'catapult' and the 'cradle' can be seen in business settings when people feel threatened. The 'catapult' is likely to be used when one person wants to intimidate another; the 'cradle' when individuals feel the need to comfort themselves. The first is a disguised form of counter-attack, while the second is a surreptitious form of self-assurance.

Face Tells

Anxiety shows on the face. An anxious smile is quite different from a genuine smile because it lacks the contraction of the *orbicularis oculi* muscles round the eyes and the wrinkled crow's feet that appear beside the eyes, which are the hallmarks of a genuine smile. Like other false smiles, anxious smiles tend to appear rather suddenly, to last longer than you'd normally expect, and then to disappear quite suddenly. Anxious smiles are also given away by unusual muscular activity round the mouth. In a genuine smile the corners of the mouth are pulled upward by the *zygomatic major* muscles, whereas in an anxious smile the corners of the mouth may be pulled sideways or even downwards. Jinni Harrigan and Dennis O'Connell at California State University at Fullerton found that when people are anxious their faces show more signs of the fear expression, and that as anxiety increases women smile less than men.[11]

We tend to think of laughter as an expression of happiness and amusement, but it can also be a sign of anxiety. A good example of this may be found in the famous experiments that Stanley Milgram conducted on obedience during the 1960s.[12] Milgram set up a bogus lab at Yale University, complete with a phoney 'experimenter' in a white coat, and an equally phoney 'learner', whose task it was to remember lists of words. People who volunteered to take part in the experiments were invited to train the learner by giving him electric shocks. The volunteers didn't realize it, but the learner was in league with the experimenter and never actually received any shocks.

The surprising discovery was that when they were urged to do so, quite ordinary people were prepared to administer powerful electric shocks to the learner, especially when he was sitting in an adjacent room where it was possible to hear, but not see him writhing about in agony. Although the volunteer subjects were prepared to administer these electric shocks, many of them were clearly uncomfortable about performing the task they'd been given. This often resulted in bouts of inappropriate laughter – in fact a third of the volunteers who took part in the experiment produced nervous laughter and smiling. When the learner made a mistake, the experimenter would instruct the subject to give the learner an electric shock, each time increasing the voltage. When the subject complied and flicked a switch, the learner would scream in pain, cry out for help, complain that he had a weak heart, or go completely silent. These cries of pain and pleas for help caused the subjects a lot of distress, but that didn't stop them giving the learner an even bigger shock a few moments later, and then laughing when they heard him screaming. When they were interviewed afterwards, the subjects could not explain why they had burst out laughing. At first glance it appeared that they were amused by the pain they were inflicting. But that was not the case – their laughter was simply a nervous reaction to the punishing regime that they had created with the help of the experimenter.

When people are feeling anxious they tend to reduce the amount of time they spend looking at others. They also spend more time searching for 'bolt holes' and 'escape hatches'. Indeed, the gaze of anxious people often focuses on how they can get out of a situation, rather than how they can make a positive contribution to what is happening. Anxious people are more likely to look away when they're in a conversation. This is largely because they're worried about the negative consequences of disagreement. In fact anxious people don't necessarily differ from confident people in terms of how much time they spend looking at the other person during a conversation – so long as there are no disagreements. However, as soon as there's any sign of disagreement, anxious people start to reduce the amount of time they spend looking at the other person.[13] For an anxious person the eyes are like a double-barrelled shotgun. Provided the safety catch is on and things are going smoothly, there's nothing much to worry about. But as soon as the atmosphere turns tense the eyes become a primed weapon – that's why it's best to keep them hidden.

Another ocular sign of anxiety is blinking. The primary purpose of blinking is to lubricate the surface of the eyes, to spread the tear film evenly over the cornea, and to keep it clean and healthy. Blink rate is affected by a variety of factors. These include features of the environment, like temperature, humidity and lighting, but they also include attentional factors, such as whether someone is reading or watching something closely. The average blink rate is about 15 blinks per minute (with women showing a higher rate than men), but this drops dramatically when people are reading. John Stern from Washington University in St Louis has studied blinking extensively. He has discovered that there is a strong link between someone's blinking rate and their emotional state – the more tired or anxious they are, the more frequent their blinking.[14] Stern points out that President Nixon was a great blinker. During the Watergate hearing, when asked questions he did not want to answer, Nixon's blinking rate rose enormously.

Mouth Tells

The most telling signs of anxiety are associated with the lips, mouth, throat, oesophagus and stomach – in fact the entire gastrointestinal tract from lips to anus. If you think of yourself as a tube through which your food passes, it's not surprising that your emotions affect the essential parts of you. The real reason why your moods are so intimately connected with your digestive system is that it has a completely integrated system of nerves called the enteric nervous system. The enteric nervous system, which is almost a brain in its own right, responds to the same neurotransmitters as the central nervous system, and that's why changes in one so often cause changes in the other. When people feel anxious, several reflexes associated with the digestive system come into play:

◆ **DRY MOUTH.** One of the early signs that someone is feeling anxious is a dry mouth. This is produced by a temporary shutdown of the saliva glands. There are visual as well as auditory cues that indicate when someone has a dry mouth – not only does the person look like he's chewing sawdust, but his voice also sounds dry and mechanical.

◆ **COUGHING.** When people become anxious they often get a tickling sensation in their throat, which makes them cough, sometimes uncontrollably. The feeling that there is an excess of saliva at the back of the throat also causes coughing.

◆ **SWALLOWING.** After President Clinton had uttered those famous words, 'I did not have sexual relations with that woman, Miss Lewinsky', he looked down and then swallowed hard. Most people, when they feel anxious, have an overwhelming desire to clear their throat by swallowing. Women can usually achieve this without being noticed, but because men have a larger Adam's apple, they tend to have more difficulty concealing this kind of nervous swallowing.

◆ **BITING LIPS**. According to Charles Bell, the Victorian anatomist, the lips are, of all the features, 'the most susceptible of action, and the most direct indices of the feelings'.[15] This can be seen both in the movement of the lips and in the ways in which they come into contact with the teeth. There are several lip-biting gestures associated with anxiety. First there's the 'lip-bite', where either the top or the bottom lip is held between the teeth. As we saw earlier, this is a gesture of self-restraint, a symbolic way of preventing oneself from saying something that one might afterwards regret. But it can also be a gesture of anxiety or embarrassment – in other words, a way of holding on to oneself with one's teeth. Then there's the 'lip-lip-bite' gesture, where both the top lip and the bottom lip are pulled inwards and held tight between the teeth. This gesture is a *trademark tell* of the great American athlete, Carl Lewis – or at least it was when he was picking up medals and in the public eye. When Lewis was interviewed on TV he would frequently reveal his discomfort by pulling his lips in and securing them between his teeth. In every other respect Lewis always came across as confident and articulate – it was only his 'lip-lip-bite' that gave him away.

◆ **NAIL-BITING**. People who habitually bite their nails tend to score low on psychological tests of self-esteem, and high on measures of anxiety. It has also been suggested that nail-biting is a sign of inhibited hostility, with nail-biters turning their aggression inwards upon themselves, rather than outwards towards other people.

◆ **MOUTHING OBJECTS**. When people feel anxious they often have a desire to put something in their mouth. This is a throwback to the comforting experience of sucking the breast and, following that, sucking the thumb. The two most common forms of oral comfort behaviour found in our society are chewing gum and smoking cigarettes. Smoking is often portrayed as a sign of coolness, and smokers as people who are in control. In fact, smokers often use cigarettes to calm their nerves and control their anxiety. The oral comfort provided by chewing gum is evident from the amount of gum that coaches and team managers get through while they're watching a game. For example, if you watch Alex Ferguson, the manager of Manchester United, you'll notice that his gum-chewing reflects the temporary fortunes of his team. When Manchester United is ahead and playing well, Ferguson's chewing is cogitative and slow. When the team is behind or playing badly, the speed and pressure of his gum-chewing increases dramatically. If you're in the stands, you don't need to watch the players to find out how Manchester United are faring – you can gauge their progress by watching Alex Ferguson's jaw movements!

Talk Tells

Anxiety is also revealed by the voice. When people are feeling anxious there's an overall increase in muscle tension, and this leads to an increase in pitch, or what linguists call 'fundamental frequency'. Perturbations in pitch – what linguists call 'jitter' and 'shimmer' – are also evidence of anxiety.[16] Loudness is another indicator – it's the opposite of slow and soft speech, which is usually a symptom of sadness or depression.[17]

When people feel anxious they tend to talk faster and to talk less. That's because they don't want to cast other people in the role of listener for any longer than necessary, and they don't want to draw attention to themselves. The best way to achieve these goals is to reduce what one has to say and to increase the speed at which one says it. Although anxious people speak faster, they are often quite slow when it comes to answering questions – that's because they spend more time thinking about what kind of answer they're going to give.[18]

The relationship between anxiety and pausing isn't straightforward, because it depends on whether people have trait or state anxiety – in other words whether they are chronically anxious or simply anxious in a particular situation. It's been found that when chronically anxious people are talking they tend to pause less – they're agitated and they want to hurry through what they're saying. On the other hand, when acutely anxious people are talking, they tend to pause more than normal – they have to deal with their immediate feelings of anxiety at the same time as deciding what to say. The pauses that are a feature of acute anxiety are often filled with speech disfluencies, like 'um' and 'er', which enable speakers to show that they have more to say, and that they want to retain the floor. Both chronically and acutely anxious people are inclined to stutter. Stutterers tend to stutter more when they're anxious, and so do non-stutterers; even people who hardly ever stutter are more likely to do so when they're feeling threatened and insecure.[19]

The thing that people dread more than anything else is public speaking. Most people experience some degree of 'speech phobia', but there are some people who are completely disabled by their fear of public speaking. It's often said that the more experience one has at public speaking, the easier it becomes. This may be true for lots of people, but for some public speaking remains a source of deep anxiety. Regardless of how often they do it, and how accomplished they've become, they continue to worry about being the centre of attention, forgetting their lines, and looking ridiculous in front of so many people.

Because anxiety is a negative emotional state it's difficult to control, and the *tells* associated with anxiety are therefore difficult to conceal. This works both ways – it makes it easy for us to detect the anxiety of other people, but it also makes it easy for them to identify our feelings of anxiety. People try to conceal their anxiety in various ways. One is by working on their state of mind so that they no longer feel anxious; another is by trying to cover up their *anxiety tells*. The only problem with this strategy is that it frequently produces a *tell-suppressing tell*, which gives the lie to the person's attempt at concealment. People who surreptitiously take a drink of water when their throat is feeling dry, or who wipe their hand on their clothes before shaking hands, often reveal more about their internal state than they would have done had they not tried to cover up their anxiety in the first place. In other words, *tell-suppressing tells* are often more revealing than the *tells* they're designed to cover up – that's because they point to the person's anxiety as well as to their desire to conceal it. So, if you don't want other people to know how anxious you feel, make sure they don't notice your *anxiety tells*. And whatever you do, don't let them catch you trying to cover up these *tells*.

9. Sexual Tells

Tells are an essential part of courtship. In fact, without them there would be no such thing as courtship or love, and sex as we know it would cease to exist. The importance of *tells* lies in the simple fact that courtship, love and sex require people to exchange signals – signals about sexual inclination, availability, readiness and compatibility. Even though we may not intend to, we are constantly sending and receiving sexual messages. While other people are looking us over and deciding how sexy, attractive, enthusiastic or desperate we are, we're busy making the same decisions about them. In this regard *sexual tells* are like grains of pollen – although they aren't always evident, they're everywhere.

Body Tells

One of the bases on which people make sexual inferences about each other is their 'secondary sexual characteristics'. Psychologists use this term to distinguish the 'primary sexual characteristics' of men and women – like the penis and testes of the male and the vagina, uterus and ovaries of the female – from their non-procreative characteristics. In men these include facial and chest hair, a deep voice, and a bigger, more muscular body. In women they include breasts, a wider pelvic girdle and the deposit of more fat on the thighs and buttocks. Nature's intention, it appears, is that these secondary sexual characteristics should serve as sexual cues, enabling men and women to assess each other's fitness as a mate. To a large extent, Nature's intentions are fulfilled – in the absence of any other information, men do find women with large breasts and an hourglass figure more attractive.[1] And women, on the whole, express a preference for men with hairy chests, square shoulders and neat bottoms.[2]

The things that men and women look for in partners are, however, highly susceptible to the influence of culture, fashion and circumstance. The physical attributes that men in our society regard as attractive in a woman are often very different from those that get men's pulses racing in other parts of the world. Within our own society there have been marked historical variations in people's notions of beauty. Compare, for example, the delicious plump ladies painted by Rubens with the scrawny models and Calista Flockharts of today.

The fact that some men prefer flat-chested women, or women with a high waist-to-hip ratio, shows that they are using alternative criteria for choosing a partner. David Buss, from the University of Texas, has conducted a large, cross-cultural survey on what men and women look for in a partner.[3] He reports that men universally prefer a woman who is young and shapely with unblemished skin. Women, on the other hand, place greater store on the man's wealth and his ability to provide security. The divergent criteria employed by men and women reflect their differing motives in the mating game – the man needs a partner who can produce lots of healthy children and who's strong enough to care for them, while the woman, it seems, needs a man to provide for her, and to protect her and the children. From an evolutionary point of view this all makes perfect sense. However, it fails to take into account the enormous fluidity in mate choice – for example the fact that some people prefer a mate who doesn't fit the evolutionary model, or that when they do find one who fits the model they adopt a completely different set of selection criteria. All things being equal, a woman may prefer a man who can provide for her. But when she has married a successful banker and had several children, she may decide that she wants to find excitement elsewhere. In searching for a sexual partner outside her marriage, she's much more likely to have a fling with her tennis coach than with a wealthy businessman. After all, when people have got what they want, they don't necessarily want more of the same – they want something new and different!

Women who possess the physical attributes that men desire are much more likely to be noticed by men. But it doesn't always follow that men are more likely to approach them, or, if they do, that they're likely to hang around if they don't get any encouragement. In fact, men are much more likely to pursue a woman who isn't beautiful but who gives off the right signals than a woman who is gorgeous but doesn't appear to be available. In contests between courtship signals and looks, courtship signals usually win hands down.[4]

It follows from this that a woman who has all the right physical attributes, and who complements these with all the right signals, is likely to be more attractive to men than one who has the attributes but doesn't produce the signals, or vice versa. The Oxford philosopher, Robert Burton, reached this conclusion in his *Anatomy of Melancholy*, first published in 1621.[5] 'It is true', he wrote, 'that those fair sparkling eyes, white neck, coral lips, turgent paps [swelling breasts], rose-coloured cheeks, &c., of themselves are potent enticers; but when a comely, artificial, well-composed look, pleasing gesture, an affected carriage shall be added, it must needs be far more forcible than it was'. Nowhere is this more evident in modern times than in the case of Marilyn Monroe – a woman who had what it takes and knew how to use it. If you've seen the movie *Some Like It Hot* you'll remember the remarkable scene where she walks down the railway platform, while Tony Curtis and Jack Lemmon stare at her undulating bottom – moving, as Jack Lemmon describes it, 'like Jell-o on springs'. The reason why Marilyn's wiggle is so effective here is that it draws attention to her feminine hips.

This brings us to the observation that the prime purpose of seductive behaviour is to accentuate secondary sexual characteristics. This in fact is the clue to why some seductive signals are used by women but not by men, and vice versa. When a woman pouts her lips, arches her back or leans forward so that her breasts are pressed together between her arms, she is accentuating the physical attributes of her sex. These actions are 'illuminations' – they give prominence to a particular feature of a woman's appearance, just like the accentuated letters in a manuscript. A man who pulls himself up to his full height in the presence of a woman, and who expands his chest or lowers his voice, is essentially doing the same thing – he's illuminating the differences between himself and the woman, making his appearance more masculine and, by contrast, hers more feminine.

Action Tells

Not being content to look different, men and women have conspired to behave differently as well. These differences in behaviour – what Ray Birdwhistell neatly referred to as 'tertiary sexual characteristics' – provide men and women with a way of emphasizing their gender and making themselves more attractive to members of the opposite sex.[6] When a man is trying to appear attractive to a woman he's more likely to engage in prototypical male behaviour – like sitting with his legs apart, extending his feet into the shared space, splaying his arms, and generally creating the impression that he needs lots of space to accommodate his enormous frame. He will also shift his body more frequently, changing postures, enlisting his hands to underline what he's saying, and moving his hands away from his body.

In contrast, the woman's gestures are likely to be towards her body. To appear feminine she's inclined to keep her movements slow, her gesticulation modest and her legs close together, and to cultivate the impression that she needs less physical space for her body, not more. When it comes to facial expression, however, the situation tends to be reversed, with the woman being lively and animated, while the man tries to give the impression that he's more controlled.

Despite increasing sexual equality, men and women try to appear attractive to the opposite sex by acting according to type – men behave in a more manly fashion, while women act in a more feminine way. One way that men try to be manlier is by being dominant. Many of the 'illuminations' of men's behaviour – like standing tall, expanding the chest, and standing or sitting with the legs apart – are in fact dominance signals, while those of women – like sitting with the ankles crossed, canting the head to one side, and touching the face – happen also to be submissive behaviours. However, this doesn't mean that during courtship men only use dominance signals, or that women restrict themselves to submissive signals. There are numerous instances where the roles become reversed, with the woman taking the role of mother and the man that of a child. These departures from socially prescribed roles, coupled with regressive excursions into the world of play, are an essential part of courtship. Laughing, tickling, and generally playing the fool give the man and woman a chance to experiment with their roles and to show each other that they're harmless and unthreatening, just like children. Fooling around also enables them to introduce the nurturing, loving activities that form part of the relationship between parent and child into their own relationship.

Availability Tells

With most mammals it's the male who does the sexual

advertising, showing females that he's strong, healthy and resourceful, and that he'll make a perfect mate. With humans, however, it's usually the other way round because most of the sexual advertising is done by women – it's women who are dressing up, styling their hair, and wearing make-up and perfume. But things weren't always this way. For example, in seventeenth-century England, during the age of the 'dandy', it was the men of polite society who dressed like gaudy peacocks and their women who looked like plain peahens. It's equally true to say that while women today do most of the sexual advertising, men are taking on an increasing share of the burden by spending money on clothes, keeping up with hairstyle fashions, and wearing aftershave and cologne. Clothes, jewellery, make-up and perfume are all worn on the person. But there are other forms of sexual advertising that don't appear on the person, like wealth and possessions. In this area of advertising it's men who usually do most of the work, investing in cars, apartments and gadgets so that they can impress members of the opposite sex.

We advertise our sexual availability in a number of ways. These include the clothes we wear, how we wear them, which parts of our body we expose, the postures we assume, the facial expressions we adopt, how we move our eyes, and what we say.

When young people enter a nightclub or a bar they usually begin by surveying the scene. Sometimes they do so innocently, to see if their friends are there, but most of the time they're making a quick assessment of the available talent. There are two main ways that they do this:

◆ **SCANNING**. People map out their social environment by scanning it visually. Monika Moore, who has made an extensive study of courtship strategies, has identified what she calls 'the room encompassing glance', where the head and eyes move together, rather like radar, tracing an arc through the room, and then returning to their original position.[7] The purpose of scanning is to perform an initial survey and not necessarily to focus on a specific person or group of people. That comes later.

◆ **PROMENADING**. Instead of casting their eyes around, people sometimes check out the room by walking around. The advantage of promenading is that it enables individuals to be noticed by other people, and to examine them at close quarters. In this way, promenading is rather similar to the Spanish and South American *paseo*, when young men and women stroll back and forth, watching each other and being seen.

With hundreds of young people milling around and checking each other out, the spectacle in a nightclub is very similar to a 'lek'.[8] Leks are the 'singles bars' of the animal world – patches of ground where males and females congregate so that the males can display to the females, and the females can decide which male to mate with. Lekking occurs in a wide range of species, including bats, antelopes, frogs, Canada geese and the greater prairie chicken. In all these species there is pronounced 'sexual dimorphism' – in other words, the males look very different from the females, and males who display at a higher rate usually manage to mate with most of the females. This, of course, is often what happens in a human 'lek' like a nightclub, where the more flamboyant and active males tend to be more successful.

If you watch people in a nightclub you'll notice that their behaviour is often extravagant. This is partly because they're competing with each other for attention. But it's also because of the low lighting, which makes it difficult to see what others are doing, and the ambient noise, which makes it difficult to hear what they're saying. People usually respond to this situation by increasing the amplitude of their signals – by raising their voice, exposing more of their body, and dancing wildly. Some people simply keep repeating themselves to the same person. Interestingly, much the same thing happens with birds. It's been discovered that birds that nest in noisy habitats deal with the problem of noise by increasing the amplitude of their signals and by singing louder.[9] They also incorporate a lot more redundancy and repetition into their songs – just like those bores in the nightclub who can't stop repeating themselves!

In order to attract each other's attention in a nightclub, men and women need to signal their sexual availability. They do this in one of two ways – either by 'broadcasting', so that everyone present knows that they're sexually available, or by 'narrowcasting' – in other words, by 'targeting' a specific individual. For example, a woman may broadcast her availability by wearing revealing clothes, exposing parts of her body, or dancing provocatively. In doing so she wants everyone to know that while she might be available to *someone*, she is definitely not available to just *anyone* – a distinction that lots of men find it difficult to understand. Women's broadcasting is often linked to their menstrual cycle – it's been found that when women are in the middle of their cycle and therefore most receptive, they are more likely to visit singles bars and nightclubs without their current partner and to wear clothes that reveal more of their body, and that they are more attracted to men with masculine features.[10] Not only are they more sexually available; they're also looking for men who are likely to be more sexually active.

Approach Tells

When it comes to romance, men like to think that they're the ones who make the first move and who decide how fast the relationship should progress. All the research on human courtship shows that this is simply not the case, and that, as Darwin put it, courtship is almost always a matter of 'female choice'. In nightclubs, bars and at parties, it's the woman who invariably makes the first move. She does this by producing an *approach tell* – a signal which is not too explicit, but which is sufficiently clear to show a man that he may approach her. It's her way of giving him 'clearance'.

When a man responds and walks across the room, he's doing so at the woman's behest. From his point of view things usually seem quite different – because he's made the effort to cross the room he's inclined to think that he's the one who's taken the initiative. Men are far less likely to engage a woman who hasn't shown that she's approachable, although there are obviously cases where men will advance on a woman who hasn't even noticed them, let alone given them clearance. When the man takes the initiative in this way his chances of success are usually reduced, simply because he's robbing the woman of a chance to be in control. He can usually get round this by appearing to be submissive or by giving the impression that his intentions are entirely non-sexual.

Women produce a variety of *approach tells* – some in 'clusters', others individually. They include the following:

◆ **THE STROBE GLANCE**. A woman who is attracted to a man will sometimes stare across the room at him until she manages to catch his eye. When this happens, she can rely on either frequency or duration of eye contact to signal her clearance.[11] She can rely on frequency by holding his gaze for a second or two and then averting her head and eyes slightly, but not so far that she appears to be removing herself from the interaction altogether. Then, while the man continues to look at her, she turns her head and eyes back towards him and repeats the cycle all over again. Monika Moore claims that it usually takes three brief glances to get the message across to the man.[12]

◆ **THE EYE-LOCK**. Instead of using several brief glances, a woman can show a man that she's approachable by holding his gaze for slightly longer than she would in other circumstances. When we look across a crowded room and happen to catch a stranger's eye, we usually avert our gaze within a second or two. This allows us to disengage before there's any suggestion that we might wish to pursue the interaction. By fixating her eyes on a man and holding his gaze for longer than normal, a woman shows the man that she's prepared to take things further.[13]

◆ **THE EYE-FLICKER**. When a woman catches the eye of an

attractive man she can usually grab his attention by performing an 'eye-flicker'. Here the upper eyelids are raised very slightly and for a fraction of a second, so that the gesture remains almost imperceptible and only evident to the person at whom it's directed. The brief elevation of the upper eyelids will sometimes cause the eyebrows to rise as well, but it's the eyes rather than the eyebrows that carry the real signal. By opening the eyes in this way, a woman shows a man that he's the person she's looking at. The flick of the eyelids also transforms the signal into a question – it makes the man feel that the woman is saying to him, 'What next?'

◆ **THE HAIR-FLICK.** Having caught a man's eye briefly, a woman will sometimes flick her hair to show him that she's approachable. She can do this either by running her hand through her hair or by tossing her head so that the hair bounces up and assumes a slightly different position. These actions serve as a 'youth display' because it's only young women who have soft, flexible hair that can convincingly be rearranged or flicked. As women get older their hair becomes less pliable and the hair-flick becomes less of an option. It's not unusual, however, to find women with lacquered or very short hair actually flicking their head when they come across a man they fancy.

◆ **THE POUT.** A woman can indicate that she is approachable by looking at a man and pouting her lips. She can convey the same message by licking her lips. These gestures draw attention to a distinctive feature of female physiology – the fact that women have larger lips than men. When boys enter puberty their body is flooded with testosterone. This encourages the growth of their jaw. Girls' faces remain fairly childlike over the same period. Increasing levels of oestrogen, however, actually discourage the growth of facial bone, and lead instead to a thickening of the lips. After puberty, fuller lips become a feature of sexual dimorphism. Consequently, when a woman pouts or licks her lips, she automatically draws attention to one of her secondary sexual characteristics, and to the fact that as people become sexually aroused their lips become engorged with blood. The same effect is of course achieved with red lipstick. When these gestures are targeted at a man they usually constitute an invitation. It's essential, however, that these gestures be subtle and brief, because although a woman might want a man to know that she's approachable, she wouldn't want him to think she's a pushover.

◆ **THE SMILE**. When a woman wants to invite a strange man to approach her, the signal that she's most likely to use is a smile – usually a brief smile that's confined to the mouth.[14] In these circumstances she's unlikely to perform a full smile, partly because full smiles tend to be reserved for friends and acquaintances. This conforms to the principle that, in order to be effective, *approach tells* should always be muted. This applies as much to smiles as it does to movements of the head, eyes and lips. It's very unlikely that a broad smile between strangers will be regarded as an invitation; it's much more likely to be interpreted as a sign of recognition. The same applies to exaggerated stares, pouts and rearrangements of the hair – because they're not muted they're likely to be seen as a joke rather than as a sincere invitation.

Flirting Tells

Flirting tells fall into three broad categories – 'come-ons', 'put-offs' and 'hang-ons'. 'Come-ons' consist of *approach tells*, which give the other person permission to make a move, and *promotion tells*, which are designed to promote sexual interest and move the relationship on to the next stage. 'Put-offs' are the exact opposite of 'come-ons' – they express a total lack of interest and are designed to reject the advances of the other person. 'Hang-ons', on the other hand, put the courtship process on hold – their purpose is to stall the relationship without discouraging the other person's interest.

In the mating game women use all three types of *tells*, while men tend to concentrate on come-ons. Men usually flatter themselves that they make most of the running in courtship, and that they control the whole process, but as we've seen it's women who are really in charge.[15] In the early stages of an encounter women produce a lot of come-ons, even when they aren't actually attracted to the man and have no intention of taking things any further.[16] They also mix come-ons with hang-ons in order to increase ambiguity and to foster the illusion that the man is in charge of proceedings. In fact men are notoriously bad decoders of women's *tells*, often assuming that a woman is interested in them when she isn't.[17] That's because a man automatically assumes that an attractive woman is aiming her availability signals at him personally, when she's actually broadcasting them to everyone. Men also have a tendency to inflate come-ons in their mind, and to assume that put-offs are only hang-ons. This tendency of men to misread women's signals is part of a more widespread insensitivity. Not only are men less observant, they are generally not as tuned in to other people's needs as women are.

Posture Tells

The postures that a man and a woman adopt when they meet for the first time often reveal their hidden feelings for each other. For example, if the woman folds her arms and coils her legs together it's very unlikely that she's about to run headlong into an affair. On the other hand, if the man sits with his legs apart and leans his body towards the woman it shows that he finds her attractive and is trying to impress her. Open postures are generally associated with positive, accepting attitudes, whereas closed postures are linked to guarded and negative ones.

Posture switching is another matter altogether. For example, when a woman repeatedly crosses and uncrosses her legs in the presence of a man, she's doing more than alternating between closed postures – she's actually drawing attention to her legs. Her motive for doing this is usually unconscious. There are times, however, when it's deliberate – like the famous scene in *Basic Instinct*, in which Sharon Stone crosses and uncrosses her legs to draw attention to the fact that she's not wearing anything under her dress! Most of the cases where women cross and uncross their legs in the presence of a man are far less dramatic than this, and a lot of the time the man isn't even aware of what's happening. Nevertheless, the way that a woman positions and moves her legs is always very informative, and the postures that the man adopts are equally telling.

Leg Tells

Women also try to make themselves attractive to men by emphasizing the length of their legs, relative to the rest of their body – trying, in this respect, to make themselves look more like a Barbie Doll. The reason why men find long legs sexy is that when girls go through puberty they have a growth spurt and this leaves their legs looking longer than the rest of their body. It's at this stage in their development that girls become women and start to get noticed by men. It is this youthful phase in their lives that women try to recover when they attempt to make their legs look longer.[18] There are three 'Barbie Doll strategies' that they can employ. The first is to wear high heels. The second is to wear a swimming costume or gym kit with a 'high leg' – this makes a woman's legs look longer by creating the illusion that they begin at her hips.

The third way that women can accentuate the length of their legs is by walking on tiptoe. This works best when they're not wearing any shoes, and it's a sure sign that they find someone attractive. Take the case where a good-looking man arrives at a house party and several people, including the host and hostess, are sitting round the swimming pool in their bathing costumes. The hostess notices the man arriving, so she gets up and goes to greet him. But notice that she's not walking flat-footed – she's moving towards him on tiptoes! And to make sure that nobody thinks she's behaving strangely, she makes a show of dodging the wet patches by the side of the pool. Observing this little scene we can see that the hostess wants everyone to think that she's trying not to slip on the puddles. But the real reason is that she's trying to impress the guest – by walking on tiptoe she's discreetly trying to make her legs look longer.

In addition to increasing the apparent length of a woman's legs, high heels also arch her back. This arching of the back is similar to 'lordosis' in the animal world. In certain animal species lordosis acts as a sexual releaser – female hamsters and guinea pigs, for example, will arch their back to show a male that they are sexually receptive. When a woman sticks out her bottom and arches her back it has the same arousing effect on a man – that's why 'girlie magazines' are full of pictures of women in this posture. When a woman finds a man attractive she sometimes reveals her feelings by arching her back. This may occur while she's standing up, sitting down, or leaning forward and supporting her weight on the table. The action may be almost imperceptible, but it shows that she's sexually attracted to him.

Spatial Tells

The way that a man and a woman arrange themselves spatially says a lot about what each of them is hoping to achieve, and about which stage they have reached in their relationship. As a rule, the closer people are to each other physically, the closer they are emotionally and sexually. This also applies to how directly or obliquely they orient their bodies towards each other. During the early stages of courtship both individuals need to treat the other person's space with caution and respect, making sure not to move in close before the other person has given them clearance. One of the moves that people use to gauge the other person's reactions is the 'quick-step'.

The last time I saw the 'quick-step' used the sequence went as follows: A young man and a woman were in conversation, with their bodies attentively oriented towards each other. They were standing some distance apart, with a large patch of no man's land between them. After a few minutes, and while she was still talking, the young woman took a big step forward, completed what she was saying, and then took an equally big step backward, ending up where she'd started. Although the man wasn't consciously aware what was happening, his response was right on cue – he started to talk and as he did so, he stepped right into the middle of the space she had just vacated. He had now become much more animated. Suddenly it was apparent that he found her attractive. What had clearly happened was that by stepping into no man's land the woman had taken the initiative and produced a very powerful *approach tell*. By stepping back she had invited him to advance towards her, and without being fully aware of what was happening, he had happily obliged – she had created a vacuum in the space between them, and he had unwittingly been drawn into it.

Watching this exchange, I knew that neither the woman nor the man realized what was happening. She didn't know that she was using the 'quick-step' or that her movements would have the desired effect on him. Equally, he didn't realize that her actions had controlled his, just as much as if she were a puppeteer and he were a puppet. I was also struck by the remarkably simple way that she had managed to move the relationship on to the next phase – by getting him to step forward she had completely changed his attitude and encouraged him to see that the situation was now full of promise.

Locomotor Tells

Walking style also plays a part in courtship – especially in the early stages when people are making snap judgements about each other. In modifying their gait to impress members of the opposite sex, women tend to accentuate their female characteristics. One way they do this is by rolling their hips. Another is by swinging their arms further back as they walk, and by turning their arms outward in order to emphasize the fact that women's arms are more 'supinated' than those of men. Men who wish to emphasize their masculinity tend to do the opposite – they swing their arms across their body and further up in the front, and they rotate their wrists inward in order to stress the fact that men's arms are more 'pronated' than those of women.

To draw attention to their youth, men and women often walk vigorously, bouncing along and generally creating the impression that they have energy to spare. This energetic style of walking, which is especially noticeable in young men, is very similar to the habit of 'stotting' found in the animal world.[19] For example, when young gazelles spot a lion nearby, they usually move away from the predator – not by running as fast as they can, but by leaping high into the air. There are several theories about why animals stot, but all agree that stotting is a highly inefficient means of escape. One theory is that animals stot in order to display their physical prowess – by leaping into the air a gazelle is, in effect, saying to the lion, 'Look at how strong I am and how much energy I have to spare! There's no way you're ever going to catch me!' These messages about strength and energy are also contained in the way that young people walk – they are a way of showing members of the opposite sex that one would make an excellent mate.

Head Tells

In the early stages of courtship people often go to extraordinary lengths to make themselves appealing and to put the other person at ease. There are several head signals that help to further these aims:

◆ **THE NOD.** Women are often very attentive listeners, nodding their head and encouraging men to keep talking – and then regretting it afterwards!

◆ **THE HAIR-FLICK.** The hair-flick sometimes serves as an *approach tell*. And in the later stages of courtship it provides women as well as men with a subtle way of displaying their youth and appearing more attractive to each other.

◆ **THE HEAD-CANT.** As we have already seen, when the head is tilted to one side the person looks helpless and appealing. The origins of head-canting can be traced to the way that babies rest their head on their parent's shoulder, and the fact that tilting the head to one side exposes a vulnerable part of the body, the neck. The head-cant is an ideal courtship signal because it sends a message of appeasement – it's a way of saying to the other person, 'Look, I trust you so much that I'm prepared to expose a really vulnerable part of my body to you'. A related appeasement gesture, often used by young women, is the 'shoulder-lift'. This is performed by raising the shoulders very quickly, and by raising the eyebrows and smiling at the same time.

◆ **THE NECK-SHOW**. In addition to the head-cant, there are other 'vulnerability displays' involving the neck that are used as come-ons. In one the chin is raised slightly; in another the head is turned, so that the other person gets an unobstructed view of the neck. Both these actions fall into the category of *show tells* – actions that are designed to expose a vulnerable or particularly appealing part of the body. A similar effect is achieved when people touch their neck. A woman who's attracted to a man may lightly run her fingers along her neck, thereby drawing his attention to her vulnerability and ultimately to her suitability as a partner. This action falls into the category of 'pointers' – that is, instances where people use a hand or a finger to draw attention to a part of their body. Another example of a *show tell* is the 'exposed wrist display', where the arm is positioned so that the inside of the wrist is presented to other people. This, like the 'neck-show', involves a vulnerable part of the body. When a woman draws attention to her neck or her wrists she's usually unaware of what she's doing. Likewise, even if the man responds positively, he's unlikely to be able to describe what she's done or what it is about her that he finds so attractive.

Eye Tells

The crucial role that the eyes play in courtship has long

been recognized. Writing in the early seventeenth century, Robert Burton called the eye 'a secret orator, the first bawd, the gateway of love'. He referred to the eyes as 'the shoeing-horns' and 'the hooks of love', pointing out that by simply looking at each other, lovers are able 'to understand one another's meanings, before they come to speak a word'.[20]

Psychologists have discovered that when people meet for the first time they often reach a decision about each other within a matter of a few seconds, and frequently before the other person has had a chance to say anything. These 'snap judgements' are therefore often based on visual information.[21] What's more, people will often cling to their snap judgements, even in the face of disconfirming evidence. During courtship the participants use their eyes to 'assess' and 'express' – in other words, see how the other person is behaving and responding, as well as to convey information about their own needs, intentions and feelings. The expressive role of the eyes is evident in a number of signals:

◆ **THE EYE-PUFF.** One way that people make themselves irresistible is by enlarging their eyes. This is especially noticeable in women. An almond-shaped face, a small chin, rounded cheeks, a pert nose and large eyes are all part of the so-called 'baby face' – those innate releasers that make us feel protective towards babies.[22] By enlarging her eyes when she's with her lover, a woman makes herself look defenceless, which in turn makes her lover feel more protective towards her. He too can achieve this effect with the eye-puff.

◆ **THE DIPPED HEAD.** When she's looking at her lover, one of the ways that a woman can make her eyes look bigger is by lowering her head. This creates a fore-shortened effect, so that her chin appears to be smaller, while the top of her face, including her eyes, seems to be bigger. But there's also another principle at work. Because children are shorter, they sometimes look at adults out of the top of their eye sockets. When a woman lowers her head while looking at her lover it auto-matically makes her seem much smaller, and therefore more in need of protection. The fact that lowering of the head is associated with submission is another reason why women are more likely to dip their head when they're flirting with a man.[23] In fact Ruth Campbell and her colleagues at University College London have found that individuals who are photographed looking down are seen as more feminine.[24]

◆ **DILATED PUPILS.** When people become aroused – either pleasantly or otherwise – their pupils tend to dilate. However, people can't consciously control the size of their pupils, and they have no way of knowing how large or small their own pupils are. People are generally more attracted to individuals with large pupils than to those with constricted pupils, although they are seldom aware of the role that pupil size plays in their preferences. But there are individuals who know about pupil dilation and who use it to gauge other people's moods. For example, it's reported that in pre-revolutionary China, jade sellers used to watch the pupils of their customers so that they could see if they liked a particular piece of jade or were happy to pay the asking price.[25] In the sixteenth century, Italian women used a tincture of belladonna to dilate their pupils. Belladonna (which means 'beautiful woman' in Italian) contains atropine, which dilates the pupils, making the person look more aroused and therefore more attractive.

◆ **THE SIDEWAYS LOOK**. This is done by looking at someone while one's head is turned away. The sideways look conveys two opposing messages – the directed gaze signals approach, while the averted head signals avoidance. The tension between approach and avoidance is partly what gives the sideways look its appeal – it's this that makes the person who is performing the sideways look appear so interesting and attractive. This is especially the case when the look is combined with a smile to create a 'turn-away smile'. The other factor behind the gesture's appeal is the implicit suggestion that the person is turning back. When a woman looks at a man with her head averted he's inclined to get the feeling that she has stopped what she was doing in order to look at him. He might even imagine that the sight of him was so arresting that the woman's head didn't have time to catch up with her eyes! Women mostly use the sideways look, although men do employ it with the same coquettish effect. Because it involves a presentation of the side of the face, the sideways look can also be seen as a form of 'flanking' – in other words, the appeasement that's signalled by offering the side of one's body can also be conveyed, in a slightly reduced form, by presenting someone with the side of one's face.

◆ **HOODED EYES**. The hooded look is achieved by lowering

the upper eyelids, raising the eyebrows slightly, and holding this expression for a while. The effect of this is to narrow the eyes, making them look like 'bedroom eyes', and to increase the distance between the eye and the eyebrow, which is one of the things that happens when people try to appear submissive. In a sense the hooded look offers the best of both worlds, because in addition to making the person appear submissive it also gives them a rather knowing and mysterious look, as if they were harbouring some secret. This, however, is not the only explanation. Paul Ekman has suggested that the reason why hooded eyes are so seductive is that they reproduce the expression that appears on people's faces just before they have an orgasm.[26] Whether or not this is true, it is certainly the case that the hooded eyes gesture is used more by women than by men – most of the time in earnest, but sometimes in jest. It was very popular during the age of the silent screen, when it became the hallmark of actresses like Greta Garbo, who sometimes combined it with the sideways look. Marilyn Monroe was also very keen on the hooded-eyes gesture, which she often combined with the 'parted-lips posture'. In this posture the jaw is relaxed and the lips are separated, as if they were inviting a kiss. With the lips parted and the eyes half-closed, a woman certainly looks like she's in the throes of sexual ecstasy. Men find this combination of tells seductive because it hints at the pleasure that they could induce in the woman if only they were given a chance.

Touching Tells

Courtship is associated with various kinds of touching. These include people touching themselves, touching the other person, and occasions when they touch or manipulate objects.

◆ **SELF-TOUCHING.** People touch themselves for all kinds of reasons when the atmosphere is sexually charged. As we have seen, when people feel anxious or self-conscious they often produce 'adaptors' by touching their face or rubbing their arm in order to comfort themselves. People also touch themselves as a way of drawing attention to a particular part of their body. Consider a young man and a woman who are out on a date in a restaurant. While the young man is talking, the young woman is leaning forward with the palms of her hands supporting her chin and her fingers wrapped round her cheeks. She's doing a 'face frame' – using her hands as a picture frame to define the image that she wants him to focus on. While the young man is talking he absent-mindedly combs his fingers through his hair. This action is a 'pointer' because, even though he doesn't know it, its purpose is to alert his date to his fine head of hair, and to set her thinking about what it would be like to run her own fingers through it. Pointers do two things – they draw someone's attention to a part of the body and they raise the issue of what it would be like to do to someone what they're doing to themselves. All this occurs outside conscious awareness – neither the person who produces the pointer nor the person to whom it's addressed are likely to recognize what's actually happening. If you

The *Neck-show*. By exposing her neck Marilyn Monroe makes herself look vulnerable *and* sexy. Here, too, she uses other 'come-ons': the *Shoulder-Lift Gesture* makes her appear submissive, while the *Hooded-eyes Look* and the *Parted-lips Posture* suggest that she's in the throes of sexual ecstasy.

watch Hugh Grant on screen you'll notice that he often produces a sheepish grin when he's running his hand through his hair. The ostensible purpose of the grin is to suggest that he's feeling embarrassed, and that's why he's running his hand through his hair. In fact, the sheepish grin is a facial decoy – it's designed to obscure the fact that he's touching his hair because, deep down, he wants the viewers to admire it.

◆ **OTHER TOUCHING.** As we saw earlier, although women tend to call the shots in courtship, it's usually the man who touches the woman first. That's because the woman has indicated that she's ready to be touched; she has, in effect, given the man the green light. The touching that takes place during the early stages of courtship is very different from the touching that occurs during the later stages, both in terms of who's likely to initiate it and what form it takes. In loving relationships women tend to get touched more than men. That's partly because women have a lower touch threshold than men and are therefore more sensitive to touch.[27] This difference emerges soon after birth. Partly for this reason, girls usually show more enjoyment of touch than boys, and this leads to their being touched more by their parents. But in addition to being more sensitive to touch, and appreciating it more, women also regard touch as more meaningful. For them, touch is an important sign of love and affection, whereas for some men it's often nothing more than a means to an end.

◆ **OBJECT TOUCHING.** People who are courting often reveal their feelings towards each other by the way they manipulate objects. In a restaurant, for example, the way that a woman caresses her wine glass or runs her fingers up and down its stem may reveal her intentions towards the man she's dining with. Equally, the way that the man reaches across the table, picks up the woman's car keys, and starts to play with them, offers strong proof that he wants to possess some part or all of her. Watching what people do to objects often shows what they would like to do to each other.

Talk Tells

Men and women often worry about what they're going to say to each other when they first meet because they know that it can have a big impact on what happens next. Men put a lot of effort into chat-up lines.[28] But because women have heard most of them before, and aren't terribly impressed with the new ones, men's opening gambits often fall flat. Men also make a lot of effort in other ways – lowering the pitch of their voice to make them sound more masculine and speaking quietly so that the conversation feels more intimate. Lowering the voice is probably a good idea because women are attracted to men with deep voices – or at least they are when they hear them on the telephone, imagining that they're tall and heavily muscled. In this respect, voice quality is actually a dishonest signal because it's an unreliable indicator of body size and it's fairly easy to fake. However, it is a fairly honest signal of dominance and sexual drive, because men with deep voices have higher levels of testosterone. Consequently, women who think that a man with a deep voice is big and muscular are likely to be disappointed, while those who expect him to be dominant and sexy are likely to have their expectations pleasantly confirmed.[29]

During the early stages of courtship men tend to ply women with compliments. Joan Manes and Nessa Wolfson, who analysed compliments in great detail, discovered that three-quarters of them include the word 'you' – which is hardly surprising – and that a third include the word 'nice'.[30] The formulaic nature of most compliments makes them very easy to compose and equally easy to comprehend. Most people are sceptical about compliments, but this doesn't stop people using them, and it certainly hasn't reduced their effectiveness.

Another thing that works is self-disclosure. Relationships between women are often characterized by intense disclosure – female friends will often know everything there is to know about each other's past, not to mention the intimate details of their sex life. A man knows where his best friend works, which football team he supports, and who he's sleeping with, but his friend's emotional life is probably a complete mystery.[31] Many women live in hope of finding a man who enjoys self-disclosure as much as she does – who wants to curl up with her on the sofa and talk about his emotions. Knowing this, a man will sometimes switch to a feminine style of interaction during the early stages of courtship – talking to the woman about his worries and concerns, and asking her about her feelings. But this doesn't always last. Once they're secure, men often revert to their old ways – they go back to talking about themselves, and dealing with facts rather than feelings.

Because language is our crowning glory there's every

reason to expect that an ability to speak clearly will be fairly high up in the list of things that men and women look for in a partner. Recent research shows that it's only men who place a premium on finding an articulate companion. Women – possibly because they know it's expecting too much – don't go looking for a mate with linguistic skills. They're much more impressed with other qualities, like a man's sense of humour.

Laughter Tells

Laughter isn't exactly an aphrodisiac, but it is a vital ingredient in cementing relationships. The research on laughter shows that when men and women are together, it's the women who do most of the laughing.[32] When women are asked what they look for in a man they usually say that they want a guy who likes a good laugh – but what they're really looking for is a man who makes *them* laugh. Robert Provine has pointed out that the aim of men is to make women laugh, not to laugh or be amused themselves. From a woman's point of view, it doesn't matter very much whether the man is given to laughter – what is important, however, is that he passes the 'laughter test' by making *her* laugh.[33]

In a research study by Karl Grammer and Irenäus Eibl-Eibesfeldt in Germany, conversations were recorded between pairs of young men and women who had met for the first time. The researchers found that the more a woman laughed during the meeting, the keener she was to meet the man again, regardless of how often he had laughed. For the men, however, it was the other way round. They were keen to get together again with the woman if they had managed to make her laugh; their enthusiasm for another meeting had nothing to do with how much they personally had laughed.[34]

When a man and a woman meet for the first time, the likelihood of them forming a relationship is not predicted by the total amount of laughter they generate, nor by how much the man laughs – it's predicted by the amount of laughter the woman produces. There are several explanations for this. One is that laughter reduces the potentially threatening nature of an encounter between a man and a woman – the woman feels that if the man is capable of being amusing then he can't be much of a threat. It might also be that the biochemical changes brought about by laughter act as a form of foreplay – in other words, women want a man who's prepared to tickle her fancy, while men want a woman who wants her fancy tickled and clearly enjoys it. Finally, there's Provine's explanation in terms of the relationship between laughter and status. He suggests that 'the desire by women for men who make them laugh may be a veiled request for dominant males. Men who pass the audition for dominance are acknowledged with women's laughter'.[35]

We don't normally consider laughter in this light. That's because we perceive people who try to make others laugh as creators of fun and levity, not as individuals who are trying to enhance their own status. I remember a situation many years ago, not long after my wife and I had met, when we spent the evening with another guy and his girlfriend. During the evening the guy switched to a comedy routine, putting on funny voices and pulling faces. Both of the girls were in stitches, but I wasn't amused at all. Later, when we were driving home my future wife said how much she'd enjoyed herself and how amusing she'd found the other guy. I said I didn't find him in the least bit funny. Of course, what I'd failed to recognize is that, by amusing the girls, he'd become more dominant. I was busy complaining that his sense of humour was infantile. I didn't realize that I was feeling grumpy and aggressive because he'd used laughter to elevate his own importance in the eyes of the two girls, and, in the process, to reduce mine.

Compatibility Tells

When people meet for the first time, they employ a mixture of come-ons, hang-ons and put-offs. When things are going well between them, most of the signals consist of come-ons. When there's doubt about the progress of the relationship the hang-ons increase in number, and when the relationship is going nowhere the put-offs start to take over. Monika Moore has made a special study of the put-offs used by women, or what she calls 'rejection signals'.[36] These include facial gestures like yawning, frowning and sneering, as well as head-shaking and manual gestures like putting her hands in her pockets or crossing her arms. All of these signals are used to deter the man, and to show him that the woman isn't interested in taking things any further.

Courting couples often reveal their compatibility through their movements and postures. There is a strong tendency for individuals who like each other, or who feel some rapport, to co-ordinate their movements and to match their postures. Studies of 'interactional synchrony' have shown that people who are on the same wavelength are more likely to synchronize their actions.[37] With our restaurant couple, for example, the man might take a drink from his glass and the woman might respond by wiping the corners of her mouth with her napkin. A few moments later she might lean on the table, and he might respond by moving his chair. What makes the interaction synchronous is the underlying rhythm of the man's and woman's activities – it's not essential that they copy each other, only that they integrate their separate contributions into the same balletic performance.

There are occasions, however, when courting couples perform the same actions. Studies of 'postural matching' show that the closer two people are emotionally, the more similar the postures that they adopt. This works in both directions – not only do people adopt similar postures when they feel more rapport, but they also feel greater rapport after they have assumed the same posture.[38] Individuals don't make a deliberate, conscious decision to copy each other. Rather, it's a matter of these processes occurring spontaneously and unconsciously, so that even after people have assumed the same posture they're not aware of what they've done.

One reason why postural matching occurs during courtship is that certain postures are linked to certain emotions, so that when two people adopt the same posture they are more likely to experience the same feelings.[39] This relationship between posture and mood is very basic. People, for example, who are hypnotized and instructed to experience a particular feeling are much more likely to comply if they are placed in a posture that is conducive to that feeling. If they are put into a posture that is inconsistent with that feeling, they may not experience it fully, or even at all. The same kind of relationship that exists between posture and emotion also occurs in everyday life. People who copy the postures of others are in a much better position to empathize with them than those who adopt very different postures. Women, it appears, have a much stronger need for postural matching than men. Geoffrey Beattie discovered, for example, that male–female and female–female pairs assume the same posture more than half the time, but that in male–male pairs the individuals only adopt the same posture for about a quarter of the time that they're together.[40] Men, it seems, are less inclined to match each other's postures. Women, on the other hand, like to copy the person they're with, regardless of whether it's a man or a woman.

If postural matching provides a measure of a couple's compatibility, it's equally true to say that its opposite, postural mismatching, offers an index of a couple's incompatibility. One of the first symptoms of trouble in a relationship is the tendency of individuals to adopt very different postures when they're together. Even when the postures are similar, they may be diametrically opposed, so that instead of facing towards each other, the two people face away from each other. The way that people use their eyes is equally telling. Think of that famous occasion when Prince Charles and Princess Diana were filmed sitting in the back of a car, just before it was announced that they were going to separate. Both of them had a rather studied, sombre countenance, but even more revealing were their postures and their gaze – each of them was oriented away from the other, and their eyes studiously avoided each other's. The rejection signals were flying in both directions.

In contrast to the signs that a relationship is disintegrating, there are *tells* which show when someone is deeply in love. These include distraction, lack of concentration, sighing, stuttering, and an inability to sleep, eat or drink. The symptoms of love and influenza are often similar – feeling hot and cold, a lack of energy, and an overpowering desire to go to bed. Lovesickness also exhibits some of the symptoms of Obsessive Compulsive Disorder – one-track thinking, strong preoccupations, fixation with routines, and the knowledge that one is behaving irrationally but can't do anything about it.

Infidelity Tells

There are four main types of infidelity. The first involves nothing more than a shared intimacy between two people where at least one of them is married. These mental acts of unfaithfulness are often conducted by letter, on the telephone or by email. Although they don't have a physical component, they can sometimes be just as dangerous as a sexual affair, especially when they generate strong attachments. The second type is the 'one-night stand', where the couple has a brief fling but doesn't consolidate the relationship. The third involves an extended affair which lasts for a few weeks or months, and the fourth consists of a long-term relationship, for example between a married man and his mistress.

Subterfuge is the essence of infidelity. People will go to enormous lengths to cover their tracks, create credible alibis and conceal their actions. In spite of their best efforts, however, they invariably leave a trail of *tells* behind them. These include changing an established routine, uncharacteristic irritability, concern about their weight or appearance, vagueness, anonymous phone calls, and an apparent loss of interest in sex. Of course many of these symptoms may appear for other reasons, so people who suspect their partner need to be doubly sure that what they see as the signs of infidelity aren't simply the projections of their own insecurity and jealousy.

Possessive Tells

People use a variety of strategies to retain their mate – these are what zoologists call 'mate-guarding' or 'mate retention' tactics. Mate retention tactics fall into two broad categories – those that are directed at the mate, and those that are addressed to potential rivals. Those directed at the mate include positive overtures, like displays of affection, gifts, promises and declarations of love. They also include 'threats', 'teases' and 'put-downs'. 'Threats' are warnings to the mate about what will happen if they're unfaithful, while 'put-downs' are ways of reducing a mate's self-esteem to the point where they don't feel worthy of anybody else's affection. 'Teases' involve flirting with other people in public so that one's mate feels jealous and more possessive.[41]

Men use threats and put-downs more than women, while women use teases more than men. Strategies that are directed at the mate tend to be private in nature. Those that are targeted at potential rivals are much more public. They include 'resource signals' – in other words, displays of wealth that try to persuade potential rivals that they don't have the resources to compete, as well as 'threats' that are intended to scare them off. 'Ownership signals' are the most common, and in some ways the most interesting of the mate retention tactics, because people aren't always aware of using them. Most ownership signals involve physical proximity – they create the impression that two people are emotionally close because they're physically close. For example, a man who puts his arm round his wife's waist, or his hand on her shoulder at a party, sends two messages – privately he reassures his wife and publicly he tells everyone that she belongs to him. The wife who removes a piece of lint from her husband's jacket, or who adjusts his tie, sends out the same messages of reassurance and ownership.

People also show that they are together by putting their arms round each other, linking arms or holding hands while they're walking along. The sociologist Erving Goffman called these actions 'tie signs'.[42] He argued that their main function was to show that the people concerned are connected, hence 'tied' to each other. One of the revealing features of an established relationship is whether the two people remain in physical contact while they are walking, and if they do, how they actually do it. Although hand-holding appears to be a fairly symmetrical activity, one person has to have his or her hand in front, while the other person has to take up the back position. With a married couple, for example, it's usually the husband who assumes the 'front hold' and the wife who has the 'back hold'. It isn't clear whether this happens because men are taller or because they prefer to lead from the front. When the wife takes up the 'front hold' position, it's usually because she's taller than her husband and therefore finds the 'back hold' uncomfortable. If she's shorter, it's usually because she likes to be in charge – even at the cost of some physical discomfort to her and her husband. There was a good example of this at the inauguration of George W. Bush in 2001. After the ceremony was over, Bill and Hillary Clinton started leaving. The two of them were walking along hand in hand, with Bill looking composed and very much in control, and Hillary looking supportive. However, if you'd looked at them more closely, you would have noticed that Hillary had the 'front hold', while Bill had the 'back hold' – an arrangement which could not be explained in terms of their height. It showed that Hillary was in charge, not Bill.

Human courtship, like that of other animals, consists of a series of stages, starting with the first meeting and progressing through to intercourse and the establishment of some kind of relationship.[43] The transition from one courtship stage to the next is inextricably bound up with *tells* which take the form of invitations to move to the next stage of intimacy. A woman might orient her body towards a man to show him that she's approachable, or a man might brush the hair from a woman's face to show that he wants to kiss her. The way that individuals respond to these overtures decides whether the courtship is going to proceed to the next phase, or whether it's going to get stuck or unwind altogether. What's critical in this whole process, of course, is the way that people read each other's *tells*. It's not enough for the participants to notice each other's *tells* – they also need to decode them correctly. People make two errors when they interpret *courtship tells*. One is to err on the side of caution, to 'mentally minimize' the *tell* by assuming that the other person's gestures of affection don't mean anything. The other error is to 'mentally expand' the *tell* by interpreting friendly behaviour as a sign of romantic or sexual interest. As we have seen, men are much more likely to mentally expand women's *tells*. Women, as a result, are often left wondering how the man got the idea that they were so keen, and doubting their ability to send the right message. The ideal situation would be one where men and women didn't mentally minimize or expand each other's *tells*. But given the need for understatement and subtlety, which are essential to courtship, this is very unlikely.

10. Lying Tells

A lot of the things that we say to other people aren't true – they're fibs, fudges, fabrications, falsehoods and barefaced lies. It has been estimated that we lie to a third of the people we meet each day. Lying is especially common when people are trying to impress each other, and that's why it's so prevalent in dating and courtship. Robert Feldman at the University of Massachusetts found that 60 per cent of the people who took part in one of his studies lied at least once during a 10-minute meeting, and that most of them told two or three lies in that time.[1]

Research on lying shows that there is no difference in the numbers of lies told by men and women, but that there are differences in the types of lies they tell – men are more likely to produce lies that are designed to make them look impressive, while women are more likely to tell lies that are intended to make other people feel good.[2] Women are generally more inclined than men to express positive opinions, both about the things they like and the things they don't like. Consequently, when women are faced with the possibility of upsetting someone – for example when they're given a present they don't want – they're more likely to try and protect the other person's feelings by telling a white lie.

Some people consider lying to be a crime, regardless of how big or small the lie is and what effect it has, while others feel that certain lies are legitimate, possibly even necessary. For example, when a woman asks her husband whether he likes her new hairstyle, she's usually inviting him to say something complimentary rather than to give an honest opinion. The husband who makes the mistake of telling his wife that he doesn't like her new hairstyle is asking for trouble. So is the wife who offers her husband less than fulsome praise when he asks her what she thinks about his performance on the sports field, or the speech he gave at the office party. Lying lubricates interpersonal relations; without lies our social life would soon grind to a complete halt.

People differ enormously in their propensity to lie. At one extreme are the 'George Washingtons', who model themselves on the American President who could not tell a lie; while at the other extreme are the 'Machiavellis', who model themselves on the Florentine statesman who advocated lying as a legitimate means of achieving one's goals. People who score high on measures of manipulation are more likely to tell lies, and not to feel bad about it. The same is true of people who are highly expressive and sociable. People who frequently lie tend to be very popular – probably because their ingratiating lies endear them to others.[3] Con artists, hoaxers and politicians have to be accomplished liars; in fact an ability to project an image of honesty, without feeling any sense of guilt about it, is an essential feature of their role. Sales people also need this ability. A few years ago Bella DePaulo from the University of Virginia performed an experiment with sales personnel who were required either to lie or to tell the truth.[4] When she examined their actions and speech she couldn't find a single difference between those who were telling the truth and those who were lying.

Detection Tells

Although lies form a large part of our exchanges with other people, we're actually not very good at telling whether someone is deceiving us or telling the truth. This isn't for lack of evidence, because 90 per cent of lies are accompanied by *tells* which, like a criminal's fingerprints, leave behind traces of deception.[5]

People often pride themselves on their ability to detect if someone is telling them a lie, especially when that person happens to be someone whom they know well. How often have you heard a mother announce that her children could never lie to her because she 'knows them too well', or a young man claim that his girlfriend could never pull the wool over his eyes because he can 'see right through her'? In fact the research on lie detection suggests that both the mother and the young man are probably mistaken, because people only detect about 56 per cent of the lies they're exposed to, which is slightly above what you'd expect by chance.[6] It's also been discovered that as people get to know each other better their ability to detect each other's lies doesn't improve – it sometimes gets worse![7]

This happens for various reasons. One is that as people get to know each other well, they become more confident in their ability to detect each other's lies. However, their accuracy doesn't necessarily increase – it's usually just their confidence that grows. Moreover, when people get to know each other well, they're more likely to allow their emotions to get in the way of their analytical skills and this reduces their ability to detect each other's lies. Finally, as each person gets to know what type of evidence of deceit the other person is looking for, they're able to modify their behaviour to reduce the chances of detection.

There are several reasons why people are so bad at detecting lies:

◆ **BLISSFUL IGNORANCE**. Even when there are clear signs that someone is lying, they may go unnoticed, not because people are insensitive to these signs, but because they don't want to admit to themselves that the other person is lying. One of the main reasons why individuals believe other people's lies is because they want to believe them, with the result that they end up as co-conspirators in their own deception. Con artists understand this principle completely and they make a point of telling people what they want to hear.[8] The desire not to discover the truth is also found in politics. The British Prime Minister Neville Chamberlain is best remembered for the way he was deceived by the German Chancellor, Adolf Hitler. When Chamberlain returned from Germany in 1938, brandishing a signed agreement with Hitler, he declared that Hitler was a man to be trusted. At the time there was evidence that Hitler intended to invade Czechoslovakia, but Chamberlain chose to ignore this evidence – had he acknowledged what was happening it would have jeopardized his attempts to secure peace.[9] People have all kinds of motives for ignoring the fact that someone is lying to them. A wife may choose to fool herself that her husband is not having an affair in the hope that he will lose interest in the other woman and return to her. Equally, parents may overlook the fact that their son is taking drugs because they don't want to have to deal with the problem.

◆ **THRESHOLD SETTINGS**. Individuals' assumptions about the prevalence of lying can affect their ability to spot liars and truth-tellers. People who are very trusting and who therefore don't expect others to deceive them are likely to set their detection threshold very high. As a result they are likely to identify the truth-tellers quite accurately, but not the liars. Highly suspicious people have the opposite problem – because they set their threshold too low, they inadvertently identify most of the liars, but fail to spot the truth-tellers. Police officers are a good example of the second type because they tend to set their lie detector threshold so low. The only reason why they are successful at spotting liars is because they think everyone is lying![10]

◆ **GUT FEELINGS**. There are two ways of identifying a liar – by looking out for clues to deception; or by relying on one's intuition. It has recently been discovered that people who use their gut feelings are less accurate in detecting liars than those who try to base their decisions on the evidence.[11] Indeed, when it comes to detecting deceit, intuition is usually more of a hindrance than a help.

◆ **MULTIPLE CAUSES**. People often make the mistake of thinking that specific actions are clues to deception, and not to anything else. It is sometimes assumed, for example, that people who touch their nose while they're talking are automatically telling a lie; that the gesture is a sign of lying, and nothing else. These assumptions overlook the fact that actions and utterances may sometimes provide clues to deception, while on other occasions they may provide clues to states of mind that have nothing to do with deception. People who rely on the polygraph lie detector often make this mistake. The polygraph measures respiration, heart rate and palmar sweating – all of which are indicators of arousal. When people become anxious, their breathing rate increases, their heart rate goes up, and their palms start to sweat more profusely. When people are lying they often become anxious, and their anxiety can be detected by the polygraph. However, there are times when people become anxious without lying, just as there are cases where people lie without experiencing any anxiety at all.

◆ **LOOKING ELSEWHERE**. People also fail to detect lies because they are looking for clues in the wrong place. Where people look is usually determined by what they believe are the giveaway signs of lying. If you ask people how they can tell if someone is lying to them, they usually mention shifty eyes or the way people fidget with their hands. The other signs of dishonesty that people mention include smiling, rapid blinking, long pauses, and talking too fast or too slow. Some of these behaviours have in fact been found to be clues to deception, but many are not. When Robert Krauss and his colleagues at

Columbia University in New York compared the signs that people use to detect lying with those that are actually associated with lying, they discovered that there was very little overlap.[12]

Eye Tells

Most people believe that gaze aversion is a sign of lying. They assume that because liars feel guilty, embarrassed and apprehensive, they find it difficult to look their victim in the eye, and they therefore look away. This is not what happens. Firstly, patterns of gaze are quite unstable – while some liars avert their eyes, others actually increase the amount of time they spend looking at the other person. Because gaze is fairly easy to control, liars can use their eyes to project an image of honesty. Knowing that other people assume gaze aversion to be a sign of lying, many liars do the exact opposite – they deliberately increase their gaze to give the impression that they're telling the truth. So, if you want to know if someone's lying to you, don't limit your attention to shifty eyes – also look out for those moments when the other person is gazing at you more intently than usual!

Another supposed sign of lying is rapid blinking. It's true that when we become aroused or our mind is racing, there's a corresponding increase in our blinking rate. Our normal blinking rate is about 20 blinks per minute, but it can increase to four or five times that figure when we feel under pressure. When people are lying they frequently become aroused, and when liars are searching for an answer to an awkward question, their thought processes speed up. In this kind of situation lying is frequently associated with blinking. However, we need to remember that there are times when people have a very high blinking rate, not because they're lying, but because they're under pressure. Also, there are times when liars show quite normal blinking rates.[13]

Body Tells

Fidgeting and awkward hand movements are also thought to be signs of deceit – the assumption being that when people are lying they become agitated and this gives rise to nervous movements of the hands. As we mentioned earlier, there is a class of gestures called 'adaptors', which consists of actions like stroking one's hair, scratching one's head or rubbing the hands together. When people tell lies they sometimes feel guilty or worried about being found out, and these concerns can cause them to produce adaptors. This tends to happen when the stakes are high or when the liar isn't very good at deception. Most of the time the exact opposite happens. Again, because liars are worried about revealing themselves, they tend to inhibit their normal gestural habits. As a result their actions are likely to become more frozen, not more animated!

Movements of the hands, like those of the eyes, tend to be under conscious control, and that's why the hands aren't a reliable source of information about lying. There are other parts of the body, however, which are also under conscious control but, because they're overlooked and neglected, often prove to be a very useful source of clues about deception. Research on lying shows that when people are asked to tell a lie they tend to produce more signs of deception in the lower part than in the upper part of their body. When video recordings of these people are shown to other people who are required to judge whether they are lying or telling the truth, the judges are more accurate if they are exposed to recordings of the lower part of the body.[14] Clearly there is something about the legs and feet which shows them to be an underrated source of information about lying. It seems that liars focus their efforts at concealment on their hands, arms and face, because they know that's what other people will be watching. Because their feet feel remote, liars don't bother about them – but it's often tiny adjustments of the legs and feet that betray them.

Nose Tells

One gesture that reveals a lie is the 'mouth-cover'. When this happens it's as if the liar were taking precautions to cover up the source of his deception, acting on the assumption that if other people can't see his mouth then they won't know where the lie has come from. Mouth-covering actions can range from full-blown versions where the hand completely covers the mouth, to gestures where the hand supports the chin and a finger surreptitiously touches the corner of the mouth. By placing a hand on or near the mouth, a liar behaves like a criminal who can't resist the temptation to return to the scene of his crime. Just like the criminal, the hand lays itself open to detection – at any moment it could become apparent to others that the act of touching the mouth is an attempt to conceal a lie.

There is, however, a substitute for touching the mouth, which is touching the nose. By touching his nose the liar experiences the momentary comfort of covering his mouth, without any risk of drawing attention to what he is really doing. In this role, nose-touching functions as a substitute for mouth-covering – it's a *stealth tell* – it looks as if someone is scratching his nose, but his real intention is to cover his mouth.

There is also a school of thought that says that nose-touching is a sign of deceit quite separate from anything to do with the mouth. One of the proponents of this idea is Alan Hirsch who, together with Charles Wolf, has done a detailed analysis of Bill Clinton's grand jury testimony in August 1998, when the President denied having had sex with Monica Lewinsky.[15] They discovered that while Clinton was telling the truth he hardly touched his nose at all, but that when he lied about his affair with Monica Lewinsky he touched his nose an average of once every four minutes. Hirsch called this the 'Pinocchio syndrome', after the famous character whose wooden nose becomes longer every time he tells a lie. Hirsch suggested that when people lie their nose becomes engorged with blood, and that this produces a sensation that is alleviated by touching or rubbing the nose.

There are at least two arguments against the 'Pinocchio syndrome'. One is that nose-touching may simply be a symptom of anxiety, rather than a sign of deceit. The other is that when people lie they often feel apprehensive and fearful about being found out, and that these emotions are associated with the blood draining away from the face – in other words, with vasoconstriction, not vasodilation. This is the view of Mark Frank of Rutgers University.[16] Frank also points out that experimental research on lying has not shown nose-touching to be a common sign of deceit. Of course it's quite possible that nose-touching does not emerge in laboratory settings, where the stakes are low and the price that people pay if they are exposed as a liar is not terribly high. It's also feasible that nose-touching isn't a sign of deceit for everyone – it might simply be the trademark *tell* of some people, including Bill Clinton.

Finally there's the possibility that nose-touching has nothing at all to do with deceit or with anxiety, but that it's an unconscious form of rejection. Ray Birdwhistell considered that when one person rubs their nose in the presence of another, it reveals the first person's dislike of the second.[17] As he put it, the 'nose rub among Americans is as much a sign of rejection as the word "No!"' Given this interpretation, Bill Clinton's nose-touching before the grand jury might be seen as an expression of his deep dislike for his interrogators, and not as a clue to the fact that he was lying to them.

Surrounding this debate there remains the unresolved question of what we mean when we say that someone is lying – is it that we know them to be lying, or do they have to believe that they're not telling the truth? As Mark Frank has pointed out, this issue is highly pertinent to the case of Bill Clinton and his testimony during the Lewinsky affair. There are some people who argue that Clinton knew that he was lying, but there are others who insist that, given his definition of 'sex' and the way he constructed his evidence, he wasn't lying at all. The interesting question that arises from this is whether people who have to persuade themselves that they're not lying behave any

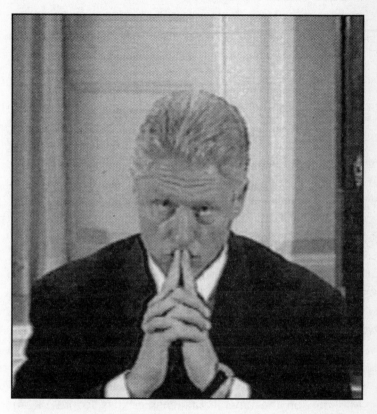

The *Mouth-cover* is an important *lying tell*. When he testified to the Grand Jury during his impeachment trial, Bill Clinton repeatedly touched his mouth. Other *lying tells*, also seen here, include excessive sweating, restrained movement of the hands, and increased levels of gaze.

differently from those who start out with the conviction that they're telling the truth.

Masking Tells

When someone knowingly tells a lie they have to hide two things – firstly the truth, and secondly any emotions that might arise out of their attempts at concealment. The emotions that liars feel are generally negative – feelings like guilt, or fear about being found out – but liars can also experience the thrill of pulling the wool over other people's eyes – what Paul Ekman has called 'duping delight'.[18] When people tell small, innocuous lies they usually don't feel any negative emotions at all. However, when they're telling big lies, and there's a lot at stake, they often experience very powerful negative emotions that need to be concealed if the lie is to remain hidden. A negative emotion can be concealed by turning away the head, by covering the face with the hands, or by masking it with a neutral or a positive emotion. The strategies of turning away and covering the face don't always work because they tend to draw attention to what the liar is trying to conceal. Masking, on the other hand, enables liars to present an exterior that isn't necessarily connected with lying.

The most commonly used masks are the 'straight face' and the smile. The straight face requires the least effort – in order to mask his negative emotions all the liar needs to do is put his face into repose. The smile is potentially more effective as a mask because it suggests that the person is feeling happy and contented – in other words, experiencing emotions that one doesn't normally associate with lying.

Smiling Tells

Of all the facial expressions, smiling is probably the easiest to produce. It's also disarming because it makes other people feel positive and less suspicious about the liar. But the thing that really recommends the smile is the fact that most people aren't very good at telling the difference between a genuine smile and a false smile, because they tend to take smiles at face value. People can usually identify 'blended smiles' which display negative emotions. They find it very easy, for example, to spot a 'miserable smile', where the inside edges of the eyebrows are raised and the corners of the mouth are either pulled up or slightly lowered. But people are notoriously bad at spotting false, unblended smiles, and that's why they're used to mask the negative emotions associated with lying.[19]

If you ask people how to spot a liar they often mention smiling. They'll tell you that when someone is lying they're more likely to use a smile to mask their true feelings. However, research on lying shows that it's the other way round – people who are lying smile less than those who are telling the truth. What appears to be happening is that liars occasionally adjust their behaviour so that it's the opposite to what everyone expects of people who are telling a lie. This doesn't mean that liars have abandoned smiling – it simply shows that they smile less than people who are telling the truth. When dissemblers do smile they often give themselves away by producing a counterfeit smile. There are several identifying features of counterfeit smiles:

◆ **DURATION**. Counterfeit smiles are sustained for much longer than genuine, heartfelt smiles.

◆ **ASSEMBLY**. Counterfeit smiles are 'put together' more rapidly than genuine smiles. They are also dismantled more quickly.

◆ **LOCATION**. Counterfeit smiles tend to be confined to the lower half of the face, whereas genuine smiles involve the muscles that pull up the corners of the mouth as well as the muscles that tighten up around the eyes and pull the eyebrows down slightly. Counterfeit and genuine smiles are controlled by different parts of the brain – voluntary centres produce counterfeit smiles, while genuine smiles are produced involuntarily.

◆ **SYMMETRY**. Genuine smiles appear on both sides of the face, whereas counterfeit smiles sometimes appear more strongly on one side of the face (usually the right side). That's because the neural pathways associated with voluntary and involuntary facial expressions are different. If you see a symmetrical smile it could be either genuine or false, but if you come across a lopsided smile there's a good chance that it's false.

Although symmetrical and lopsided smiles are quite different to look at, people tend to react to lopsided smiles as if they were genuine. That's why we are so unconcerned about the authenticity of smiles – provided other people smile at us, we don't much care what kind of smile we're offered.

Micro-tells

When people try to mask their emotions their face receives two opposing sets of instructions – while involuntary processes in the brain are instructing the face to show their true feelings, voluntary processes are instructing the face to display the masked expression. For masking to work, voluntary processes need to have the upper hand, so that the person's real emotions remain hidden. Successful masking depends on several factors, including the ability to mask one's emotions, and the strength of the emotion that is being suppressed. When an emotion is very strong it can sometimes overwhelm attempts to suppress it, so that the masked expression gives way to the real emotion. There are times, however, when the real emotion momentarily breaks through, and the masked expression then reinstates itself immediately. These glimpses of people's real feelings are called 'micro-momentary expressions' or *micro-tells*.[2] They are extremely fast and short-lived – typically less than a second, and sometimes as short as one twenty-fifth of a second – the equivalent of a single frame in a standard video recording! People don't know it when they produce *micro-tells*, and the vast majority don't notice it when they're exposed to them. However, people like the police can be trained to spot them, and they can also be taught how to use them to interpret other people's behaviour.

When people lie they sometimes produce *micro-tells* that reveal their true feelings. A person might, for example, be telling a story about how he managed to fight his way out of a burning building, giving the impression that he was completely in command during the incident. While he's telling the story his face remains composed. But all of a sudden his expression changes to one of fear, and then it immediately switches back to its normal composure. If you were watching this, and you didn't know about *micro-tells*, you probably wouldn't notice what had happened, and you almost certainly wouldn't spot the brief exposure of fear. To the trained observer this *micro-tell* would be a useful source of information about the person telling the story – it would show that he is trying to give the impression of being in control, but that during the incident he actually experienced a great deal of fear.

Because *micro-tells* are completely involuntary they are rather like traitors – without our knowing it, they betray what we're thinking, but only to those who understand what they mean. Mark Frank and Paul Ekman have shown that these fleeting glimpses of people's real emotions can be a valuable tool in the detection of deceit.[21] Although they aren't common, *micro-tells* can be extremely informative. For example, after the Falklands war the British Prime Minister, Margaret Thatcher, appeared on a television programme and a member of the audience asked her why a British submarine had been given orders to torpedo the Argentine battleship, the *Belgrano*. Mrs Thatcher replied that the *Belgrano* was inside the British exclusion zone and was therefore a legitimate target. In fact this was not true – the *Belgrano* was outside the exclusion zone and was actually sailing away from the Falkland Islands when it was attacked. When Mrs Thatcher gave this untruthful reply she appeared composed, and at one point even produced a false smile. There was a moment, however, when her masked expression dropped, and an extremely brief expression of anger, with the eyes bulging and the jaw thrust forward, appeared on her face. The anger that Mrs Thatcher had managed to hide broke through. But no sooner had it appeared, than it was removed and her masked expression was reinstated.

The way that people react when they are no longer required to convince others that they're telling the truth can also provide subtle clues to deceit. For example, most travellers passing through customs have nothing to fear because they're not carrying any contraband. The smuggler, on the other hand, needs to keep up the pretence of appearing normal, and usually manages to carry it off. What often distinguishes the smuggler as he walks through customs is the muscular tension in his body. Because it's not apparent how he normally walks, these tensions are very difficult to spot. What is noticeable, however, is what happens when the smuggler has gone past the customs officials. It's at this point, when he has nothing more to worry about, that the smuggler is likely to relax his body and to produce a *tension release tell*. The change that occurs is seldom dramatic – it usually takes the form of a slight lowering of the shoulders – but it's possible to detect. The fact that someone relaxes as he passes through customs suggests that he sees the customs officials as a threat and that he has something to hide. Inevitably, there are some people who feel tense about going through customs even when they have nothing to hide, and who are therefore likely to exhibit the same *tension release tell* as the guilty smuggler. This only goes to show that while *tells* are highly informative, they don't always offer a perfect guide to what is happening in people's heads.

Talking Tells

Most people believe that liars give themselves away by what they do, rather than what they say or how they say it. In fact, it's the other way round – the best indicators of lying are to be found in people's speech rather than in their behaviour. Aldert Vrij from Portsmouth University has suggested that when people try to catch liars they pay too much attention to their non-verbal behaviour and not enough to speech.[22] This, he points out, is reflected in the tendency to overestimate the chances of detecting deceit by watching someone's behaviour, and to underestimate the chances of catching liars by listening to what they say.

Several features of talk provide clues to lying. Some involve the verbal content of what people say, others the way that people articulate what they're saying.

◆ **CIRCUMLOCUTION**. Liars often beat about the bush. They tend to give long-winded explanations with lots of digressions, but when they're asked a question they're likely to give a short answer.[23]

◆ **OUTLINING**. Liars' explanations are painted with broad brushstrokes, with very little attention to detail. There's seldom any mention of time, place or people's feelings. For example, a liar will tell you that he went for a pizza, but he probably won't tell you where he went or what kind of pizza he ordered. When liars do provide details they are seldom in a position to elaborate on them. So, if you ask a liar to expand on his account, it's very likely that he'll simply repeat himself. When a truth-teller is asked the same question, he usually offers lots of new information.

◆ **SMOKESCREENS**. Liars often produce answers that are designed to confuse – they sound as if they make sense, but they don't. Examples of remarks that don't make sense include Bill Clinton's famous response during the Paula Jones harassment case, when he was asked about his relationship with Monica Lewinsky, and answered, 'That depends on what the meaning of "is" is.' Another example is the justification that the ex-mayor of New York City, David Dinkins, gave when he was accused of failing to pay his taxes: 'I haven't committed a crime. What I did was fail to comply with the law.'

◆ **NEGATIVES**. Political lies are frequently couched in the form of a denial – remember Bill Clinton's famous denial, 'I did not have sexual relations with that woman, Miss Lewinsky.' When a politician denies that he is going to introduce a new measure, like raising taxes, you can usually take this as a sign that the measure is about to be introduced. As Otto von Bismarck said, 'Never believe anything in politics until it has been officially denied.' Liars are more likely to use negative statements. For example, during the Watergate scandal, President Nixon said, 'I am not a crook.' He didn't say, 'I am an honest man.'

◆ **WORD CHOICE**. Liars make fewer references to themselves – they use words like 'I', 'me' and 'mine' less frequently than people who are telling the truth. Liars also tend to generalize by making frequent use of words like 'always', 'never', 'nobody' and 'everyone', thereby mentally distancing themselves from the lie.

◆ **DISCLAIMERS**. Liars are more likely to use disclaimers such as 'You won't believe this', 'I know this sounds strange, but' and 'Let me assure you'. Disclaimers like these are designed to acknowledge any suspicion the other person may feel in order to discount it.

◆ **FORMALITY**. When people are telling the truth in an informal situation they are more likely to use an elided form – for example, to say 'don't' instead of 'do not'. Someone who is telling a lie in the same situation is more likely to say 'do not' instead of 'don't'. That's because people become more tense and formal when they lie.

◆ **TENSE**. Without realizing it, liars have a tendency to increase the psychological distance between themselves and the event they're describing. As we have seen, one way they do this is by their choice of words. Another is by using the past tense rather than the present tense.

◆ **SPEED**. Telling a lie requires a lot of mental work because, in addition to constructing a credible line, the liar needs to keep the truth separated from the lie. This places demands on the capacities of the liar, which in turn can slow him down. That's why people pause before producing a lie, and why lies tend to be delivered at a slower pace than the truth – unless, of course, the lie has been carefully rehearsed, in which case there should be no difference in speed.

◆ **PAUSES**. Liars also produce more pauses between their words and sentences, and some of these pauses are filled with speech disfluencies like 'um' and 'er'. The cognitive work involved in producing a spontaneous lie also gives rise to more speech errors, slips of the tongue and false starts, where the person starts a sentence and then abandons it for another sentence.

◆ **PITCH**. The pitch of someone's voice is often a very good indicator of their emotional state, because when people get upset the pitch of their voice starts to rise. Emotions are closely connected to vocal pitch, and the changes that occur when people become emotional are very difficult to mask or conceal. Although increases in pitch are fairly consistent, they are sometimes quite small, and it is usually necessary to have heard someone speaking in other situations before one can decide whether the pitch of their voice has risen.

There is a lot of talk nowadays about actions that are supposedly associated with lying – people will tell you that if someone scratches their nose or responds to a question by looking to the left, then it proves that they are telling a lie. None of this is true – there are no specific behaviours that show that someone is lying. They may show that someone is in a state of conflict, under the influence of strong emotions or trying to cover up their feelings of discomfort, but it doesn't follow that they are therefore telling a lie. As Paul Ekman has remarked, 'There is no sign of deceit itself – no gestures, facial expression, or muscle twitch that in and of itself means that a person is lying'.[24] Another authority on lying, Bella DePaulo, echoes this opinion when she points out that behavioural and speech indicators have a 'problematic association' with deception: 'They correlate with deception, but not perfectly'.[25]

Although there is no guaranteed method of detecting lies, there are certain things that you can do to increase your chances of spotting a liar:

◆ To detect a lie successfully you need to set your criteria so that they're neither too high nor too low. That way you'll avoid coming to the conclusion that nobody ever tells a lie, or that everybody lies all the time.

◆ Where possible, the actions that someone performs while they are supposedly lying should be compared with how they behave when they are telling the truth.

◆ To be a good lie detector you should also concentrate on behaviour that falls outside conscious control or that people are likely to ignore.

◆ Given the opportunity, focus your attention on what people say and how they say it, rather than on what they do.

◆ It's important to work out whether the lie is likely to be spontaneous or rehearsed, and whether it's a high-stakes or a low-stakes lie. When the stakes are low or the lie has been rehearsed, the task of detecting the lie is much more difficult.

◆ To spot a lie you should always focus on a broad range of behavioural and speech clues. If you think you can spot a liar on the basis of a single clue, you're deceiving yourself.

11. Foreign Tells

When people speak the same language it's often very difficult to tell where they come from simply on the basis of their vocabulary, grammar or accent. However, there is sometimes a 'shibboleth', a test that shows where they come from. The word 'shibboleth' is mentioned in the Book of Judges in the Old Testament. After the Ephraimites had been defeated in battle by the Gileadite army, they tried to sneak back across the River Jordan. The Gileadites, who wanted to make sure that none of them escaped, stopped every man who was trying to cross the river and asked him if he was an Ephraimite. If he said 'no', he was asked to say 'shibboleth', which was the Hebrew word for 'river'. Gileadites pronounced the word 'shibboleth', but Ephraimites said 'sibboleth'. Anyone who pronounced the word with an initial 'sh' was spared; those who used 's' were immediately executed.

Talk Tells

There are other ways of identifying people's nationality,

usually with less bloody consequences. Europeans often have difficulty telling Canadians and Americans apart. But there are some giveaway pronunciations that enable them to spot a Canadian. Canadians, for example, tend to pronounce words like 'shout' and 'about' as 'shoot' and 'aboot', while Americans are inclined to pronounce 'house' as 'hayouse'.[1] Americans are likely to greet you with 'It's a great day'. Canadians, on the other hand, are more likely to say, 'It's a great day, eh?' While the Americans opt for an upbeat, declarative form, the Canadians prefer to phrase their statements as questions.

Although Australians and New Zealanders have no trouble telling each other apart, outsiders often find it very difficult to distinguish them because they sound so similar. However there are differences between Australian and New Zealand English. Some of the differences are in vocabulary – New Zealand English, for example, has borrowed many more words from the indigenous Maori people than Australian English has from the Aborigines. There are also differences in the pronunciation of certain vowels. Australians pronounce words such as 'air' and 'ear' differently, whereas New Zealanders pronounce both as 'ear'. There are also instances where the New Zealanders make distinctions but the Australians don't – Australians, for example, pronounce 'moan' and 'mown' the same, whereas New Zealanders distinguish the two by pronouncing 'mown' as 'mow-an'. But the big difference is in the way they pronounce 'i'. New Zealanders pronounce 'bat' as 'bet', 'bet' as 'bit', and 'bit' as 'but'. The English talk of 'fish and chips'. The Australians, on the other hand, elongate the vowel and talk about 'feesh and cheeps', while the New Zealanders, who like to turn 'i' into 'u', talk about 'fush and chups'.[2]

Action Tells

Shibboleths can also take the form of actions. To identify someone's nationality it's sometimes enough to watch their table manners. The English, for example, will normally eat with the fork in their left hand and the knife in their right, cutting the food with the knife and transferring it to their mouth with their fork. Americans also hold the fork in their left hand and the knife in their right – but only while they're cutting up their food. As soon as the food has been cut up, they put the knife to one side, shift the fork to their right hand, and use their right hand to transfer the food to their mouth. In Canada the convention is again quite different. The Canadians only resort to their knife when the situation demands it; otherwise they're happy to dispose of the knife and to use the fork to cut up the food and to transfer it to their mouth.

Where people come from is also indicated by tiny gestures, like the way they signal 'yes' and 'no' with their head. The most common head signals for 'yes' and 'no' are the nod and the head-shake respectively – in the nod the head is moved up and down, and in the shake it's rotated from side to side. The 'nod–shake' code is found all round the world, but it's by no means the only one. The Greeks and Turks, for example, use the 'dip–toss' code, where the head is dipped down for 'yes' and tossed sharply upward for 'no'. The 'head-toss', as it is called, is often accompanied by closed eyes, raised eyebrows and a click of the tongue. The remnant of the 'dip–toss' code may be found in southern Italy and Sicily, having been introduced to the region by the ancient Greeks when they set up trading posts there during the second millennium BC.[3]

If you visit Rome today, you'll find that the Romans use the 'nod–shake' code. However, if you travel 200 kilometres south, to Naples, you'll enter a region where the locals use the nod for 'yes' and either the head-shake or the head-toss for 'no'.[4] The head-toss consists of a single upward movement of the head, which could easily be confused with a brief nod that begins with an upward movement. In order to avoid this confusion, southern Italians initiate their head-nod with a downward movement. In this respect they're similar to the Greeks, who use a single, downward movement of the head for 'yes'. Because their nod doesn't conflict with any other signals, northern Italians don't have to worry about whether to begin their nods with an upward or a downward movement. In fact, when we look more closely, we find that northerners initiate their nods in either direction.[5] So if you want to play the role of Professor Henry Higgins and identify where Italians come from, you can simply watch how they signal 'yes' with their head. If they start with a downward movement they could be either from the north or the south. But if they start with an upward movement, they're almost certainly from the north.

Greeting Tells

The way that people greet each other also provides clues to where they come from. The handshake, for example, can differ cross-culturally in terms of who uses it, the situations where it's employed, how long the hands are clasped, how vigorously the hands are pumped, and in many other ways. Handshakes in Africa are often executed with a very light grip, and they can extend for several minutes while the participants exchange niceties and make enquiries about each other's relatives. West African handshakes often include embellishments, like a click of the fingers as the hands are released.[6] It's possible that the constant elaboration of hand-shaking practices in African-American communities owes something to the central role that hand-shaking plays in West African societies.

Although the English have helped to export the handshake to other parts of the world, during the seventeenth century the handshake, or handclasp, was used exclusively for sealing agreements.[7] It was only later that it became a greeting and started to spread to other countries. According to Theodore Zeldin, author of *The French*, the handshake was exported from England to France, where it became known as 'Le Handshake'.[8] Today the French have a very strong attachment to the handshake. While British colleagues might shake hands when they arrive at work, their French counterparts are likely to shake each other's hand several times during the same day. The Russians also shake hands with the same person several times a day, and so do the Italians and the Spaniards. The British and the Germans, on the other hand, tend to confine themselves to one handshake on meeting and another on parting – if in fact they ever shake hands at all.

There are also differences in the way that the handshake is executed. The French, for example, tend to produce a single, determined pump of the hand, whereas the Italians are inclined to draw out the handshake by holding on to the other person's hand. The social rules governing who should shake hands with whom also differ from one country to the next. While in France people shake hands regardless of their sex, in Britain hand-shaking is more likely to occur between two men than between a man and a woman or two women. The preponderance of male–male hand-shaking in Britain could be a hangover from the days when men used the handshake to seal agreements.

When people perform a non-contact greeting they often accompany their verbal salutations with a slight dip of the head. The British have developed their own version, which is the 'head-cock'. This is performed by shifting the chin to one side while the top of the head is lowered – in other words, by dipping and twisting the head at the same time. This greeting often mystifies visitors to Britain, who wonder what it could conceivably mean. Its origins are rather obscure. It is possible that the head-cock emerged from the practice of tugging the forelock, a submissive gesture used during medieval times. It's also possible that the head-cock originated from the now defunct practice of doffing or touching the hat. Winking is another possible source, because it often involves an involuntary tilt of the head to one side. The collusive message conveyed by winking is also to be found in the head-cock. Finally, the head-cock may be a hybrid gesture – a cross between the head-dip and head-canting, both of which, as we saw earlier, are signals of submissiveness.

Another form of greeting that varies cross-culturally is the kiss. The practice of kissing a lady's hand has all but disappeared, but before the Second World War it was used extensively throughout Europe, especially in countries like Poland and Hungary, which once formed part of the Austro-Hungarian Empire. If you find a man kissing a woman's hand nowadays, the chances are he's joking around. If he's serious he probably has some connection with Eastern Europe.

Cheek-kissing varies geographically in terms of the number of times people kiss each other on the cheek. Scandinavians tend to make do with a single kiss, while the French go in for the double kiss. The Dutch and the Belgians often employ a multi-kiss, with at least three separate kisses. In all these countries kissing is a standard feature of the greeting ritual. As a result everyone knows how many kisses to expect and which cheek to kiss first. In countries like Britain, Australia, Canada and the United States – where greeting practices are in the process of evolving – there is often a lot of fumbling and bumping of noses when people try to greet each other with a kiss. These problems aren't so critical for the Welsh or the Irish because historically Celtic communities have been quite uncomfortable about social kissing.[9]

Hugging is another practice that is on the increase – partly because the hug has shed its political connotations and been accepted as something that men can do to express their affection towards each other. But there are still enormous cultural differences in people's attitudes to hugging. Edmund Hillary tells the story that when he and Tenzing Norgay reached the peak of Everest they stood there facing each other, elated at being the first people to have climbed the world's highest mountain. In Anglo-Saxon fashion, Hillary extended his hand to congratulate Tenzing. Tenzing ignored the hand, flung his arms around Hillary and embraced him.[10] That was the proper way to celebrate their achievement!

Face Tells

Nationality is sometimes revealed in facial expressions. Research by Paul Ekman and his colleagues shows that facial expressions that depict the basic emotions – like happiness, sadness, fear, surprise, disgust and anger – are recognized throughout the world, suggesting that the relationship between these emotions and their facial expressions is innate.[11] There are cultural differences, however, in the conventions governing the expression of emotions, as well as differences in how frequently they are displayed, where and to whom they are displayed, and the detailed expression of these emotions. Ray Birdwhistell has observed that smiling in the United States is much more frequent above the Mason-Dixon line than it is below the line, leading him to conclude that smiling means different things to people in the northern and southern states.[12] Of course it doesn't follow that people who smile more are necessarily happier, or that smiling has a different meaning for them than it does for people who smile less. What it does suggest, however, is that the conventions governing smiling, or the expression of happiness, may differ between communities.

This is borne out by Henry Seaford's research on facial expressions in Virginia. Seaford studied historic portraits and photographs in yearbooks. When he compared his Virginia material with material from Pennsylvania, he found a 'facial dialect' in Virginia.[13] This consisted of several expressions, including an 'orbicular clamp' and a 'purse-clamp'. In both these expressions the muscles above and below the mouth are tightened and this clamps the lips together. In the 'purse-clamp' the muscles at the side of the mouth are also tightened, so that the lips become clamped and pursed together at the same time. Seaford observed that, since people from the British Isles colonized Virginia, the facial expressions of Virginians may have descended from expressions that were once found in Britain.

The English have a long reputation for being cold and unemotional. They are also reputed to have a 'stiff upper lip'. This is generally intended to refer to the stoical character of the English, but it could equally apply to their facial habits. When they smile the English are much more likely to keep their teeth hidden, and to pull the corners of their mouth sideways rather than up. When the face is in repose, there is also a tendency for the English to purse their lips. This goes back to the sixteenth century, when a small mouth was considered to be desirable. We can see this very clearly in Holbein's portraits of Henry VIII, and more strikingly in his wedding portrait of Jane Seymour, where the King and his future Queen are shown with tightly pursed lips.[14]

Facial habits too are shaped by language. French, for example, is articulated very differently from other languages. Visitors to France often remark on the unusual way that the French move their mouth, and particularly the way they protrude their lips, when they are talking. According to Theodore Zeldin, this is because the French language has more sounds that require the rounding of the lips than other languages. 'Nine out of the sixteen French vowels', he tells us, 'involve strong lip-rounding, compared to only two out of the twenty English vowels. (Germans have five lip-rounding vowels.) The degree of lip-rounding in French is moreover greater because vowels following consonants often have to be prepared before the consonant is uttered.'[15]

Related observations have been made about the German language. Robert Zajonc and his colleagues were interested in the idea that different speech sounds differentially affect blood flow to the brain and that this may affect people's mood. To test this they asked a group of German-speakers to read out a story which either had a lot of 'ü' sounds or very few 'ü' sounds.[16] Participants who read the story with lots of 'ü' sounds were found to have hotter foreheads; they also rated the protagonist in the story less positively. The authors of the study took these findings as support for the notion that 'ü' sounds affect blood flow to the brain, which in turn affects mood.

Although this particular effect has not been replicated, psychologists have discovered that mouth postures can affect people's moods in other ways. For example, people who are asked to hold a pencil between their teeth while they're looking at cartoons (and who therefore inadvertently replicate the extended mouth posture of a smile) are likely to rate the cartoons as funnier than people who hold the pencil either between their lips or in their hand. This study supports the 'facial feedback theory' – the idea that people's moods can be shaped by the facial expressions that they adopt.[17]

Conversation Tells

Countries differ widely in their enthusiasm for conversation. The French have always struck the English as overly garrulous. 'A Frenchman', declared Dr Johnson, 'must be always talking, whether he knows anything of the matter or not; an Englishman is content to say nothing, when he has nothing to say.' The Italians also have a reputation for being talkative, and so do the Irish. At the opposite extreme are the Finns and the northern Swedes, who are happy to enjoy the presence of others without saying a word.

The Finnish attachment to silence is also evident in the way they organize their conversations. Although the Finns have a wide range of vocal signals that they can use as back-channel when they're in the listener role, they prefer to use visual signals, like nods, to encourage the speaker and to show that they understand what the speaker is saying. This avoidance of audible back-channel ensures that the only person who's got anything to say is the person who's occupying the speaker role. It also has the effect of making Finnish conversations sound rather stilted and one-sided – something that foreigners, who are used to giving and receiving audible back-channel, often find rather uncomfortable. This is reinforced by the fact that Finnish conversations have very few interruptions. Consequently, when foreigners talk to a Finn they often get the impression that the Finn doesn't really want the floor, that he's not being attentive, and that he's not really interested.[18]

The same could hardly be said of the foreigner's experience in Italy, where conversation is more of a free-for-all. In Italy conversations often take on the appearance of a contest, especially where friends are concerned. In these cases the speaker will often fix his eyes on the listener while the listener looks away. This, of course, is the opposite of what we find in other countries, where the listener looks more intently at the speaker than the speaker does at the listener. In an Italian conversation it's not unusual to find the listener looking around, affecting an air of boredom, while the speaker is constantly moving around so that he's in front of the listener and using his hands to try and capture the listener's attention.

Turn-taking in Italy is based on the 'conch shell model' – so called after the famous scene in William Golding's *Lord of the Flies*, where a group of English schoolboys are marooned on an island.[19] At their first meeting on the island all the boys start to talk at once, so they make a rule that from that point onwards only one person will be allowed to speak at a time – the boy who is holding the large conch shell that was found on the beach. Italian conversations conform to the conch shell model, not because the Italians want to eliminate overlap talk – there's very little chance of that – but because the person who has his hands in the air is deemed to be the speaker.[20]

In Italy a speaker who wants to retain her role needs to ensure that her hands are in the air, and that they are gesticulating and holding the other person's attention. The listener, on the other hand, does not produce a lot of backchannel, partly because the speaker doesn't need that much encouragement to keep talking, and partly because the listener is less keen about remaining in the role, and therefore is less interested in offering the speaker a lot of support. In Italian conversations the listener often withholds his approval by looking away while the other person is talking. This can sometimes create a rather theatrical spectacle, where the speaker is in hot pursuit, trying to ensnare the listener with wild gesticulations, while the listener refuses to ratify the speaker by giving the speaker

Conversation Tells. Italians use their hands to hold the other person's attention and to retain the speaker role during conversations.

his undivided attention. To show that she intends to continue, the speaker needs to keep her hands up and to ensure that the listener doesn't get his hands up and thereby lay claim to her role. When I first visited Italy I was struck by how often people would touch each other while they were talking. When two people were talking and I saw the speaker touch the listener on the arm I assumed that she was being affectionate. What I failed to notice at first was that these are 'controlling touches'. They're not intended to reassure the listener – they're designed to hold the floor by making sure that the listener can't get his hands up!

When Italians want to relinquish the speaker role, they simply lower their hands. This shows that they no longer wish to continue talking. The other termination signal that speakers use is to shrug their shoulders, which is very similar in meaning to such expressions as 'I don't know' that speakers elsewhere sometimes use to relinquish the floor. Listeners who want to take the floor can do so either by interrupting the speaker or by grabbing the speaker's arm, pulling it down, and getting their own gesticulating hands into the air. The listener who wants to signal that he has no desire to take over the speaker's role can do so by keeping his arms folded or by placing his hands behind his back. This serves as an 'unintention display' – it shows that the listener is not in a position to start talking. After all, how could he if his hands are hidden?

Hand Tells

Someone's nationality can often be identified at a

distance, simply by observing how they use their hands. That's partly because some nations gesticulate more than others. If there were a league table for gesture, the Italians would win hands down. The identification of Italy with wild gesticulation goes back a long way. In 1581 the author of *A Treatise of Daunces* noted that 'The Italian in his ... speeche ... intermingleth and useth so many gestures, that if an Englishman should see him afar off, not hearing his words, [he] would judge him to be out of his wit, or else playing some comedy upon a scaffold.' By contrast, the author observed, a German preaching from a pulpit would look as though he was physically paralysed.[21]

We tend to assume that nations that gesticulate a lot have always been animated, and that nations that gesticulate very little, like the English, have always been reticent and undemonstrative. This isn't entirely correct. It is generally accepted, even by the English themselves, that they are not a particularly expressive people and they don't go in for elaborate displays of gesticulation. However, there was a time when gesture played a much more prominent role in their lives. A thorough knowledge of posture and gesture was a requirement for all Elizabethan actors, and Shakespeare's plays are full of references to expressive postures and movements of the hands. Hogarth's drawing of scenes from English life show that gesticulation was also popular during the eighteenth century, and that it was not restricted to specific sectors of society. The 'grand manner' of oratory, which appeared in Parliament and the pulpit in the nineteenth century, also relied on extravagant use of the hands. It was during this period, however, that a more demure style of social behaviour started to become fashionable, and the English began to lose interest in gesture.[22]

Historically the French have moved in the opposite direction. The French are enthusiastic gesticulators, but this wasn't the case during the sixteenth century. Before Catherine de Medici of Florence arrived in France to marry Henry II, French courtiers made very little use of gesture, regarding the spectacle of flailing arms as rather common and vulgar. By the Restoration, however, the French had joined the ranks of the gesticulating nations, and they have remained there ever since.

If you compare an Italian with a Frenchman, you'll notice that their expressive gestures differ in several ways. First of all, the Italian moves his hands around much more than the Frenchman. What's more revealing, however, are the positions that the fingers assume while the hands are gesticulating. As a rule the French tend to use more open postures of the hand, while the Italians show a preference for 'precision grips', where the thumb and forefinger, for example, are pressed against each other, or the tips of all five digits are joined together. Another clue to nationality is to be found in the rhythm of gesticulation – French movements tend to be more languid and even-paced, whereas Italian gesticulation is more staccato and varied in its pace. Then there's the geometry of gesticulation – in other words, the space through which the hands move when they're gesticulating. Here we find that the French tend to confine their movements to the hands and forearms, while the Italians enlist the upper arms as well. As a result, Italian gestures are more expansive and expressive.

Another group that gesticulates a lot, but who don't use

expansive movements, are Eastern European Jews. David Efron, who completed a special study of gesture in New York City during the Second World War, noticed that when people from Eastern European Jewish communities gesticulate they tend to keep their elbows tucked in and their arms close to their chest – the hands are always busy but they are never far from the body.[23] This is the gestural style of an oppressed people – they want to connect with each other, but they're worried about lowering their defences. The hands reach out, but the arms and elbows wait in reserve, protecting the body from attack. In contrast to the restricted, almost apologetic circumference of Jewish gesticulation, Italian gestures are wide-ranging. Because the elbows aren't tucked in, the hands are free to make long excursions away from the body, and the performance is therefore much more spectacular.

There are also national differences in the meanings that people attach to certain gestures. The 'thumbs-up' gesture, which most people recognize as a sign of approval or good luck, doesn't always have positive connotations. In Greece, and in parts of Australia, where there are large Greek communities, the thumbs-up gesture is an insult. It's an emasculatory gesture, rather similar in meaning to the middle finger gesture, and it's often associated with the expression, 'Sit on this!' It is worth remembering this if you're planning to hitchhike in Greece.[24] Whatever you do, don't present approaching cars with a raised thumb or you'll never get a ride!

Another gesture that is open to misinterpretation is the famous Greek insult, the *moutza*. This is performed by splaying the fingers and presenting the palm of the hand to the person whom you want to insult. The moutza owes its origins to the ancient Byzantine practice of dragging chained criminals through the streets, while the local populace picked up dirt and rubbish and thrust it into their faces. Fortunately this demeaning practice has long since disappeared, but the moutza lives on as a highly charged insult, often accompanied by expressions like 'Take five!' or 'Go to hell!' Of course to foreigners the moutza looks like an innocent presentation of five fingers, so it's liable to be interpreted as a gesture for the number '5'. This is reputed to have happened several years ago when the English football club Nottingham Forest were playing a Greek club in Athens.[25] The sports correspondent for a British newspaper reported that young Greek fans had approached the coach that was transporting the English players, and that they had indicated with their hands what they thought the final score for the match was likely to be – five–nil! What the poor journalist had failed to realize was that this was a deep insult, not some pre-match prediction.

A similar misunderstanding could occur with the famous V-for-Victory gesture. This, as most of us know, is performed by separating the index and the middle fingers, keeping the rest of the hand in the shape of a fist, and presenting the palm of the hand to the other person. In most countries the position of the palm doesn't matter, and the Victory gesture can be performed with the palm facing either forward or back. However, in countries like Greece and the United Kingdom, the position of the palm is crucial. In Greece there is a miniature version of the moutza where just the index and middle fingers are extended, with the palm facing forward. This insulting gesture is sometimes accompanied by the expression,

'Take two!' or 'Go half-way to hell!' Just like the Churchillian V-sign for Victory, the miniature moutza is performed with the palm facing forward. That's why, in order to avoid any confusion, the Greeks perform their Victory gesture with the palm facing backward. This gesture, however, is identical to the famous insulting V-sign of the British. When the British want to insult each other, they make a V-sign with the palm facing backward. The fact that the Britons and the Greeks have chosen the same gestures to convey very different messages can very easily lead to international misunderstanding – when a Greek performs a palm-back V-sign he thinks he's signalling Victory, but the British man thinks he's being insulting, whereas with the palm-front V-sign the situation is reversed. Here the Briton thinks he's signalling Victory, but the Greek thinks that he's being insulting.[26]

Some gestures are confined to one country, others to a specific region within a country. There are also gestures that span several countries – like drinking gestures. When people offer you a drink by miming the act of drinking, you can often tell where they come from, simply by looking at how they arrange their fingers. People from beer-drinking countries like Britain, Germany, Holland and Belgium tend to wrap their fingers round an imaginary beer glass, with the four fingers curled and facing the thumb. People from vodka-drinking countries like Russia, Ukraine and Poland use a gesture that mimics the shape of a short vodka glass. Here the first and second fingers are placed opposite the thumb, and the hand is rapidly tilted once or twice to simulate the act of pouring the contents down the throat. People from wine-drinking countries like France, Italy and Spain usually mimic a wine bottle by forming their hand into a fist, extending the thumb, and pointing it towards their mouth. This gesture is sometimes performed by raising the hand above the mouth so that the neck of the 'bottle' faces downwards. This, of course, mimics the old practice of drinking from a leather bottle, where the bottle was held above the head and the wine was squirted into the mouth. It is therefore very likely that the wine-drinking gesture is a 'relic tell' – in other words, a gesture that owes its origins to an ancient practice that has since become extinct.

A comparison of nationalities shows that some gesticulate more than others, and that they fall into three broad groups. In the first group are the Nordic peoples – the Swedes, Finns, Norwegians and Danes – who make very little use of gesticulation and who, compared with other countries, are gesturally illiterate. This category also includes the Japanese, Koreans and Chinese, all of whom make very little use of gesticulation. The second group includes the British, Germans, Dutch, Belgians and Russians, who use gesture in moderation. People who fall into this category tend only to use their hands when they become excited, when they need to communicate over long distances, and when they feel the need to threaten or insult each other. The third group of nations includes the Italians, French, Greeks, Spaniards and Portuguese. It also includes South American nations like the Argentinians and Brazilians, who have been heavily influenced by the Italians, the Spanish and the Portuguese. These three groupings work fine for countries that are culturally uniform or have a dominant cultural group. The scheme works less well with multi-ethnic countries like the United States because some ethnic groups within the country are more gesturally expressive than others. This shows that culture often plays a much bigger part than nationality in shaping people's behaviour.

Some *tells* are universal, others are local. Universal *tells* spring from the common biology that people share with each other – the wide-eyed facial expression of fear, for example, is an innate feature of our human make-up, and that's why it's found on every continent. However, some *tells* are extremely widespread, not because they're innate, but because they've been copied and borrowed by people all round the world. The fact that in almost every country young people wear baseball caps facing backwards has nothing to do with biology – it's simply part of fashion culture. Then there are local *tells*, which are confined to specific groups of people. These too owe their existence to cultural invention, and that's why they're much more susceptible to change than *tells* which are biologically programmed. It's sometimes quite difficult to distinguish universal from local *tells*, and in the absence of evidence to the contrary we may assume that the meanings we attach to certain actions are similar to the meanings that people in other parts of the world attach to those actions. But, as we have seen, there are numerous cases where people in different parts of the world attach quite different meanings to the same actions. When we ignore this fact it's very easy for international misunderstandings to occur. While some of these misunderstandings may be amusing and insignificant, others may have far-reaching consequences.

12. Smoking Tells

The way someone smokes says a lot about who they are, what they feel, and how they want other people to see them. Smoking is full of *tells* about the smoker, their attitude to smoking, and their relationship to other people. By learning to decipher these *tells* we can identify what smokers are saying about themselves – where they come from, their personality, their state of mind, and what they're trying to achieve, even if they're not aware of it. If you're a smoker, gaining an understanding of these *tells* will help you to see what kinds of messages you're sending out, and what your smoking style might be telling other people about you.

Scientific investigations of smoking style – what's called 'smoking topography' – have examined the mechanics of smoking in some detail.[1] They've looked at how long it takes people to smoke a cigarette or cigar, how many puffs they take, how long each puff lasts, its volume, how long the smoke is held in the mouth before it's inhaled, how fast it's inhaled, how long it's held in the lungs, and the interval between successive puffs. The way these features vary tells us a great deal about the act of smoking and how smokers regulate their intake of nicotine. In addition, the way people light their cigarette or cigar, how they hold it, how they position it in the mouth, what they do between puffs – all these features provide clues about the impression that smokers are trying to convey.

Scientific attempts to understand the attraction of smoking are usually couched in purely chemical terms. Most smoking, however, happens to be enjoyed in the company of other people, and it's therefore heavily influenced by the social impression that smokers are trying to convey.

Holding Tells

For most of the time that a cigarette or cigar remains lit, it's not actually being smoked – it's either left in the mouth, placed in an ashtray, or held. The three main ways of holding are the 'pincer hold', the 'dart hold' and the 'legs hold'. In the 'pincer hold' the cigarette or cigar is held between the index finger and the thumb, while in the 'dart hold' it's held between the thumb, forefinger and middle finger – just as you hold a dart that you're about to throw at the dartboard. In the 'legs hold' the cigarette or cigar is grasped between the forefinger and the middle finger – in other words, between the two fingers we use when we mimic the act of walking with our hands.

Basically, there are two ways of grasping with the hand – the 'power grip' and the 'precision grip'.[2] In the 'power grip' the thumb and all four fingers are wrapped round the object, whereas in the 'precision grip' just the thumb and forefinger are used. One of the things that sets humans apart from chimpanzees and other primates is the 'opposability' of our thumb, and the fact that we can grasp with greater deftness than our non-human relatives. The 'power grip' doesn't play a part in smoking, but the 'precision grip' appears in the shape of the 'pincer hold' and the 'dart hold'. What's interesting about the 'legs hold' is that it doesn't fit into the 'power/precision grip' scheme at all. In fact it's unique to smoking – the only time that people ever grip something between their forefinger and middle finger is when they're holding a cigarette or a cigar. The attraction of the 'legs hold' is that it positions the cigarette or cigar where it doesn't interfere with other activities – it allows the smoker, if necessary, to hold something else with the same hand. This helps to give the impression that smoking is a secondary activity.

There are other ways of holding a cigarette or a cigar. For example, it can be held between the thumb and the ring finger, the middle finger and the ring finger, or the ring finger and the little finger. These holds, however, are rare, and that is why they are sometimes used to identify villains or foreigners in films. The message they convey is clear – someone who can't be trusted to smoke properly can't be trusted at all.

Gender Tells

In several respects, the smoking topography of men and women is very similar – on average they take the same number of puffs, and the duration and interval between puffs is the same. However there are ways that the sexes differ – most notably in terms of the delay between puffing and inhaling, with men holding the smoke in their mouth much longer, which is one of the reasons why they absorb more nicotine than women.

The most dramatic gender differences are to be found not in smoking topography but in how men and women manipulate their cigarette – how they light it, hold it with their fingers, and position it in their mouth. Both men and women use the 'pincer hold', but usually quite differently. Men tend to use an 'open' pincer hold by forming a circle between the thumb and forefinger, while women are more likely to use a 'closed' pincer hold by flattening the space between the two fingers. The 'closed' pincer hold is widely used by marijuana smokers, largely because it enables them to smoke the roach right up to the end. In fact the association is so strong that the gesture alone is widely recognized as referring to marijuana.

There are several variants of the 'legs hold'. One is the 'bent-leg hold', where the cigarette is positioned between the index and middle finger and both are curled; in the 'straight-leg hold' the two fingers are kept straight. Because the curl of the fingers makes it easier to grip the cigarette, the 'bent-leg hold' is more comfortable, and that is why both men and women use it. The 'straight-leg hold' is marginally more difficult to perform, but it's also more elegant, which is why women favour it.

Men and women tend to hold cigarettes at different points in the gap between the forefinger and the middle finger. Each finger has three bones. If you imagine that the bones at the end are feet, the middle bones are calves, the bones near the palm are thighs, and the point where the fingers meet is the crotch, then you'll notice that most

The 'bent-leg hold'

people use a 'calf hold' – in other words, they use the middle bones of their fingers to hold the cigarette. Women are also fond of the 'foot hold', with the fingers straight, and the same is true of men who wish to convey an impression of sophistication. Men who work with their hands, however, are inclined to use a 'thigh hold' or even a 'crotch hold', with the fingers bent.

The most dramatic gender differences in smoking style are to be found in the location of the hand and the position of the wrist. Here we find that men are more likely to keep the hand holding the cigarette close to their body, to keep the wrist straight, and to curl the fingers inwards towards the palm. These conventional postures conform to a primitive rule which requires men to remain vigilant: that's why the wrist is kept straight, the hands are kept down and the fingers are curled in preparation for attack or defence. There are occasions when men hold

The 'straight-leg hold'

their cigarette in a relaxed fashion with their wrist flexed (i.e. with the hand bent towards the wrist), but unless they're trying to appear camp or effete, men don't usually hold their cigarette with their wrist extended (i.e. with the hand bent away from the wrist). As Richard Klein points out, the cigarette held between thumb and index finger 'allows the tough guy to smoke and to show his knuckles. Whenever two men are engaged in a relation of competition or rivalry, whether sexual or political, they are scrupulous to show each other the back of their hands, usually balled into a fist'.[3] But even when there's no rivalry, men like to hold their cigarette with a 'knuckle display'. Having an excuse to present their knuckles in this way appears to makes them feel more manly.

For women, the arrangement of the hand holding the

The 'dart hold'

cigarette is quite different. Here the fingers are likely to be extended, so that the palm is exposed, and the hand is likely to be held up and away from the body, rather than down and close to the body, thereby creating an overall impression of defencelessness. While the man's wrist is typically rigid, the woman's wrist can be either flexed or extended. When a woman has her wrist straight it's often part of an 'exposed-wrist display'. Here the hand is held up and away from the body, the palm is exposed, and the inside of the wrist is presented for everyone to see. Women unconsciously use this posture to draw attention to their wrist because it's a soft and vulnerable part of their body. By holding her cigarette with an 'exposed wrist display' a woman shows submissiveness, and this supposedly makes her attractive to men. There are cases where men use the same display as a camp gesture – both Oscar Wilde and Noël Coward liked to hold their cigarette in this position.

334

Gender is displayed in other ways. When a woman taps the ash off the end of her cigarette she tends to do so lightly with an extended forefinger, the man more vigorously with his forefinger bent. Likewise, when extinguishing a cigarette: a woman is more likely to stub it out lightly, while the man is more likely to fold it over and crush it under his thumb![4]

Background Tells

Smoking can provide clues to someone's occupation. People who work outdoors, for example, tend to use the 'bunker gesture' when lighting a cigarette. This is done by forming the hands into a bowl, so that the flame is shielded from the wind and rain. Those who work out-doors also hold their cigarettes differently – typically by using a 'cup hold', where the cigarette is clasped between the ends of the thumb, index and middle finger, and where the lit end faces towards, instead of away from, the palm of the hand. Both the 'bunker gesture' and the 'cup hold' have evolved as a defence against the elements, but smokers who employ them often use them indoors as well. Practically, these gestures provide protection; symbolically they shield the act of smoking from prying eyes. That's why they're also favoured by schoolchildren who smoke behind the bicycle shed – the illicit nature of the act and the thrill it provides are reinforced by the secretive way the cigarette is held.

Courtship Tells

Up until a few years ago a woman who took out a cigarette at a social gathering could reasonably expect a man to offer her a light. The ritual of lighting a woman's cigarette still provides men and women with an opportunity to exchange courtship signals – the man can position his body and the lighter to convey his interest, and he is able to check her out at close quarters while she's busy lighting her cigarette. For her part, the woman can reciprocate by lightly touching his hand, ostensibly to steady herself but really so that she can make physical contact. She can also show her interest in the man by disengaging slowly and looking him in the eye for longer than normal when she thanks him. The beauty of this ritual is that it enables people to exchange suggestive signals very rapidly and with all the ambiguity that courtship requires.

Generally speaking, the courtship signals that men and women exchange are based on the secondary sexual characteristics that distinguish them. Individuals who want to attract members of the opposite sex do so by emphasizing and exaggerating these differences, while people who wish to discourage attention do so by downplaying and disguising them. It's the same with courtship and smoking. A woman who wants to emphasize her femininity usually does so by accentuating the smoking style of women – by adopting a straight-leg hold, displaying the wrist, using the ends of the fingers, and smoking slowly. Men react unconsciously to these signals – they know there's something sexy about the woman who's using them, but they can't explain why they find her so attractive.

There are several reasons why smoking is seen as sexy. Firstly, because smoking wasn't traditionally part of the female role, women who smoked were regarded as sexually liberated. This was very noticeable in the 1920s, when young 'flappers' scandalized society by taking up the smoking habits of men, and doing it in public! Although this association probably no longer holds, lots of men believe that a woman who smokes is sexier than one who doesn't. Then there's the phallic symbolism of cigarettes and cigars, and the strong connection between smoking and sex, with cigarettes playing a central role immediately prior to sexual foreplay and immediately afterwards in the shape of the post-coital smoke.

The act of smoking surreptitiously raises the issue of seduction. 'We must not forget,' said Jean Cocteau, 'that a pack of cigarettes, the ceremony of taking one out, igniting the lighter, and the strange cloud which surrounds us, have seduced and conquered the world.' Whenever smokers light up they show themselves to be seduced. By smoking suggestively they can also be seductive. The languid, unhurried way that the cigarette is raised to the mouth and held between the lips, the way the smoke is savoured and dispelled from the mouth – all of these movements are reminiscent of the acts of love. Although people don't realize it, they often draw conclusions about how someone is likely to behave in bed from the way they smoke a cigarette. That's why flirtatious smoke signals are so successful – they suggestively shape people's impressions of each other without them knowing.

Coping Tells

Cigarettes and cigars can be used as a prop, supporting a totally artificial social performance. For someone who feels uneasy in the company of other people, smoking can provide a distraction, a disguise and a sense of security. Cigarettes serve as 'transitional objects', mediating between the inner and the outer world and performing the same role as a security blanket or a teddy bear.[5] They also help people to cope with life's problems. People can be divided into three groups on the basis of their coping strategies – those who seek help from their friends, those who seek advice from experts, and those who prefer to solve problems on their own. Of the three, the last group is most likely to 'self-medicate' – faced with a problem they're more likely to reach for a cigarette to help them cope.[6]

A major concern of self-conscious individuals is what to do with their hands when they're with other people. Smoking solves the problem by occupying the hands and giving them something to do. As we have seen, anxious people need to reassure themselves, and they often do so by touching their face or covering part of their face with their hand. The problem with these 'self-comforting gestures' is that they can sometimes draw attention to the person who's feeling anxious. Smoking, however, provides self-conscious individuals with a perfectly legitimate reason to touch their face and cover it with their hands. It also gives them a chance to envelop themselves in smoke, creating a protective smokescreen against other people. Interestingly, smokescreens can also perform the opposite function. For example, when a woman creates a veil of smoke around her face, she makes herself appear more mysterious. Here the smokescreen is designed, not defensively, but as a sexual lure.

Smoking also provides a defence against the world because it is regressive – it takes smokers back to the oral phase of their psychosexual development, when comfort was mediated through the mouth. When Freud said, 'Let there be no doubt that smoking is a form of oral pleasure', he was referring, not only to his own attachment to tobacco, but to the fact that oral pleasures are reassuring because of their association with breast-feeding. When smokers place their lips round a cigar or a cigarette, they're not just smoking; they're connecting themselves to the security they once experienced at their mother's breast. Not only has it been found that smokers who were denied the breast early in infancy have greater difficulty giving up smoking in later life, but it has also been discovered that heavy smokers have more oral pre-occupations than light smokers – they're more likely, for example, to suck the end of their pencil and to bite their nails.[7]

Conversation Tells

Smoking plays a role in conversation too. Take the case where two men are talking, and where one is smoking while the other isn't. When the person who isn't smoking stops talking for a moment, the smoker is likely to assume that he's finished his turn, and that it's therefore all right for him to take over. But when the person who's smoking hesitates for a moment, the non-smoker is likely to give him the benefit of the doubt and allow him to continue holding the floor. The floor-holding role of smoking was recognized by William Thackeray in the nineteenth century. 'Honest men with cigars in their mouths,' he observed, 'have great physical advantages in conversation. You may stop talking if you like – but the breaks of silence never seem disagreeable, being fuelled up by the puffing of smoke.'[8]

Cigarettes also help to initiate conversations and consolidate relationships. Before smoking started to become unfashionable, cigarettes were often used to strike up a conversation – one person offered a cigarette and provided a light, the other accepted, and a bond of friendship and trust was immediately formed. Nowhere is this process more evident than in war, where cigarettes are the currency of comradeship and where smoking binds soldiers powerfully together. The act of offering a cigarette, both in this situation and elsewhere, is a very primitive gesture, not only because it represents a gift, but because it's Promethean – it's a gift of the distinctively human ability to make fire. The other reason why cigarettes bind people together is that they provide a way of modifying mood. As Richard Klein has pointed out, the gift of a cigarette is always a gift of composure.[9] It offers the person a means to relax, to take stock, and to obscure their worries in smoke.

Personality Tells

Cigarettes and cigars can be used aggressively. Watch a group of smokers and you'll often see a dominant person waving his cigarette around like a sword. Notice the 'rapier hold', where the cigarette is held between the thumb and forefinger, with the lit end facing away and the palm facing up. The fact that this posture makes smoking difficult provides an essential clue to its latent aggression; the fact that the cigarette is held like a rapier is another. When someone says something the smoker doesn't like, he can always 'parry' the remark by raising his cigarette – just as if he were physically blocking an attack. This can be followed by a 'thrust', where the lit end of the cigarette is aimed and then prodded at the head or chest of the other person. With a good aim and careful timing a verbal duel can often be settled with a cigarette or a cigar. When the other person isn't smoking it's usually no contest at all.

The way people smoke is linked to other aspects of personality. Studies of smoking topography, for example, show that Type A individuals (people who are competitive and impatient) don't necessarily differ from Type B individuals (people who are co-operative and patient) in terms of the number of puffs or puff volume. But Type A individuals inhale the smoke for 70 per cent longer than Type Bs.[10] This enables Type As, who are more anxious, to calm themselves down.

The way people exhale when they're in the company of others also provides valuable clues to their personality.[11] 'Fronters', who blow the smoke forward, enclosing other people in it, tend to be dominant and aggressive. Then there are 'uppers', who exhale the smoke upwards and who tend to be considerate and confident. 'Downers', who blow the smoke downwards, are usually submissive and unassuming, rather like 'siders', who blow the smoke out of the side of their mouth and tend to be lacking in confidence. Then there are the 'nasals', who blow smoke out of their nose. Like 'fronters', they tend to be dominant and aggressive, rather like a bull. 'Fronters' and 'uppers' like to announce their presence by filling the atmosphere with their smoke; 'downers' and 'siders' are more considerate. They don't like to intrude on others by enveloping them with their smoke, so they direct it away.

In addition to the way that people smoke cigarettes, the fact that they smoke – and how heavily they smoke – can also provide clues to what kind of person they are. Psychologists have discovered that there are moderate but significant differences in personality between smokers and non-smokers – smokers, for example, tend to be more extraverted, impulsive and neurotic.[12] Extraverts, it seems, are drawn to cigarettes because they have lower levels of arousal than introverts, and need the boost provided by nicotine. It has also been suggested that the reason why so many extraverts are smokers is that they find it harder to give up smoking – the idea being that the difference between the numbers of extraverts and introverts who take up smoking is not that pronounced, but that because the introverts find it relatively easy to give up, there are always more extravert than introvert smokers.[13] It's also worth noting that the social pressure to conform to the smoking habits of one's friends and colleagues is much greater for extraverts, because they spend more time in company and are more eager than introverts to please other people. The link between impulsivity and smoking is fairly straightforward – people who are uninhibited and who seek out new experiences are much more likely to take up smoking. The mood swings that occur between smoking a cigarette and being without a cigarette may also appeal, in a perverse fashion, to people who are high on impulsivity. Finally, neurotics are attracted to cigarettes because they promise to provide relief from the heightened anxiety and worry that they experience. Cigarettes offer them a social prop, a means of appearing busy, and a way of concealing themselves, both figuratively and literally, behind a cloud of smoke.

Mood Tells

The unique feature of tobacco is its ability to produce totally opposite physiological states – on the one hand it can be used as a means of arousal, a way of waking oneself up, while on the other it can be used to calm oneself down. This 'biphasic' property of tobacco is due entirely to the way that people actually smoke – when they want to relax they try to absorb lots of nicotine, and when they want to be aroused they try to absorb much less.[14] That's because small doses of nicotine act as a stimulant, mimicking the effect of acetylcholine, a neurotransmitter that sends messages from the nerves to the muscles, while larger doses of nicotine act as a sedative. By watching how people smoke we can see, therefore, which kind of mood they are trying to create – a state of relaxation when they're drawing heavily or inhaling for longer, or a state of arousal when they're taking smaller puffs and inhaling less.

Smokers claim that smoking helps them to feel relaxed, but there is increasing evidence that smokers are more stressed and tense when they're not smoking, and that

Smoke Signals. The *Exposed Wrist Display*, as demonstrated by Jane Fonda (above), is an alluring sign of femininity and flirtation. The position of the cigarette in the mouth also reveals the smoker's mood – as we can see (below) in the upbeat 'FDR', the menacing 'Clint Eastwood' and the brooding 'Bogart'.

smoking simply provides them with a temporary respite from the stress that they experience between cigarettes.[15] The positive relationship between neuroticism and smoking may be due to the fact that anxious people are more likely to take up smoking, but it may also have something to do with the fact that smoking actually induces a feeling of generalized anxiety because of the discomfort associated with nicotine deprivation. With the combination of these two effects, it's not surprising that smokers register higher neuroticism scores than non-smokers. It's almost as if smokers assume a Jekyll-and-Hyde personality – tense and potentially irritable between cigarettes, and relaxed or energized when they're smoking. With non-smokers there's much more equanimity. Their moods may vary, but the swings are less pronounced, and they're not connected to the presence or absence of nicotine in the bloodstream.

Watching how smokers hold the cigarette or cigar in their mouth can provide more clues to their mood and the impression they're trying to create. With men there are several revealing mouth-hold postures. One is the 'Clint Eastwood', where the cigar or cigarette is located horizontally between the lips or teeth. This is how Clint Eastwood held his cigar in his mouth in his role as 'The Man With No Name' in the spaghetti westerns – it's a mouth-hold posture that conveys a strong impression of masculinity. Then there's the 'FDR posture', named after President Franklin Delano Roosevelt, where the cigar, cigarette, or in his case the cigarette holder, assumes an erect, upbeat position, rather like that of a New Guinean penis sheath. The underlying mood of the 'FDR posture' is confidence and optimism in the face of adversity.

Finally there's the 'Bogart', named after Humphrey Bogart, where the cigarette hangs down from the mouth. Here the mood is preoccupied and brooding, sometimes menacing. There was a time, several decades ago, when every male who wanted to look cool had to employ the 'Bogart'. This included several famous movie stars, like James Dean, John Wayne, and Humphrey Bogart himself. As a smoke signal of coolness, the 'Bogart' has all but disappeared, except in France, where it has become a distinguishing feature of the way Frenchmen smoke their cigarettes – a sign, not so much of coolness, but of *égalité* and *fraternité*. In their time most of the French presidents – De Gaulle, Pompidou, Mitterrand, Chirac – have been photographed with a proletarian cigarette dangling from their lower lip – something no self-respecting politician in Britain or America would ever dream of doing.

Mouth-hold smoking postures convey a variety of messages for men. But women seldom use them. That's because women don't usually leave cigarettes in their mouth between puffs — unless, of course, they're trying to look like some *femme fatale* or like Dot Cotton from *EastEnders*. The essential difference between these two archetypes is that while Dot Cotton always speaks with a cigarette in her mouth, a convincing *femme fatale* never does. Instead, she allows the cigarette to speak on her behalf. After all, that's what cigarettes and cigars do all the time – they tell us about the people who smoke them.

13. Tell-tales

You're going to work in the morning. You walk out the front door, you get in your car, you drive through the traffic, you park the car and walk into the building. The man in reception greets you as you enter and you say hello to him. You go up to your office and sit down. Your secretary comes in, says good morning and hands you your mail. You say good morning and thank her, and then she leaves. You're ready to start the day.

You're obviously an observant person because on your way to work you spotted things that very few people would have noticed. You saw that the clock face on the railway station had been changed, that the flag at City Hall was flying at half-mast, and that the lanes in the car park have been given a new coat of paint. But there are several things that you missed. You didn't notice, for example, that the man in reception, whose face is normally beaming, could only manage a lopsided smile this morning, or that your secretary, who's been with you for twelve years, had a smudge of mascara under her right eye. How were you to know that the man in reception had been to the dentist early this morning, and that your secretary had been crying because her boyfriend walked out on her last night?

There are several reasons why you failed to spot these tell-tale signs. Like most other people, you're quick to notice changes to your physical environment, but slow to spot changes in the people around you. It's not that they're unimportant – in fact they mean a lot to you. It's just that you've come to take them for granted. You're comforted by the knowledge that they don't change, and that – like the characters in the film *Groundhog Day* – they're always there, doing the same thing day after day.

This is all linked to what psychologists call 'change blindness'. Change blindness takes several forms, one of which is the inability to notice how people have changed. In a clever experiment conducted by Daniel Simons and Dan Levin at Harvard, the experimenter approached strangers on the campus and innocently asked them for directions.[1] Imagine for a moment that you're one of the unsuspecting subjects who took part in the experiment. You're walking across the campus when a stranger approaches you and asks you for directions. While you're talking to him, two workmen walk between you and the stranger, carrying a large wooden door. Naturally you feel irritated by this interruption, but after the workmen have moved on you continue giving directions to the stranger. When you've finished, the stranger thanks you and informs you that you have just taken part in an experiment. 'Did you notice anything different after the two men passed by with the door?' he asks. 'No,' you reply, 'I didn't notice anything at all.' He then explains that he's not the same man who originally approached you for directions. The original man walked off behind the door, leaving the present man behind in his place to continue the conversation! At this point the first man walks over and joins you. Looking at the two of them, standing there together, you can see how very different they are. Not only do they differ in height and build, but they're also dressed differently and have very different voices.

If you had behaved in this way, you would not have been alone, because more than half of the people who took part in the experiment failed to notice the difference between the two men. After the workmen had disappeared and the switch had taken place, the subjects continued to give directions as though nothing unusual had happened. This experiment shows that while we think we notice what's happening around us, a lot of the time we don't. Not only are we oblivious to the changes that take place in people's appearance, but we're also insensitive to the words, gestures and expressions they use. In addition to suffering from 'change blindness', we're also afflicted with *tell blindness*.

There are three reasons why we don't notice *tells*. The first is a 'failure of observation' – we simply don't pay enough attention to what people say and do. The second is a 'failure of recognition' – we notice that people are behaving in certain ways, but we don't recognize their actions as being informative. The third is a 'failure of interpretation' – we recognize that there's something informative about someone's behaviour, but we can't see what it reveals about them; in other words, we can't read the *tells*. These failures can be remedied by developing what Charles Darwin called the 'habit of minute observation' – watching people closely, paying attention to details, comparing people in different situations, and basing our conclusions on what we observe about people, rather than what they tell us about themselves.

When we're looking out for *tells*, there are several principles that we need to follow. These form the basis of *telleology*.

◆ **LOOK FOR MULTIPLE TELLS**. It's often tempting to draw inferences about people on the basis of a single *tell* – especially when you're trying to decide whether someone is lying or telling the truth. This temptation should always be resisted, because the strength of *tells* is always in direct proportion to their number – the more *tells* someone displays, the more certain you can be about what they're thinking or feeling.

◆ **DON'T JUMP TO CONCLUSIONS**. It's also tempting to assume that *tells* always reveal the same things about people. Unfortunately, that's not always the case, because a *tell* can sometimes convey quite different meanings. For example, if you were to meet someone with sweaty palms you'd probably conclude that they were nervous about something. But you could be wrong – the person might have hyperhidrosis, a genetic condition which has nothing to do with anxiety. The moral here is that you should always make your inferences conditional until you've had a chance to check them out.

◆ **COMPARE PEOPLE WITH THEMSELVES**. In order to interpret someone's *tells* it's sometimes necessary to compare that person in several different settings, rather than to compare him or her with lots of other people in one setting. For example, if you arrived at a party and your host greeted you effusively, you'd want to know whether you'd been singled out or if everyone was getting the same treatment. To find out, you'd need to watch how he greeted the other guests – in other words, you'd have to compare him with himself. That way you'd be able to find out whether your host was especially pleased to see you, or whether he's equally enthusiastic with everybody.

One reason why we're so blind to *tells* is that they seem so small and insignificant. We're so busy concentrating on what people are saying to us that we fail to notice their choice of words, the inflection of their voice, and the way they move their hands and feet. One of the most important lessons to emerge from *telleology* is the fact that, where *tells* are concerned, size doesn't matter. In fact, it's often the tiny, almost imperceptible actions that provide clues to people's thoughts and personality. This is most noticeable in situations where people act unintentionally and where they aren't aware of their actions. As Arthur Schopenhauer pointed out, 'It is with trifles, and when he is off guard, that a man best reveals his character.'

It was attention to detail that formed the basis of Sherlock Holmes's legendary ability to understand people's motives and to solve mysteries. 'You know my method', said Holmes: 'it is founded upon the observance of trifles.' His advice was 'Never to trust general impressions – but concentrate upon the details'.[2] It's often in the tiny *tells* and in the details of their unintended actions that people are most revealing about themselves – in slips of the tongue, minute hand movements, and the fleeting, almost tachistoscopic *micro-tells* that flicker across their face when they're trying to conceal their true feelings.

Telleology promises to play an increasingly important role in forensic science. In the old days the only tools available to a detective were his keen senses. There have been enormous changes since Sherlock Holmes looked out of his window, noticed how a woman hesitated before crossing the road, and informed Dr Watson that 'oscillation upon the pavement always means an *affaire du coeur*'.[3] Although today's detectives recognize the need for a trained eye, their task is made easier by the opportunity to record people's actions, to view them repeatedly, and to subject them to detailed analysis. A good example is John Napier's analysis of the famous cinefilm of 'Bigfoot', where he was able to show that the style of walking was entirely humanoid.[4]

Whether we like it or not, we're all involved with *tells* – there's no escaping them. An enormous number of *tells* is produced whenever we interact with other people, and even when we remain silent in their company. Some of these *tells* are under our control – they're the ones that we use to present a particular image of ourselves. But there are also *tells* that we cannot control, like blushing and pupil dilation, as well as *tells* that we can control, but don't, like preening, posture matching, and certain facial expressions. As we noticed earlier, there are differences in the way that we relate to unintended *tells*, because while we may be painfully aware of the fact that we're blushing, there's no way we could know that our pupils are dilated; we are only ever aware of the treachery of our cheeks, never that of our eyes. Equally, while we are quite capable of positioning our limbs or moving our hands in ways that are likely to give a certain impression, we often fail to consciously control these features of our behaviour, allowing them instead to reveal moods and thoughts that we wish to conceal from other people.

Although we're often blind to other people's *tells*, this doesn't mean that we're unaffected by them. In recent years psychologists have discovered that features of their social environment can unconsciously shape people's moods. For example, Sheila Murphy and Bob Zajonc found that people's moods are affected very differently, depending on whether they are exposed to a smiling or a scowling face. In both instances, their subjects were only exposed to these faces for four milliseconds, which was too short for them to be aware of what they had seen.[5] Ulf Dimberg and his colleagues at Uppsala University have gone one step further by showing that our facial responses are influenced by other people's facial expressions, even when we're unaware of what they're doing with their face. Dimberg and his colleagues placed electrodes on their subjects' faces and then exposed them to subliminal images of smiling, angry or neutral faces.[6] They found that subjects were more likely to frown when they were presented with an angry face, and more likely to raise the corners of their mouth when they were exposed to the smiling face, even though they were completely unaware that they'd seen a face.

These studies suggest that other people's *tells* can affect us in ways of which we are entirely unaware. They also raise the possibility that the way we respond to other people has more to do with the tiny, almost subliminal features of their demeanour than to the gross, more obvious aspects of their behaviour. I was very struck by this when I watched Bill Clinton address the Labour Party Conference in Blackpool in October 2002. At the time

Tony Blair was having trouble persuading Labour members that it would be necessary for Britain to support the United States if it decided to go to war against Iraq, and it was thought that Bill Clinton would be able to bring the doubters into line behind Blair. The speech was vintage Clinton – he flattered the delegates, exposed both sides of the argument and showed that he was fallible. But more importantly, he interspersed his remarks with Clintonian *tells* – that upward-looking smile, the magisterial wave, the carefully timed hesitations to remind everyone that politics was about making tough decisions. When he said that war is indiscriminate – 'I do not care how precise your bombs and your weapons are, when you set them off innocent people will die' – he did his trademark *lip-bite tell*, reminding the gathering that he was a man of feeling. At the end of the speech there was thunderous applause. When conference members were interviewed on TV after-wards, they were all ecstatic – MPs of every political hue said that Clinton was on their side. There was of course no mention of the various oratorical devices that he'd used, even though it was these devices that had electrified the conference, rather than anything Clinton had said. The delegates thought they were responding to his arguments, but they weren't. They were reacting to the *tells* that he had produced, those little signals that he'd marshalled to show that he was thoughtful and sensitive, a man of political conviction with strong emotions. It was the *tells* – the medium, not the message – that had won the day.

In Chapter 1 we saw that the word *tell* comes from poker, where it is used to describe any action or speech mannerism that reveals what kind of hand someone is holding or what kind of strategy they're using. The ensuing chapters have shown that the notion of *tells* isn't exclusive to the game of poker, and that it can profitably be applied to a wide range of everyday pursuits. Poker is like life in some respects, and different in others. Part of the similarity lies in the fact that we need to conceal our thoughts, feelings and intentions from others, just as poker players need to keep their hand and their motives hidden.

The other similarity lies in individuals' attempts to understand each other, and to use their observations as a guide to what the other person is thinking. When you're playing poker there are two sources of information about the kind of hand another player is holding – one is the cards you're holding, and the other is the way he or she is behaving. The trouble with the latter is that there's no way of knowing whether the inferences you draw about the other person's hand are based on what he or she is failing to conceal, or what they are doing in order to deceive you. In many respects, life's the same – it's not always clear whether the conclusions we draw about other people are based on actions that they can't control or actions that they've deliberately produced in order to mislead us. In poker this conundrum is solved by comparing the various hands that a player has with the way that he or she behaves during each round. Although life isn't neatly parcelled into discrete deals, it's still possible to link individuals' circumstances to the way they behave, and in this way to identify their *tells*.

When you're playing poker with someone for the first time there's no way of knowing what their *tells* are – the only thing you can do is assume that the *common tells* apply to them as much as they do to anyone else. After watching another player for several rounds, it should be possible to identify their *signature tells*. The same thing applies outside the game of poker – it takes several occasions to recognize the distinctive features of some-one's behaviour and to link these to what they're feeling. In the meantime one can always resort to one's knowledge of *common tells* in order to work out what that person is thinking.

The study of *tells* promises to enrich our lives in many ways. By focusing our attention on the tiny details and fleeting aspects of other people's behaviour we are exposed to the enormous complexity of our social world, and this can only encourage us to be more sensitive towards other people. Observing other people's *tells* also turns our attention back on ourselves – it sensitizes us to our own behaviour and helps us to recognize that while we are using other people's *tells* to draw inferences about their feelings and intentions, they're doing exactly the same to us. In addition, the study of *tells* is potentially liberating because it reveals how people try to manipulate others and how they give themselves away; being armed with these insights helps to protect us from the dangers of being manipulated ourselves. Finally, the study of *tells* invites us to see the world differently, and to recognize that people are constantly conveying information about themselves in the form of *tells*. Unpacking these *tells* enables us to read their minds and to understand them more fully.

Notes

1. Tells

1 Caro, M. (1994) *The Body Language of Poker: Caro's Book of Tells*. Secaucus, NJ: Carol Publishing Group.

2 Haggard, E. A., and Isaacs, K. S. (1966) 'Micromomentary facial expressions as indicators of ego mechanisms in psychotherapy'. In L. A. Gottschalk and A. H. Auerbach (eds), *Methods of Research in Psychotherapy*. New York: Appleton-Century-Crofts.

3 Hess, E. (1975) *The Telltale Eye*. New York: Van Nostrand Reinhold.

4 Ekman, P., and Friesen, W. (1969) 'Nonverbal leakage and clues to deception'. *Psychiatry*, 32, 88–106.

5 Freud, S. (1905) 'Fragments of an analysis of a case of hysteria'. *Collected Papers*, Vol. 3. New York: Basic Books (reprinted 1959).

6 Ro, K. M., Cantor, R. M., Lange, K. L., and Ahn, S. S. (2002) 'Palmar hyperhidrosis: evidence of genetic transmission'. *Journal of Vascular Surgery*, 35(2), 382–86.

7 Dryden, J., and Clough, A. H. (eds) (1902) *Lives of Noble Grecians and Romans*, Vol. 3. Boston: Little, Brown.

8 Bulwer, J. (1644) *Chirologia; or the Natural Language of the Hand*. London.

9 Mahl, G. F., Danet, B., and Norton, N. (1959) 'Reflections of major personality characteristics in gestures and body movements. Research Report to A.P.A. Annual meeting'. Cited in B. Christiansen (1972) *Thus*

Speaks the Body. New York: Arno Press.

10 LaFrance, M. (1985) 'Postural mirroring and intergroup relations'. *Personality and Social Psychology Bulletin*, 11(2), 207–17; Bernieri, F., and Rosenthal, R. (1991) 'Interpersonal coordination: behavioural matching and interactional synchrony'. In R. S. Feldman and B. Rime (eds), *Fundamentals of Nonverbal Behavior*. Cambridge: Cambridge University Press.

11 Provine, R. R. (1996) 'Contagious yawning and laughter: Significance for sensory feature detection, motor pattern generation, imitation, and the evolution of social behavior'. In C. M. Heyes and B. G. Galef (eds), *Social Learning in Animals: The Roots of Culture*. New York: Academic Press.

12 Krebs, J. R. and Dawkins, R. D. (1984) 'Animal signals: mind-reading and manipulation'. In J. R. Krebs and N. B. Davies (eds), *Behavioral Ecology: An Evolutionary Approach*. Sunderland, MA: Sinauer.

13 Gottman, J. M., and Silver, N. (1999) *The Seven Principles for Making Marriage Work*. New York: Crown Publishers.

2. Dominant Tells

1 Kalma, A. (1991) 'Hierarchisation and dominance assessment at first glance'. *European Journal of Social Psychology*, 21, 165–81.

2 Cassidy, C. M. (1991) 'The good body: when big is better'. *Medical Anthropology*, 13, 181–213; Ellis, L. (1994) 'The high and the mighty among man and beast: how universal is the relationship between height (or body size) and social status?' In L. Ellis (ed.), *Social Stratification and Socioeconomic Inequality*, Vol. 2, Westport, CT: Praeger.

3 Gunnell, D., Rogers, J., and Dieppe, P. (2001) 'Height and health: predicting longevity from bone length in archaeological remains'. *Journal of Epidemiology and Community Health*, 55, 505–7.

4 Ellis, B. J. (1992) 'The evolution of sexual attraction: evaluative mechanisms in women'. In J. H. Barkow, L. Cosmides and J. Tooby (eds), *The Adapted Mind: Evolutionary Psychology and the Generation of Culture*. New York: Oxford University Press; Pierce, C. (1996) 'Body height and romantic attraction: a meta-analytic test of the male-taller norm'. *Social Behavior and Personality*, 24(2), 143–50; Pawlowski, B., Dunbar, R., and Lipowicz, A. (2000) 'Evolutionary fitness: tall men have more reproductive success'. *Nature*, 403 (6766), 156.

5 Tremblay, R. E., Schaal, B., Boulerice, B., Arseneault, L., Soussignan, R. G., Paquette, D., and Laurent, D. (1998) 'Testosterone, physical aggression, dominance, and physical development in early adolescence'. *International Journal of Behavioral Development* 22(4), 753–77.

6 Cassidy, C. M. (1991) 'The good body: when big is better'. *Medical Anthropology*, 13, 181–213; Pinker, S. (1997) *How the Mind Works*. New York: W. W. Norton.

7 Hensley, W. E. (1993) 'Height as a measure of success in academe'. *Psychology: A Journal of Human Behavior*, 30(1), 40–6.

8 Weisfeld, G. E., and Beresford, J. M. (1982) 'Erectness of posture as an indicator of dominance or success in humans'. *Motivation and Emotion*, 6(2), 113–31; Weisfeld, G. E., and Linkey, H. E. (1985) 'Dominance displays as indicators of a social success motive'. In S. L. Ellyson and J. F. Dovidio (eds), *Power, Dominance, and Non-verbal Behavior*. New York: Springer Verlag.

9 Riskind, J. H. (1983) 'Nonverbal expressions and the accessibility of life experience memories: a congruence hypothesis'. *Social Cognition*, 2(1), 62–86; Riskind, J. H. (1984) 'They stoop to conquer: guiding and self-regulatory functions of physical posture after success and failure'. *Journal of Personality and Social Psychology*, 47(3), 479–93.

10 Lott, D. F., and Sommer, R. (1967) 'Seating arrangement and status', *Journal of Personality and Social Psychology*, 7(1), 90–5; Sommer, R. (1969) *Personal Space*. New York: Prentice Hall.

11 Schnurnberger, L. (1991) *40,000 Years of Fashion: Let There Be Clothes*. New York: Workman Publishing.

12 Spicer, J. (1991) 'The Renaissance elbow'. In J. Bremmer and H. Roodenburg (eds), *The Cultural History of Gesture*. Cambridge: Polity Press.

13 From the English edition of Desiderius Erasmus' *De Civilitate Morum Puerilium* (1532), translated by Robert Whitinton (1540) and cited by Joaneath Spicer (1991), ibid.

14 Mueller, U., and Mazur, A. (1997) 'Facial dominance in Homo Sapiens as honest signalling of male quality'. *Behavioural Ecology*, 8, 569–79; Mazur, A., and Booth, A. (1998) 'Testosterone and dominance in men'. *Behavioral and Brain Sciences*, 21, 353–98.

15 Keating, C. F. (1985) 'Human dominance signals: the primate in us'. In S. L. Ellyson and J. F. Dovidio (eds), *Power, Dominance, and Non-verbal Behavior*. New York: Springer Verlag.

16 Keating, C. F., Mazur, A., and Segall, M. H. (1981) 'A cross-cultural exploration of physiognomic traits of dominance and happiness', *Ethology and Sociobiology*, 2, 41–8.

17 Tiedens, L. Z. (2001) 'Anger and advancement versus sadness and subjugation: the effect of negative emotion expressions on social status conferral'. *Journal of Personality and Social Psychology*, 80(1), 86–94.

18 Dabbs, J. M. (1992) 'Testosterone, smiling and facial appearance'. *Journal of Nonverbal Behavior*, 21, 45–55. See also Mazur, A., and Booth, A. (1998) 'Testosterone and dominance in men'. *Behavioral and Brain Sciences*, 21, 353–98.

19 Schniter, E. (2000) 'The evolution of yawning: why do we yawn and why is it contagious?' MA thesis, Department of Anthropology, University of Oregon.

20 Schino, G., and Aureli, F. (1989) 'Do men yawn more than women?' *Ethology and Sociobiology*, 10, 375–8.

21 Ridgeway, C. L., Berger, J., and Smith, L. (1985) 'Nonverbal cues and status: an expectation states approach'. *American Journal of Sociology*, 90(5), 955–78; Schwartz, B., Tesser, A., and Powell, E. (1982) 'Dominance cues in nonverbal behavior'. *Social Psychology Quarterly*, 45(2), 114–20.

22 Gregory, S., and Webster, S. (1996) 'A nonverbal signal in the voices of interview partners effectively predicts communication accommodation and social status'. *Journal of Personality and Social Psychology*, 70(6), 1231–40. See also Bilous, F. R., and Krauss, R. M. (1988) 'Dominance and accommodation in the conversational behaviors of same and mixed-gender dyads'. *Language and Communication*, 8(3/4), 183–95.

23 Ohala, J. J. (1994) 'The frequency code underlies the sound-symbolic use of voice pitch'. In L. Hinton, J. Nichols and J. J. Ohala (eds), *Sound Symbolism*. Cambridge: Cambridge University Press.

24 Krebs, J. R., and Dawkins, R. D. (1984) 'Animal signals: mind-reading and manipulation'. In J. R. Krebs and N. B. Davies (eds), *Behavioral Ecology: An Evolutionary Approach*. Sunderland, MA: Sinauer; Collins, S. (2001) 'Men's voices and women's choices'. *Animal Behavior*, 60, 773–80.

25 Elliot, A. J. (1981) *Child Language*. Cambridge: Cambridge University Press.

26 Pemberton, C., McCormack, P., and Russell, A. (1998) 'Have women's voices lowered across time? A cross-sectional study of Australian women's voices'. *Journal of Voice*, 12(2), 208–13.

27 Henley, N. (2001) 'Body politics'. In A. Branaman (ed.), *Self and Society*. Malden, MA: Blackwell.

28 Chance, M. R. A. (1967) 'Attention structure as the basis of primate rank orders'. *Man*, 2(4), 503–18 (reprinted in M. R. A. Chance and R. R. Larsen (eds) (1976) *The Social Structure of Attention*. London: Wiley.

29 Strongman, K. T., and Champness, B. G. (1968) 'Dominance hierarchies and conflict in eye contact'. *Acta Psychologia*, 28, 376–86; Argyle, M., and Cook, M. (1976) *Gaze and Mutual Gaze*. Cambridge: Cambridge University Press; Rosa, E., and Mazur, A. (1979) 'Incipient status in small groups'. *Social Forces*, 58, 18–37; Webbink, P. (1986) *The Power of the Eyes*. New York: Springer Verlag.

30 Ellyson, S. L., Dovidio, J. F. and Fehr, B. J. (1981) 'Visual behavior and dominance in women and men'. In C. Mayo and N. M. Henley (eds), *Gender and Nonverbal Behavior*. New York: Springer Verlag; Dovidio, J. F., and Ellyson, S. L. (1982) 'Decoding visual dominance: attributions of power based on relative percentages of looking while speaking and looking while listening'. *Social Psychology Quarterly*, 45(2), 106–13.

31 Mehrabian, A. (1969) 'Significance of posture and position in the communication of attitude and status relationships'. *Psychological Bulletin*, 71(5), 359–72.

3. Submissive Tells

1 Darwin, C. (1872) *The Expression of the Emotions in Man and Animals*. London: John Murray.

2 Efron, D. (1942) *Gesture and Environment*. New York: Kings Crown Press.

3 Brault, G. J. (1963) 'Kinesics and the classroom: some typical French gestures'. *The French Review*, 36, 374–82.

4 Gilbert, P. (2000) 'Varieties of submissive behavior as forms of social defense: their evolution and role in depression'. In L. Sloman and P. Gilbert (eds), *Subordination and Defeat: An Evolutionary Approach to Mood Disorders and Their Therapy*. Mahwah, NJ: Erlbaum.

5 Collett, P., and Contarello, A. (1987) 'Gesti di assenso e di dissenso'. In P. Ricci Bitti (ed.), *Communicazione e Gestualità*. Milano: Franco Angeli; Collett, P. (1993) *Foreign Bodies: A Guide to European Mannerisms*.

London: Simon & Schuster.

6 Goffman, E. (1976) 'Gender advertisements'. *Studies in the Anthropology of Visual Communication*, 3, 69–154 (reprinted as Goffman, E. (1979) *Gender Advertisements*. New York: Harper & Row; Morris, D. (1979) *Manwatching: A Field Guide to Human Behaviour*. London: Jonathan Cape; Regan, J. M. (1982) 'Gender displays in portrait photographs'. *Sex Roles*, 8, 33–43; Halberstadt, A. G. and Saitta, M. B. (1987) 'Gender, nonverbal behavior, and perceived dominance: a test of a theory'. *Journal of Personality and Social Psychology*, 53, 257–72; Wilson, A., and Lloyd, B. (1990) 'Gender vs. power; self-posed behavior revisited'. *Sex Roles*, 23, 91–8.

7 Costa, M., Menzani, M., and Ricci Bitti, P. E. (2001) 'Head canting in paintings: an historical study'. *Journal of Nonverbal Behavior*, 25(1), 63–73.

8 Chance, M. R. A. (1962) 'An interpretation of some agonistic postures: the role of "cut-off" acts and postures'. *Symposium of the Zoological Society of London*, 8, 71–89.

9 Zebrowitz, L.A. (1997) *Reading Faces: Window to the Soul?* Boulder, CO: Westview Press.

10 Hall, J. A., Smith LeBeau, L., Gordon Reinoso, J., and Thayer, F. (2001) 'Status, gender, and nonverbal behavior in candid and posed photographs: a study of conversations between university employees'. *Sex Roles*, 44, 677–91; Hall, J. A., Carter, J. D., Jimenez, M. C., Frost, N. A., and Smith LeBeau, L. (2002) 'Smiling and relative status in news photographs'. *Journal of Social Psychology*, 142, 500–10.

11 Van Hooff, J. A. R. A. M. (1972) 'A comparative approach to the phylogeny of laughter and smiling'. In R. A. Hinde (ed.), *Nonverbal Communication*. Cambridge: Cambridge University Press.

12 Hecht, M., and LaFrance, M. (1988) 'License or obligation to smile: the effect of power and gender on amount and type of smiling'. *Personality and Social Psychology Bulletin*, 24, 1326–36; LaFrance, M., and Hecht, M. A. (1999) 'Option or obligation to smile: the effects of power and gender on facial expression'. In P. Philippot, R. S. Feldman and E. J. Coats (eds), *The Social Context of Nonverbal Behavior*. Cambridge: Cambridge University Press.

13 Duchenne de Boulogne, G. (1862) *Mécanisme de la physionomie humaine*. Paris: Jules Renard (reprinted in English as *The Mechanism of*

Human Facial Expression, edited and translated by R. A. Cuthbertson, Cambridge, Cambridge University Press, 1990).

14 Cashdan, E. (1998) 'Smiles, speech and body posture: how women and men display sociometric status and power'. *Journal of Nonverbal Behavior*, 22(4) 209–28; LaFrance, M., and Hecht, M. (2000) 'Gender and smiling: a meta-analysis of sex differences in smiling'. In A. H. Fisher (ed.), *Gender and Emotion*. Cambridge, Cambridge University Press, 1990; Hall, J. A., Carney, D. R., and Murphy, N. M. (2002) 'Gender differences in smiling'. In M. H. Abel (ed.), *An Empirical Reflection on the Smile*. New York: Edwin Mellen Press.

15 Dabbs, J. M. (1992) 'Testosterone, smiling and facial appearance'. *Journal of Nonverbal Behavior*, 21, 45–55.

16 Darwin, C. (1872) *The Expression of the Emotions in Man and Animals*. London: John Murray.

17 Ricks, C. (1974) *Keats and Embarrassment*. Oxford: Clarendon Press.

18 Leary, M. R., Britt, T. W., Cutlip, W. D., and Templeton, J. L. (1992) 'Social blushing'. *Journal of Personality and Social Pychology*, 112(3), 446–60.

19 Halberstadt, A., and Green, L. R. (1993) 'Social attention and placation theories of blushing'. *Motivation and Emotion*, 17(1), 53–64; De Jong, P. J. (1999) 'Communicative and remedial effects of social blushing'. *Journal of Nonverbal Behavior*, 23(3), 197–217.

20 Smith, W. J., Chase, J., and Lieblich, A. K. (1974) 'Tongue showing: a facial display'. *Semiotica*, 11, 201–246.

21 Dolgin, K. M., and Sabini, J. (1982) 'Experimental manipulation of a human nonverbal display: the tongue show affects an observer's willingness to interact'. *Animal Behaviour*, 30, 935–6; Jones, N., Kearins, J., and Watson, J. (1987) 'The human tongue show and observers' willingness to interact: replication and extensions'. *Psychological Reports*, 60, 759–64.

22 Kendon, A. (1975) 'Some functions of the face in a kissing round'. *Semiotica*, 15, 299–334.

23 Festinger, L., and Carlsmith, M. (1959) 'Cognitive consequences of forced compliance'. *Journal of Abnormal and Social Psychology*, 58, 203–10.

24 Jones, E. E. (1964) *Ingratiation*. New York: Appleton-Century-Crofts; Gordon, R. A. (1996) 'Impact of ingratiation on judgements and evaluations: a meta-analytic investigation'. *Journal of Personality and*

Social Psychology, 71(1), 54–70; Stengel, R. (2000) *You're Too Kind: A Brief History of Flattery*. New York: Simon & Schuster.

25 Judge, T. A., and Bretz, R. D. (1994) 'Political influence behavior and career success'. *Journal of Management*, 20(1), 43–65.

26 Colman, A., and Olver, K. R. (1978) 'Reactions to flattery as a function of self-esteem: self-enhancement and cognitive consistency theories'. *British Journal of Social and Clinical Psychology*, 17(1), 25–9.

4. Conversation Tells

1 Walker, M. (1982) 'Smooth transitions in conversational turn-taking: implications for theory'. *Journal of Psychology*, 110, 31–7.

2 Sacks, H., Schegloff, E., and Jefferson, G. (1974) 'A simplest systematics for the organization of turn-taking in conversation'. *Language*, 50, 696–735; Beattie, G. (1983) *Talk: An Analysis of Speech and Non-verbal Behaviour in Conversation*. Milton Keynes: Open University Press.

3 Yngve, V. J. (1970) 'On getting a word in edgewise'. *Papers from the 6th Regional Meeting of the Chicago Linguistic Society*, Chicago: Chicago Linguistic Society.

4 Meltzer, L., Morris, W. N., and Hayes, D. (1971) 'Interruption outcomes and vocal amplitude: explorations in social psychophysics'. *Journal of Personality and Social Psychology*, 18, 392–402.

5 Anderson, K. J., and Leaper, C. (1998) 'Meta-analyses of gender effects on conversational interruptions: who, what, when, where and how'. *Sex Roles*, 39(3/4), 225–52.

6 Tannen, D. (1981) 'New York Jewish conversational style'. *International Journal of the Sociology of Language*, 30, 133–49.

7 Kendon, A. (1967) 'Some functions of gaze-direction in social inter-action'. *Acta Psychologia*, 26, 2–63; Argyle, M., and Cook, M. (1976) *Gaze and Mutual Gaze*. Cambridge: Cambridge University Press; Beattie, G. (1978) 'Sequential temporal patterns of speech and gaze in dialogue'. *Semiotica*, 23(1/2), 29–52.

8 Harrigan, J. A., and Steffen, J. J. (1983) 'Gaze as a turn-exchange signal in group conversations'. *British Journal of Social Psychology*, 22(2), 167–8; Kalma, A. (1992) 'Gazing in triads: a powerful signal in floor apportion-ment'. *British Journal of Social Psychology*, 31, 21–39.

9 Duncan, S. (1972) 'Some signals and rules for taking speaking turns in conversations'. *Journal of Personality and Social Psychology*, 23(2), 283–92.

10 Caspers, J. (2000) 'Looking for melodic turn-holding configurations in Dutch'. *Linguistics in the Netherlands 2000*, Amsterdam: John Benjamins; Wichmann, A., and Caspers, J. (2001) 'Melodic cues to turn-taking in English: evidence from perception'. In J. van Kuppeveldt and R. Smith (eds), *Proceedings of the 2nd SIGdial Workshop on Discourse and Dialogue.* Aalborg, Denmark.

11 Walker, M., and Trimboli, C. (1983) 'The expressive function of the eye flash'. *Journal of Nonverbal Behavior*, 8(1), 3–13.

12 Scheflen, A. E., and Scheflen, A. (1972) *Body Language and Social Order.* Englewood Cliffs, NJ: Prentice-Hall; Scheflen, A. (1973) *How Behavior Means.* New York: Gordon & Breach.

13 Sebba, M., and Tate, S. (1986) 'You know what I mean? Agreement marking in British Black English'. *Journal of Pragmatics*, 10, 163–72.

14 Commins, S. (1935) *The Complete Works and Letters of Charles Lamb.* New York: Modern Library.

15 Feldman, S. (1959) *Mannerisms of Speech and Gestures in Everyday Life.* New York: International Universities Press; Weintraub, W. (1989) *Verbal Behavior in Everyday Life.* New York: Springer Verlag.

16 Weinstein, E. A. (1966) 'Toward a theory of interpersonal tactics'. In C. Backman and P. Second (eds), *Problems in Social Psychology: Selected Readings.* New York: McGraw-Hill.

17 Lakoff, G. (1973) 'Hedges: a study in meaning criteria and the logic of fuzzy concepts'. *Journal of Philosophical Logic*, 2, 458–508; Schiffrin, D. (1988) *Discourse Markers.* Cambridge: Cambridge University Press; Holmes, J. (1990) 'Hedges and boosters in women's and men's speech'. *Language and Communication*, 10(3), 185–205.

18 Malmstrom, J. (1960) '*Kind of* and its congeners'. *English Journal*, 44, 288–90.

19 Holmes, J. (1986) 'Functions of *you know* in women's and men's speech'. *Language in Society*, 15, 1–22.

20 Lockard, J. S., Allen, D. J., Schiele, B. J., and Wiemer, M. J. (1978) 'Human postural signals: stance, weight-shifts and social distance as intention movements to depart'. *Animal Behaviour*, 26, 219–24.

21 Wildeblood, J., and Brinson, P. (1965) *The Polite World.* London:

Oxford University Press; Rockwood, J. (1992) *The Craftsmen of Dionysus: An Approach to Acting.* New York: Applause Books.

5. Political Tells

1 Gregg, G. L. (1998) 'Liberals, conservatives and the presidency'. *The Intercollegiate Review*, Spring, 26–31.

2 Blum, M. D. (1988) *The Silent Speech of Politicians.* San Diego: Brenner Information Group.

3 Henton, C. G., and Bladon, R. A. W., (1985) 'Breathiness in normal female speech: inefficiency versus desirability'. *Language and Communication*, 5, 221–7; W. Hardcastle and J. Laver (eds) (1995) *The Handbook of Phonetic Sciences.* Oxford: Blackwell.

4 Gregory, S. W., and Gallagher, T. J. (2002) 'Spectral analysis of candidates' nonverbal vocal communication: predicting U.S. presidential election outcomes'. *Social Psychology Quarterly*, 65(3), 298–308.

5 Masters, R. D. (1988) 'Nice guys don't finish last: aggressive and appeasement gestures in media images of politicians'. In M. R. A. Chance and D. R. Omark (eds), *Social Fabrics of the Mind.* Hove: Lawrence Erlbaum.

6 Chance, M. R. A. (1962) 'An interpretation of some agonistic postures: the role of "cut-off" acts and postures'. *Symposium of the Zoological Society of London*, 8, 71–89.

7 Atkinson, M. (1986) *Our Masters' Voices: The Language and Body Language of Politics.* London: Methuen.

8 Harris, S. (1991) 'Evasive action: how politicians respond to questions in political interviews'. In P. Scannell (ed.), *Broadcast Talk.* London: Sage.

9 Bull, P., and Mayer, K. (1993) 'How not to answer questions in political interviews'. *Political Psychology*, 14(4), 651–66; Bull, P. (1998) 'Political interviews: television interviews in Great Britain'. In O. Feldman and C. De Landtsheer (eds), *Politically Speaking.* Westport, CT: Praeger.

10 Bull, P., and Mayer, K. (1988) 'Interruptions in political interviews: a study of Margaret Thatcher and Neil Kinnock'. *Journal of Language and Social Psychology*, 7(1), 35–45.

11 Beattie, G. (1982) 'Turn-taking and interruption in political interviews: Margaret Thatcher and Jim Callaghan compared and contrasted'. *Semiotica*, 39(1/2), 93–114.

12 Schegloff, E. A. (1989) 'From interview to confrontaton: observations on the Bush/Rather encounter'. *Research on Language and Social Interaction,* 22, 215–40.

6. Greeting Tells

1 Kendon, A., and Ferber, A. (1973) 'A description of some human greetings'. In R. P. Michael and J. H. Crook (eds), *Comparative Ethology and Behavior of Primates.* New York: Academic Press.

2 Wildeblood, J., and Brinson, P. (1965) *The Polite World.* London: Oxford University Press; Rockwood, J. (1992) *The Craftsmen of Dionysus: An Approach to Acting.* New York: Applause Books.

3 Bulwer, J. (1644) *Chirologia; or the Natural Language of the Hand.* London.

4 Doran, G. D. (1998) 'Shake on it'. *Entrepreneur Magazine,* July.

5 Givens, D. (1977) 'Greeting a stranger: some commonly used nonverbal signals of aversiveness'. *Semiotica,* 19(1/2), 13–28; Hall, P. M., and Hall, D. A. S. (1983) 'The handshake as interaction'. *Semiotica,* 45(3/4), 249–64.

6 Collett, P. (1983) 'Mossi salutations'. *Semiotica,* 45(3/4), 191–248.

7 Chaplin, W. F., Phillips, J. B., Brown, J. D., and Clanton, N. R. (2001) 'Handshaking, gender, personality, and first impressions'. *Journal of Personality and Social Psychology,* 79(1), 110–17.

8 Stephanopoulos, G. (1999) *All Too Human: A Political Education.* New York: Little, Brown.

9 Goffman, E. (1971) *Relations in Public.* Harmondsworth: Penguin; Greenbaum, P. E., and Rosenfeld, H. M. (1980) 'Varieties of touch in greetings: sequential structure and sex-related differences'. *Journal of Nonverbal Behavior,* 5(1), 13–25.

10 Collett, P. (1993) *Foreign Bodies: A Guide to European Mannerisms.* London: Simon & Schuster.

11 Erasmus, D. (1540) *Opera Omnia,* 9 vols. Basle.

12 Bakken, D. (1977) 'Saying goodbye: an observational study of parting rituals'. *Man–Environment Systems,* 7, 95–100; Summerfield, A., and Lake, J. A. (1977) 'Nonverbal and verbal behaviours associated with parting'. *British Journal of Psychology,* 68, 133–6; Albert, S., and Kessler, S. (1978)

'Ending social encounters'. *Journal of Experimental Social Psychology*, 14, 541–53.

13 Knapp, M. L., Hart, R. P., Friedrich, G. W., and Shulman, G. M. (1973) 'The rhetoric of goodbye: verbal and nonverbal correlates of human leave-taking'. *Speech Monographs*, 40, 182–98.

7. Royal Tells

1 Nicolson, H. (1968) *Diaries and Letters, 1945–1962*, edited by N. Nicolson, London: Collins.

2 Lacey, R. (1977) *Majesty: Elizabeth II and the House of Windsor.* London: Hutchinson.

3 Provine, R. R. (2000) *Laughter: A Scientific Investigation.* London: Penguin.

4 Castiglione, B. (1528) *Libro del Cortegiano.* Venice (translated by Sir Thomas Hoby as *The Book of the Courtier.* London, 1561).

5 Naunton, R. (1641) *Fragmenta Regalia* (reprinted in H. Walpole (ed.), *Paul Hentzner's Travels in England.* London, 1797).

6 Hoggart, S. (1986) 'Caribbean Queen'. In T. Grove (ed.) *The Queen Observed.* London: Pavilion Books.

7 Tooley, S. A. (1896) *The Personal Life of Queen Victoria.* London: S. H. Bousefield.

8 Windsor, E. (1987) *Wallis and Edward: Letters 1931–1937: The Intimate Correspondence of the Duke and Duchess of Windsor*, edited by M. Bloch. Bath: Chivers.

9 Henley, N. (2001) 'Body politics'. In A. Branaman (ed.), *Self and Society.* Malden, MA: Blackwell.

10 Windsor, E. (1951) *A King's Story: The Memoirs of H.R.H. the Duke of Windsor.* London: Cassell.

11 Bloch, M. (1973) *The Royal Touch: Sacred Monarchy and Scrofula in England and France*, translated by J. E. Anderson. London: Routledge & Kegan Paul.

12 Holden, A. (1979) *Charles: Prince of Wales: A Biography.* London: Little, Brown.

13 Mehrabian, A. (1969) 'Methods and designs: some referents and measures of nonverbal communication'. *Behavioral Research Methods and*

Instrumentation, 1, 203–7; Beebe, S. S., Beebe, S. J., and Redmond, M. V. (2002) *Interpersonal Communication: Relating to Others.* Boston: Allyn & Bacon.

14 Montagu, A. (1971) *Touching: The Human Significance of the Skin.* New York: Columbia University Press.

15 Darwin, C. (1872) *The Expression of the Emotions in Man and Animals.* London: John Murray.

8. Anxiety Tells

1 Marks, I. M., and Nesse, R. M. (1994) 'Fear and fitness: an evolutionary analysis of anxiety disorders'. *Ethology and Sociobiology*, 15, 247–67.

2 Christiansen, B. (1972) *Thus Speaks the Body.* New York: Arno Press; Fried, R., and Grimaldi, J. (1993) *The Psychology and Physiology of Breathing: In Behavioral Medicine, Clinical Psychology and Psychiatry.* New York: Plenum.

3 James, W. (1980) *The Principles of Psychology*, 2 vols. New York: Henry Holt.

4 Perera, J. (1988) 'The hazards of heavy breathing'. *New Scientist*, 3 December, 46–8.

5 Reich, W. (1949) *Character Analysis.* New York: Farrar, Strauss & Giroux; Lowen, A. (1958) *Physical Dynamics of Character Structure.* New York: Grune & Stratton.

6 Lowen, A. (1958) *Physical Dynamics of Character Structure.* New York: Grune & Stratton.

7 Middlemist, R. D., Knowles, E. S., and Matter, C. F. (1976) 'Personal space invasion in the lavatory: suggestive evidence for arousal'. *Journal of Personality and Social Psychology*, 33, 541–6.

8 Hinde, R. (1982) *Ethology: Its Nature and Relations to Other Sciences.* Oxford: Oxford University Press.

9 Ekman, P., and Friesen, W. A. (1969) 'The repertoire of nonverbal behavior: categories, origins, usage, and coding'. *Semiotica*, 1, 49–98.

10 Waxer, P. (1977) 'Nonverbal cues for anxiety: an examination of emotional leakage'. *Journal of Abnormal Psychology*, 86, 306–14; Daly, J. A., Hogg, E., Sacks, D., Smith, M., and Zimring, L. (1983) 'Sex and relationship affect social self-grooming'. *Journal of Nonverbal Behavior*, 7, 183–9; Shreve, E. G., Harrigan, J. A., Kues, J. R., and Kagas, D. K. (1988) 'Nonverbal expressions of anxiety in physician–patient interactions'.

Psychiatry, 51 (4), 378–84; Kenner, A. N. (1993) 'A cross-cultural study of body-focused hand movement'. *Journal of Nonverbal Behavior*, 17(4), 263–79; Morris, D. (1994) *Bodytalk: The Meaning of Human Gestures*. New York: Crown Publishers.

11 Harrigan, J. A., and O'Connell, D. M. (1996) 'How do you look when feeling anxious?' *Personality and Individual Differences*, 21(2), 205–12. See also Leventhal, H., and Sharp, E. (1965) 'Facial expressions as indicators of distress'. In S. Tomkins and C. Izard (eds), *Affect, Cognition and Personality*. New York: Springer Verlag.

12 Milgram, S. (1974) *Obedience to Authority*. New York: Harper & Row.

13 Farabee, D. J., Holcom, M. L., Ramsey, S. L., and Cole, S. G. (1993) 'Social anxiety and speaker gaze in a persuasive atmosphere'. *Journal of Research in Personality*, 27(4), 365–76.

14 Stern, J. A. (1992) 'The eye blink: affective and cognitive influences'. In D. G. Forgays, T. Sosnowski and K. Wrzesniewski (eds), *Anxiety: Recent Developments in Cognitive, Psychophysiological and Health Research*. Washington: Hemisphere.

15 Bell, C. (1847) *The Anatomy and Philosophy of Expression, as Connected with the Fine Arts*. London: John Murray.

16 Jackson, D. D. (1985) 'From the lungs to larynx to lip, it's jitter, shimmer and blip'. *Smithsonian*, 6 (July), 78.

17 Ellgring, H., and Scherer, K. R. (1996) 'Vocal indicators of mood change in depression'. *Journal of Nonverbal Behavior*, 20(2), 83–110.

18 Siegman, A. W. (1987) 'The telltale voice: nonverbal messages of verbal communication'. In A. W. Siegman and S. Feldstein (eds), *Nonverbal Behavior and Communication*. Hillsdale, NJ: Erlbaum; Siegman, A. W., and Boyle, S. (1993) 'Voices of fear and anxiety and depression: the effects of speech rate and loudness on fear and anxiety and depression'. *Journal of Abnormal Psychology*, 102(3), 430–7.

19 Murray, D. C. (1971) 'Talk, silence and anxiety'. *Psychological Bulletin*, 75, 244–60; Rochester, S. R. (1973) 'The significance of pauses in spontaneous speech'. *Journal of Psycholinguistic Research*, 2, 51–81.

9. Sexual Tells

1 Eibl-Eibesfeldt, I. (1971) *Love and Hate: The Natural History of Behavior Patterns*. New York: Holt, Rinehart & Winston; Morris, D. (1971) *Intimate Behaviour*. London: Jonathan Cape; Singh, D., and Young, R. K. (1995) 'Body weight, waist-to-hip ratio, breasts, and hips: role in judgments of

female attractiveness and desirability for relationships'. *Ethology and Sociobiology*, 16, 483–507; Furnham, A., Dias, M., and McClelland, A. (1998) 'The role of body weight, waist-to-hip ratio, and breast size in judgments of female attractiveness'. *Sex Roles*, 3/4, 311–26.

2 Lloyd-Elliott, M. (1995) *Secrets of Sexual Body Language*. London: Hamlyn.

3 Buss, D. (1994) *The Evolution of Desire*. New York: Basic Books.

4 Perper, T. (1985) *Sex Signals: The Biology of Love*. Philadelphia: ISI Press; Perper, T. (1989) 'Theories and observations on sexual selection and female choice in human beings'. *Medical Anthropology*, 11(4), 409–54.

5 Burton, R. (1621) *The Anatomy of Melancholy*. Oxford: Henry Cripps.

6 Birdwhistell, R. (1970) *Kinesics and Context*. New York: Ballantine.

7 Moore, M. M. (1985) 'Nonverbal courtship patterns in women: context and consequences'. *Ethology and Sociobiology*, 6, 237–47.

8 Wiley, R. H. (1991) 'Lekking in birds and mammals; behavioral and evolutionary issues'. *Advances in the Study of Behavior*, 20, 201–91.

9 Krebs, J. R., and Dawkins, R. D. (1984) 'Animal signals: mind-reading and manipulation'. In J. R. Krebs and N. B. Davies (eds), *Behavioral Ecology: An Evolutionary Approach*. Sunderland, MA: Sinauer.

10 Grammer, K., Jutte, A., and Fischmann, B. (1997) 'Der Kampf der Geschlecter und der Krieg der Signale'. In B. Kanitscheider (ed.), *Liebe, Lust und Leidenschaft: Sexualität im Spiegel der Wissenschaft*. Stuttgart: Hirzel; Penton-Voak, I. S., Perrett, D. I., Castles, D. L., Kobayashi, T., Burt, D. M., Murray, L. K., and Minamisawa, R. (1999) 'Menstrual cycle alters face preferences'. *Nature*, 399, 741–2.

11 Walsh, D. G., and Hewitt, J. (1985) 'Giving men the come-on: effect of eye contact and smiling in a bar environment'. *Perceptual and Motor Skills*, 61, 873–4.

12 Moore, M. M. (1985) 'Nonverbal courtship patterns in women: context and consequences'. *Ethology and Sociobiology*, 6, 237–47.

13 Kleinke, C. L. (1986) 'Gaze and eye contact: a research review'. *Psychological Bulletin*, 100(1), 78–100; Lizuka, Y. (1992) 'Eye contact in dating couples and unacquainted couples'. *Perceptual and Motor Skills*, 75, 457–61.

14 Walsh, D. G., and Hewitt, J. (1985) 'Giving men the come-on: effect of eye contact and smiling in a bar environment'. *Perceptual and Motor Skills*, 61, 873–4.

15 Givens, D. B. (1978) 'The nonverbal basis of attraction: flirtation, courtship, and seduction'. *Psychiatry*, 41, 346–59; Givens, D. B. (1983) *Love Signals: How to Attract a Mate*. New York: Crown.

16 Grammer, K., Krück, K., Juette, A., and Fink, B. (2000) 'Non-verbal behavior as courtship signals: the role of control and choice in selecting partners'. *Evolution and Human Behaviour*, 21, 371–90.

17 Abbey, A. (1987) 'Misperceptions of friendly behavior as sexual interest: a survey of naturally occurring incidents'. *Psychology of Women Quarterly*, 11(2), 173–94; Shotland, R. L., and Craig, J. M. (1988) 'Can men and women differentiate between platonic and sexually interested behavior?' *Social Psychology Quarterly*, 51(1), 66–73.

18 Morris, D. (1977) *Manwatching: A Field Guide to Human Behaviour*. London: Jonathan Cape.

19 Caro, T. M. (1986) 'The function of stotting: a review of the hypotheses'. *Animal Behaviour*, 34, 649–62; Zahavi, A., and Zahavi, A. (1997) *The Handicap Principle: A Missing Piece of Darwin's Puzzle*. Oxford: Oxford University Press.

20 Burton, R. (1621) *The Anatomy of Melancholy*. Oxford: Henry Cripps.

21 Ambady, N., Hallahan, M., and Conner, B. (1999) 'Accuracy of judgments of sexual orientation from thin slices of behavior'. *Journal of Personality and Social Psychology*, 77, 538–47; Ambady, N., LaPlante, D., and Johnson, E. (2001) 'Thin slice judgments as a measure of interpersonal sensitivity'. In J. Hall and F. Bernieri (eds), *Interpersonal Sensitivity: Measurement and Applications*. Hillsdale, NJ: Lawrence Erlbaum.

22 Berry, D. S., and McArthur, L. A. (1985) 'Some components and consequences of a babyface'. *Journal of Personality and Social Psychology*, 48, 312–23; McArthur, L. Z., and Berry, D. S. (1987) 'Cross-cultural consensus in perceptions of babyfaced adults'. *Journal of Cross Cultural Psychology*, 18, 165–92.

23 Eibl-Eibesfeldt, I. (1971) *Love and Hate: The Natural History of Behavior Patterns*. New York: Holt, Rinehart & Winston.

24 Campbell, R., Wallace, S., and Benson, P. J. (1996) 'Real men don't look down: direction of gaze affects sex decisions on faces'. *Visual Cognition*, 3(4), 393–412.

25 Hess, E. (1975) *The Telltale Eye*. New York: Van Nostrand Reinhold; Aboyoun, D. C., and Dabbs, J. M. (1998) 'The Hess pupil dilation findings: sex or novelty?' *Social Behaviour and Personality*, 26(4), 415–19.

26 Paul Ekman, personal communication.

27 Montagu, A. (1971) *Touching: The Human Significance of the Skin*. New York: Columbia University Press; Lockard, J. S., and Adams, R. M. (1980) 'Courtship behaviors in public: different age/sex roles'. *Ethology and Sociobiology*, 1, 245–53; McCormick, N. B., and Jones, A. J. (1989) 'Gender differences in nonverbal flirtation'. *Journal of Sex Education and*

Therapy, 15(4), 271–82.

28 Perper, T. (1985) *Sex Signals: The Biology of Love*. Philadelphia: ISI Press; Murray, T. E. (1985) 'The language of singles bars'. *American Speech*, 60(1), 17–30.

29 Krebs, J. R., and Dawkins, R. D. (1984) 'Animal signals: mind-reading and manipulation'. In J. R. Krebs and N. B. Davies (eds), *Behavioral Ecology: An Evolutionary Approach*. Sunderland, MA: Sinauer; Dabbs, J. M., and Mallinger, A. (1999) 'Higher testosterone levels predict lower voice pitch among men'. *Personality and Individual Differences*, 27, 801–4; Collins, S. (2001) 'Men's voices and women's choices'. *Animal Behaviour*, 60, 773–80.

30 Manes, J., and Wolfson, N. (1980) 'The compliment formula'. In F. Coulmas (ed.), *Conversational Routine*. The Hague: Mouton. See also Herbert, R. K. (1990) 'Sex-based differences in compliment behaviour'. *Language in Society*, 19, 201–24; Holmes, J. (1995) *Women, Men and Politeness*. London: Longman.

31 Dindia, K., and Allen, M. (1992) 'Sex differences in self-disclosure: a meta-analysis'. *Psychological Bulletin*, 112, 106–24.

32 Grammer, K. (1990) 'Strangers meet: laughter and non-verbal signs of interest in opposite-sex encounters'. *Journal of Nonverbal Behavior*, 14(4), 209–36.

33 Provine, R. R. (2000) *Laughter: A Scientific Investigation*. London: Penguin.

34 Grammer, K., and Eibl-Eibesfeldt, I. (1990) 'The ritualization of laughter'. In W. A. Koch (ed.), *Natürlichkeit der Sprache und der Kultur*. Bochum: Brockmeyer.

35 Provine, R. R. (2000) *Laughter: A Scientific Investigation*. London: Penguin.

36 Moore, M. M. (1998) 'Nonverbal courtship patterns in women: rejection signalling – an empirical investigation'. *Semiotica*, 118(3/4), 201–14.

37 Grammer, K., Krück, K. B., and Magnusson, M. S. (1998) 'The courtship dance: patterns of nonverbal synchronization in opposite-sex encounters'. *Journal of Nonverbal Behavior*, 22(1), 3–27.

38 Bernieri, F. J., and Rosenthal, R. (1991) 'Interpersonal coordination: behavior matching and interactional synchrony'. In R. S. Feldman and B. Rime (eds), *Fundamentals of Nonverbal Behavior*. Cambridge: Cambridge University Press.

39 LaFrance, M. (1979) 'Nonverbal synchrony and rapport: analysis by the cross-lag panel technique'. *Social Psychology Quarterly*, 42, 66–70;

Bavelas, J. B., Black, A., Lemery, C. R., and Mullett, J. (1987) 'Motor mimicry as primitive empathy'. In N. Eisenberg and J. Strayer (eds), *Empathy and its Development*. Cambridge: Cambridge University Press; Bernieri, F. (1988) 'Coordinated movement and rapport in teacher–student interactions'. *Journal of Nonverbal Behavior*, 12, 120–38; Dijksterhuis, A. (2000) 'Automatic social influence: the perception–behavior link as an explanatory mechanism for behavior matching'. In J. Forgas and K. D. Williams (eds), *Social Influence: Direct and Indirect Processes*. Philadelphia: Psychology Press.

40 Beattie, G. (1988) *The Candarel Guide to Beach Watching*. Hove: Rambletree.

41 Buss, D. M., and Shackelford, T. K. (1997) 'From vigilance to violence: mate retention tactics in married couples'. *Journal of Personality and Social Psychology*, 72, 346–61; Buss, D. (2000) *The Dangerous Passion: Why Jealousy Is as Necessary as Love and Sex*. London: Bloomsbury.

42 Goffman, E. (1971) *Relations in Public*. Harmondsworth: Penguin.

43 Givens, D. B. (1983) *Love Signals: How to Attract a Mate*. New York: Crown; Perper, T. (1985) *Sex Signals: The Biology of Love*. Philadelphia: ISI Press.

10. Lying Tells

1 Feldman, R. S., Forrest, J. A., and Happ, B. R. (2002) 'Self-presentation and verbal deception: do self-presenters lie more?' *Basic and Applied Social Psychology*, 24(2), 163–70.

2 DePaulo, B. M., Epstein, J. A., and Wyer, M. M. (1993) 'Sex differences in lying: how women and men deal with the dilemma of deceit'. In M. Lewis and C. Sarrni (eds), *Lying and Deception in Everyday Life*. New York: Guilford Press; DePaulo, B. M., Kashy, D., Kirkendol, S. E., Wyer, M. M., and Epstein, J. A. (1996) 'Lying in everyday life'. *Journal of Personality and Social Psychology*, 70(5), 979–95; Feldman, R. S., Forrest, J. A., and Happ, B. R. (2002) 'Self-presentation and verbal deception: do self-presenters lie more?' *Basic and Applied Social Psychology*, 24(2), 163–70.

3 Feldman, R. S., Tomasian, J. C., and Coats, E. J. (1999) 'Nonverbal deception abilities and adolescents' social competence: adolescents with higher social skills are better liars'. *Journal of Nonverbal Behavior*, 23(3), 237–49; Kashy, D., and DePaulo, B. M. (1996) 'Who lies?' *Journal of Personality and Social Psychology*, 70(5), 1037–51.

4 DePaulo, P. J., and DePaulo, B. M. (1989) 'Can attempted deception by

salespersons and customers be detected through nonverbal behavioral cues?' *Journal of Applied Social Psychology*, 19, 1552–77.

5 Ekman, P. (2001) *Telling Lies*. New York: W. W. Norton.

6 Ekman, P. (2001) Ibid.

7 McCormack, S. A., and Parks, M. R. (1990) 'What women know that men don't: sex differences in determining the truth behind deceptive messages'. *Journal of Social and Personal Relationships*, 7, 107–18; Millar, M. G., and Millar, K. (1995) 'Detection of deception in familiar and unfamiliar persons: the effects of information restriction'. *Journal of Nonverbal Behavior*, 19(2), 69–84.

8 Burton, S. (2000) *Impostors: Six Kinds of Liar*. London: Viking.

9 Ekman, P. (2001) *Telling Lies*. New York: W. W. Norton.

10 Vrij, A. (2001) *Detecting Lies and Deceit*. Chichester: John Wiley.

11 Seager, P. (2001) 'Improving the ability of individuals to detect lies'. Unpublished Ph.D. thesis, University of Hertfordshire.

12 Krauss, R. M. (1981) 'Impression formation, impression management, and nonverbal behaviors'. In E. T. Higgins, C. P. Herman and M. Zanna (eds), *Social Cognition: The Ontario Symposium*, Vol. 1. Hillsdale, NJ: Erlbaum. See also: Vrij, A., and Semin, G. R. (1996) 'Lie experts' beliefs about nonverbal indicators of deception'. *Journal of Nonverbal Behavior*, 20, 65–80; Anderson, D. E., DePaulo, B. M., Ansfield, M. E., Tickle, J. J., and Green, E. (1999) 'Beliefs about cues to deception: mindless stereotypes or untapped wisdom'. *Journal of Nonverbal Behavior*, 23, 67–89; Vrij, A. (2001) *Detecting Lies and Deceit*. Chichester: John Wiley.

13 Vrij, A. (2001) *Detecting Lies and Deceit*. Chichester: John Wiley.

14 Ekman, P., and Friesen, W. V. (1969) 'Nonverbal leakage and clues to deception'. *Psychiatry*, 32, 88–106.

15 Hirsch, A. R., and Wolf, C. J. (1999) 'A case example utilizing practical methods for detecting mendacity'. AMA Annual Meeting, Washington, DC [Abstract], NR505: 208; Hirsch, A. R., and Wolf, C. J., (2001) 'Practical methods for detecting mendacity: a case study'. *Journal of the American Academy of Psychiatric Law*, 29(4), 438–44.

16 Davis, K. (1999) 'Clinton and the truth: on the nose?' *USA Today*, 19 May, 4; Dribben, M. (2002) 'In your face'. *The Philadelphia Inquirer*, 19 October.

17 Birdwhistell, R. (1955) 'Do gestures speak louder than words?' *Collier's*, 4 March, 56–7.

18 Ekman, P. (2001) *Telling Lies*. New York: W. W. Norton.

19 Ekman, P., Friesen, W. V., and O'Sullivan, M. (1988) 'Smiles when lying'. *Journal of Personality and Social Psychology*, 54, 414–20; Ekman, P. (2001) *Telling Lies*. New York: W. W. Norton; Frank, M., Ekman, P., and

Friesen, W. (1993) 'Behavioral markers and recognizability of the smile of enjoyment'. *Journal of Personality and Social Psychology*, 64(1), 83–93.

20 Haggard, E. A., and Isaacs, K. S. (1966) 'Micromomentary facial expressions as indicators of ego mechanisms in psychotherapy'. In L. A. Gottschalk and A. H. Auerbach (eds), *Methods of Research in Psychotherapy*. New York: Appleton-Century-Crofts; Ekman, P., and O'Sullivan, M. (1991) 'Who can catch a liar?' *American Psychologist*, 46, 913–20.

21 Frank, M. G., and Ekman, P. (1997) 'The ability to detect deceit generalizes across different types of high-stake lies'. *Journal of Personality and Social Psychology*, 72, 1429–39.

22 Vrij, A. (2001) Ibid.

23 Anoli, L., and Ciceri, R. (1997) 'The voice of deception: vocal strategies of naïve and able liars'. *Journal of Nonverbal Behavior*, 21(4), 259–84.

24 Ekman, P. (2001) *Telling Lies*. New York: W. W. Norton.

25 DePaulo, B. M. (1994) 'Deception'. In T. Manstead and M. Hewstone (eds), *Blackwell Encyclopaedia of Social Psychology*, pp 164–8. Oxford: Blackwell.

11. Foreign Tells

1 Chambers, J. (1973) 'Canadian rising'. *Canadian Journal of Linguistics*, 18, 113–35; Penner, P., and McConnell, R. (1980) *Learning English*. Toronto: Gage Publishing.

2 Bell, A. (1997) 'The phonetics of fish and chips in New Zealand: marking national and ethnic identities'. *English World-Wide*, 18(2), 243–70; Scott, A. W., and Starks, D. (2000) ' "No-one sounds like us?" A comparison of New Zealand and other southern hemisphere Englishes'. In A. Bell and K. Kuiper (eds), *New Zealand English*. Wellington: Victoria University Press.

3 Collett, P., and Contarello, A. (1987) 'Gesti di assenso e di dissenso'. In P. Ricci Bitti (ed.), *Communicazione e Gestualità*. Milano: Franco Angeli; Collett, P. (1993) *Foreign Bodies: A Guide to European Mannerisms*. London: Simon & Schuster.

4 Morris, D., Collett, P., Marsh, P., and O'Shaughnessy, M. (1979) *Gestures: Their Origins and Distribution*. London: Jonathan Cape.

5 Collett, P. (1993) *Foreign Bodies: A Guide to European Mannerisms*. London: Simon & Schuster.

6 Collett, P. (1983) 'Mossi salutations'. *Semiotica*, 45(3/4), 191–248.

7 Bulwer, J. (1644) *Chirologia: or the Natural Language of the Hand*. London.

8 Zeldin, T. (1988) *The French*. London: Collins Harvill.

9 Collett, P. (1993) *Foreign Bodies: A Guide to European Mannerisms*. London: Simon & Schuster.

10 Hillary, E. (1999) *View from the Summit*. London: Doubleday.

11 Ekman, P. (1982) *Emotion in the Human Face*. Cambridge: Cambridge University Press.

12 Birdwhistell, R. (1970) *Kinesics and Context*. New York: Ballantine.

13 Seaford, H. W. (1981) 'Maximizing replicability in describing facial behavior'. In A. Kendon (ed.), *Nonverbal Communication, Interaction, and Gesture*. The Hague: Mouton.

14 Collett, P. (1993) *Foreign Bodies: A Guide to European Mannerisms*. London: Simon & Schuster.

15 Zeldin, T. (1988) *The French*. London: Collins Harvill.

16 Zajonc, R. B., Murphy, S. T., and Inglehart, M. (1989) 'Feeling and facial efference: implications of the vascular theory of emotions'. *Psychological Review*, 96, 395–416.

17 Strack, F., Martin, L., and Stepper, S. (1988) 'Inhibiting and facial conditions of the human smile: a nonobtrusive test of the facial feedback hypothesis'. *Journal of Personality and Social Psychology*, 54, 768–77. See also Cappella, J. N. (1993) 'The facial feedback hypothesis in human interaction: review and speculation'. *Journal of Language and Social Psychology*, 12, 13–29; McIntosh, D. N. (1996) 'Facial feedback hypothesis: evidence, implications, and directions'. *Motivation and Emotion*, 20, 121–47.

18 Lehtonen, J., and Sajavaara, K. (1985) 'The silent Finn'. In D. Tannen and M. Saville-Troike (eds), *Perspectives on Silence*. Norwood, NJ: Ablex.

19 Golding, W. (1954) *Lord of the Flies*. London: Faber & Faber.

20 Collett, P. (1993) *Foreign Bodies: A Guide to European Mannerisms*. London: Simon & Schuster.

21 Anon. (1581) *A Treatise of Daunces*. London.

22 Efron, D. (1942) *Gesture and Environment*. New York: Kings Crown Press.

23 Efron, D. (1942) Ibid.

24 Morris, D., Collett, P., Marsh, P., and O'Shaughnessy, M. (1979) *Gestures: Their Origins and Distribution*. London: Jonathan Cape.

25 Collett, P. (1982) 'Meetings and misunderstandings'. In S. Bochner (ed.), *Cultures in Contact*. Oxford: Pergamon.

26 Collett, P. (1993) *Foreign Bodies: A Guide to European Mannerisms*. London: Simon & Schuster.

12. Smoking Tells

1 Hatsukami, D., Morgan, S. F., Pickens, R. W., and Hughes, J. R. (1987) 'Smoking topography in a nonlaboratory environment'. *International Journal of the Addictions*, 22(8), 719–25; Miller, P. M., Fredrickson, L. W., and Hartford, R. L. (1979) 'Social interaction and smoking topography in heavy and light smokers'. *Addictive Behavior*, 4, 147–53.

2 Napier, J. R. (1962) 'The evolution of the hand'. *Scientific American*, 207(6), 56–62.

3 Klein, R. (1995) *Cigarettes Are Sublime*. London: Picador. See also Starr, M. E. (1984) 'The Marlboro man: cigarette smoking and masculinity in America'. *Journal of Popular Culture*, 17(4) 45–57.

4 Danesi, M. (1999) *Of Cigarettes, High Heels, and Other Interesting Things*. London: Macmillan.

5 Hyllienmark, G. (1986) 'Smoking as a transitional object'. *British Journal of Medical Psychology*, 59, 263–7.

6 Revell, A. D., Warburton, D. M., and Wesnes, K. (1985) 'Smoking as a coping strategy'. *Addictive Behaviors*, 10, 209–24.

7 McArthur, C., Waldron, E., and Dickinson, J. (1958) 'The psychology of smoking'. *Journal of Abnormal and Social Psychology*, 56, 267–75; Howe, M., and Summerfield, A. (1979) 'Orality and smoking'. *British Journal of Medical Psychology*, 52, 85–90.

8 Thackeray, W. M. (1856) *Sketches and Travels in London*. London: Bradbury & Evans.

9 Klein, R. (1995) *Cigarettes Are Sublime*. London: Picador.

10 Lombardo, T., and Carreno, L. (1987) 'Relationship of Type A behavior pattern in smokers to carbon monoxide exposure and smoking topography'. *Health Psychology*, 6(5), 445–52.

11 Pease, A. (1997) *Body Language*. London: Sheldon Press.

12 Gilbert, D. G. (1995) *Smoking: Individual Differences, Psychopathology, and Emotion*. London: Taylor & Francis; Canals, J., Blade, J., and Domenech, E. (1997) 'Smoking and personality predictors among young Swedish people'. *Personality and Individual Differences*, 23(5), 905–8; Acton, G. S. (2003) 'Measurement of impulsivity in a hierarchical model of personality traits: implications for substance use'. *Substance Use and Abuse*, in press.

13 Helgason, A. R., Fredrikson, M., Dyba, T., and Steinbeck, G. (1995) 'Introverts give up smoking more often than extraverts'. *Personality and Individual Differences*, 18, 559–60.

14 Golding, J. F. and Mangan, G. F. (1982) 'Arousing and de-arousing

effects of cigarette smoking under conditions of stress and mild sensory isolation'. *Psychophysiology*, 19, 449–56; Mangan, G. F., and Golding, J. F. (1984) *The Psychopharmacology of Smoking*. Cambridge: Cambridge University Press.

15 Parrott, A. C. (1998) 'Nesbitt's Paradox resolved? Stress and arousal modulation during cigarette smoking'. *Addiction*, 93, 27–39; Parrott, A. C. (1999) 'Does cigarette smoking *cause* stress?' *American Psychologist*, 54(10), 817–20.

13. Tell-tales

1 Simons, D., and Levin D. (1998) 'Failure to detect changes to people during a real-world interaction'. *Psychonomic Bulletin & Review*, 5, 644–9.

2 Truzzi, M. (1973) 'Sherlock Holmes: applied social psychologist'. In M. Truzzi (ed.), *The Humanities as Sociology*. Columbus, OH: Charles E. Merrill.

3 Doyle, A. C. (1891) 'A case of identity'. In W. S. Baring-Gould (ed.) (1967), *The Annotated Sherlock Holmes*. New York: Clarkson N. Potter.

4 Napier, J. R. (1973) *Bigfoot: The Yeti and Sasquatch in Myth and Reality*. London: E. P. Dutton.

5 Murphy, S. T., and Zajonc, R. B. (1993) 'Affect, cognition, and awareness: affective priming with optimal and suboptimal stimulus exposures'. *Journal of Personality and Social Psychology*, 64, 723–39.

6 Dimberg, U., Thunberg, M., and Elmehed, K. (2000) 'Unconscious facial reactions to emotional facial expressions'. *Psychological Science*, 11, 86–9.

Index

Aborigines 308
accommodation 61–2
action (sending sexual
  messages) 248–9
actions, and nationality 309–10
activity tells 59
adaptors 228, 229–31, 269,
  291
'adoring wife' role 144–7
adulation 144–7
affection, public displays of
  207–8
Africa 310–11
African Americans 64, 311
aggression 147–54, 234
agonistic stare 56
agreement marker 115
AIDS sufferers 209
Alabama, University of 169
alerting signals 107
Allen, Woody 87
Americans 308, 309, 313
  314–5
Andrew, Prince 198
anger 300–1

Anne, Princess Royal 198, 199
Anne, Queen 207
Annie Hall 87
anthropomorphic insults 153
antithesis, principle of 71–3
anvil posture 45
anxiety tells 28, 212, 219–43,
  293, 345
appeasement 67, 141–2
applause 144–5
approach tells 253–6
Arafat, Yasser 177–8
Argentinians 326
arms
  akimbo posture 47–51
  arm grip 79
  bandoleer posture 79
  crossing 79, 276
  in handshaking 174–6
  raised 74
  splayed 248
  swinging 132–3, 262
  used in gesticulation 322
  waving 164
asides 213

Atkinson, Max, *Our Masters'
Voices* 144
attached tells 12
attack, responses to 220
attempt-suppressing strategies
114
attentiveness display 106
Attlee, Clement 153
attractors 117–8
Australians 65, 308, 313, 323
auto-contact 77
autonomous tells 11–12
availability 249–53

babies 78–9
baboons 39, 42, 59–60,
142–3
baby face 265
back, arching 260
back of body, attention to
194–5
back-channel signals and back-
calling 105, 107, 114–15,
121, 162, 191, 317, 318
negative back-channel 108,
161–2
Balzac, Honoré de 46
Barbie Doll strategies 259
Basic Instinct 258
Beattie, Geoffrey 278
beauty, notions of 245–6
Belgians 313, 325, 326
Belgrano 300
Bell, Charles 239
Benn, Tony 150
bent-leg hold 331, 332
bent blade stance 76, 124–5
'Bigfoot' 352
Birdwhistell, Ray 248, 294,
314

Bismarck, Otto von 303
Blair, Cherie 145, *146*
Blair, Tony 135, 136, 145,
146, 175, 212, 221, 354
blood, flow to brain 316
blushing 21, 22, 25, 34, 93–6,
214, 221, 352
body 244–8
orientation 51–3, 142, 282
body armour 224
body-builders 133
Bogart, Humphrey *344*, 346
boredom signals 58
Bosanquet, Reginald 160
bows and curtseys 166
Brazilians 326
breathing
heavy or shallow 28, 222–4
rate 289
British 325, 326
and cheek-kissing 313
and gesture 321–2, 326
and handshake 311
and smiling 315
and V-sign 324–5
broadcasting 252–3
Bruno, Frank 115
Bull, Peter 155
Bulwer, John 29, 166
Burkina Faso 69–70
Burton, Robert 265
Anatomy of Melancholy 247
Bush, George, Sr 33, 128, 160
Bush, George W. 128, 129,
134–5, 136, 161, 162, 175,
182–3, 282
Buss, David 245–6
button-holing 116–17
buttress stance 124, 125–6

Caesar, Julius 26
California State University, Fullerton 235
California, University of, San Francisco 23
calling 164
Camp David meeting 135
Campbell, Ruth 266
Canadians 308, 309, 313
Caro, Mike 13–14
carrying angle 132
Carter, Jimmy 129, 137
Caspers, Johanneke 112
Castiglione, Baldassare, *The Book of the Courtier* 201
Castro, Fidel 130–1, 177
catapult posture 234
Catherine de Medici, Queen 322
Chamberlain, Neville 287–8
Chance, Michael 84
change blindness 348–9
Chaplin, William 169
Charles, Prince of Wales *81*, 198, 199–200, 202–3, 205, 208, 210–13, 217, 218, 278
chest, expanding 249
Chesterfield, Earl of 103
chimpanzees 36–7, 67, 69, 88–9, 138
chin
    muscles 136
    shape 53
    stroking 227, 228
China 266
Chinese 326
Chirac, Jacques 346
chopping 150
Churchill, Winston 152, 153
CIA 130–1

cigarettes
    exhaling 341–2
    lighting ritual 336
    as props 338–9, 343
    ways of holding 329–35, 341
    see also smoking
circumlocution 302
Clinton, Bill *295*
    debate with Bush 33
    denial 303
    handshake 177–9
    health 128
    and Hillary 145, 282
    at Labour Party conference 353–4
    lip-biting 25, 354
    nose-touching 293–4
    oratorical devices 354
    'oxbow' mouth 136
    smile 137, 178, 354
    smokescreens 303
    swallowing 238
    walking style 134
    waving 147, 354
Clinton, Hillary 145, 282
closure signals 191
Cocteau, Jean 337
codpieces 42
cold insults 152
Coleridge, Samuel Taylor 116–17
Coloureds (South Africa) 64
Columbia University, New York 289–90
come-ons 257, 276
common tells 25–6, 355–6
Commons, House of, Question Time 141–2, 150–1
comparisons 350–1

compatibility 276–9
compliments 273
comprehension marker 115
conch shell model 318
conclusions, jumping to 350
continuity talk 192
contrastors 118–19
conversation 104–126
    and nationality 316–20
    and smoking 339–40
coping strategies 338–9
Costa, M., Menzani, M. and
    Ricci Bitti, P. 83
coughing 238
counterfeit tells 23–5
courtship signals 246–8, 282–3
    see also lovers, signals
    between
Coward, Noël 334
cradle posture 230–4
crane posture 204
crotch-yank 44
crying 24–5
Cuba 177
cuff-link fiddle 210–12, 213
Curtis, Tony 247
cut-off 84, 143

Danes 326
Darwin, Charles 80, 215, 253,
    349
    and blushing 93–4, 95
    The Expression of the
    Emotions in Man and
    Animals 71–2
David, Jacques-Louis 27
Day, Robin 160–1
De Gaulle, Charles 346
Dean, James 346
defensive tells 75–7

deflectors 118
DePaulo, Bella 286, 305
Diana, Princess of Wales 27,
    208–10, 213–16, 278
Dimberg, Ulf 353
dimorphism, sexual 251
Dinkins, David 303
disclaimers 304
displacement activities 59, 165,
    210–13, 227–8
Disraeli, Benjamin 152, 189
distance signals 164–5, 200–3
dogs
    body orientation of 52, 142
    dominance and submission
    in 71–2
dominance 36–70, 71, 158,
    172, 196, 199, 249, 340–1
drinking gestures 325–6
Duchenne de Boulogne,
    Guillaume, Mécanisme de la
    physionomie humaine 90–1
Duncan Smith, Iain 130
Duncan, Starkey 111
Dutch 313, 326

earlobe rub 212–13, 227
EastEnders 346
Eastern Europe 179
Eastwood, Clint 55, 344, 345
Eden, Anthony 159
Edward the Confessor, King
    207
Edward, Prince 198
Edward VIII, King (later Duke
    of Windsor) 197, 202, 206
Efron, David 74, 323
Eisenhower, Dwight D. 174
Ekman, Paul 23, 268, 296,
    300, 305, 314

elbows 46–51
  tucking in 74, 323
Elizabeth I, Queen 201
Elizabeth II, Queen 66, 198, 199, 201–2, 203, 204, 206, 208
Elizabeth, Queen, the Queen Mother 197–8, 209
emasculating insults 152
embarrassment 22, 93–6
emotions 53
English see British
Erasmus, Desiderius 48, 183
European Championship (1996) 230–1
evaluation talk 192
exposed wrist display 264, 334, 344
extraverts and introverts 342
eye-flicker 254–5
eye-lock 254
eye-shuttle 85
eyebrows
  plucked 54
  raising or lowering 54, 73–74, 86–8, 164, 200
eyes 83–6
  averting 290–1, 305
  blinking 237, 289, 290–1
  eye-cover 229
  eye-dip 84–5
  eye-flash 27, 114, 161
  eye-puff or narrowing 54, 55, 85, 161, 164, 198, 200, 214, 265, 267–8
  gazing intently 290
  glancing from side to side (shuttle) 85
  hooded 267–8
  looking sideways 236, 267

and lying 289, 290
pupil dilation 21–2, 266–7, 352
and sexual signals 254–5, 264–8
shifty 289, 290
and smiling 90–1
winking 139, 245
wiping 11, 20

face tells 53–7, 234–7
  actions 53–4
  attributes 53–4
  expressions 34, 53, 248–9, 353
  face-cover 229, 338
  facial decoy 271
  and nationality 314–16
  straight 296
  touching 228
Falklands war 300
false tells 21, 23–5
farewells 189, 195
fausse sortie 193–4
FDR 344
fear 76, 92, 300
feet 122–6
  adjusting 292
  extended 248
  tapping 27–8, 225
Feldman, Robert 284
Ferguson, Alex 240
fight or flight 223
fight, flight and freeze 220, 224–7
figure four posture 45
fillers, verbal 121–2
fingers 149
Finns 317, 326
flanking 142

flattery 99–103
flattery trap 99–100
flight reflex 150
flirting 257–8
Flockhart, Calista 245
Fonda, Jane *344*
football 230–4, *232–3*, 240
Ford, Gerald 153
foreign tells 113, 307–27
foretells 174
formality 304
Frank, Mark 293–4, 300
freezing 76
French 75, 186, 311–12, 313,
    315–17, 322, 325–6
Freud, Sigmund 23, 339
friendliness 137–9, 197–200
frowning 276

Gallagher, Timothy 140–1
Garbo, Greta 268
gaze, patterns of 67–8
gender differences
    arm movement 132–3, 262
    breathing 222–3
    choice of partner 245–6
    conversations 107, 110
    handshakes 168–9
    interruptions 110, 159
    lying 284–5
    sensitivity to touch 271
    smiling 92–3
    smoking 330–5, 336
    use of 'you know' 121
    see also men; women
genitals
    display of 77
    protecting 26, 226
genuine tells 21–3, 63
George V, King 197

George VI, King 197, 207
Germans 311, 315, 316, 321,
    325, 326
gestures *see* hands,
    gestures of
Gimme Shelter concert 50
glasses
    playing with 229
    worn on head 85–6
Goffman, Erving 281
Golding, William 318
*The Good, the Bad and the
    Ugly* 55
Gore, Al 182–3
Gore, Tipper 182
Grammer, Karl and Eibl-
    Eibesfeldt, Irenäus 274–5
Grant, Hugh 271
gratitude escalation 192–3
Greeks 309, 310, 323–5
greetings 163–95
    in business firms 68
    and nationality 310–13
    of respect 165–6
    of solidarity 165–6
Gregory, Stanford 62, 140–1
gripping 149
grooming 98
grooming talk 99–103
Groundhog Day 348
gum-chewing 240
gut feelings 288

Hague, William 130
Haile Selassie, Emperor 128
hair
    flicking 255, 263
    lack of 130
    pulling 28
    stroking 78, 228, 291

touching 165, 227, 269, 271, 282
Hall, Jerry *81*
handbags 204
hands 227–34
  clammy 170
  clasping 203, 227
  dovetail 79
  fidgeting with 289, 291
  framing face 269
  gestures of 29, 113, 147–51, 191, 225, 318–27
  on hips 46–51
  holding 281–2
  kissing 184, 312–13
  palm press 79
  palms exposed 74, 164
  in pockets 205, 218, 276
  royal family's ways of holding 203–5
  rubbing 291
  steepling 79
  sweating 289, 350
  in waistcoat 26–7
  and ways of holding cigarettes 329–35
  see also handshakes
handshakes 165, 166–72
  huddled 175
  and nationality 310–12
  open 176
  and personality 169
  in politics 172–9
  position of hands 171–5
  relocated 171, 175–6
  royal 206, 207–8
  secret 18
  types 168–72
hang-ons 257, 276
Harrigan, Jinni, and O'Connell, Dennis 235

Harris, Sandra 154–5
Harry, Prince 209, 210
Harvard University 348–9
head
  canting 27, 73, *81*, 82–3, 215, 263–4, 312
  clasp 230
  dip-toss 309–10
  head-cock 312
  kissing on 184
  lowering (dipping) 80–2, 164, 266, 312
  micro-nod 161
  nodding 82, 105–6, 164, 191, 263, 309–10
  shaking 106, 276, 309–10
  tossing 309–10
  touching 228
  twisting 27, 138–9
Healey, Denis 153
health tells 127–9
heart rate, increase in 222, 289
Hecht, M. and LaFrance, M. 89–90
hedges 120–2
height, physical 127–8, 216
helplessness 72, 74
Henley, Nancy 205–6
Henry II, King of France 322
Henry VIII, King *49*, 216, 315
Hepburn, Audrey 139
hesitation 15, 354
Heston, Charlton 57
Hillary, Edmund 313
hind-hide tell 195
hips
  hands on 46–51
  rolling 262
Hirsch, Alan and Wolf, Charles 293

Hitler, Adolf 26, 287
Hogarth, William 321
Hoggart, Simon 201
Holbein, Hans 48, 49, 315
hormones 256
House of Games 14
Howard, Michael 160
Howe, Sir Geoffrey 153, 154
hugging 21, 79, 165, 179–82,
    194, 210
    types of 179–82
humour 198–9
hybrid expressions 215
hyperhidrosis 170, 350
hyperventilation 223–4

iconic hand gestures 147,
    148
illuminations 247–8, 249
impatience 27–8
inactivity 75–6
India 80
indignation 72
infidelity 279–80
ingratiation 100–3, 188
    strategies 101–3
insults, political 151–4
intention displays 31–2, 106,
    191
intention movements 31–3
interactional synchrony
    276–7
interpretation, failure of 349
interruptions 108–10, 113–14,
    158–9, 320
interviews, political 154–62
intimidation 161–2
introductions 186–9
involuntary tells 34
Irish 313, 317

Italians 43, 74, 186, 267,
    309–10, 311, 317–20, 321,
    323, 325–6

Jackson, Michael 44
Jagger, Mick 50, *81*, 114
James, William 223
Japanese 48, 326
jaws 54, 55
    dropping 164
Jews 74–5, 110, 322–3
Johnson, Lyndon B. 143, 153
Johnson, Samuel 316–17
Judges, Book of 307
justification talk 191–2

Keating, Paul 66, 206
Kendon, Adam 97
Kennedy, Bobby 129
Kennedy, Jacqueline 145–7
Kennedy, John F. 129, 131,
    147, *173*, 174, 175–6
Khrushchev, Nikita 175–6
Kinnock, Neil 130, 156, 158
kissing 182–6, 210
    in 15th-century England
        183–4
    at parting 194
    of babies 142–3
    on cheek 12, 183, 184–5,
        313
    feigned 185
    as greeting 165, 166, 194
    hand 184, 312–13
    on head 184
    on lips 183–4
    social 183–6, 313
    types of 184–6
    vacuum 185
    vocalised 186

Kissinger, Henry 161
Klein, Richard 333, 340
kneeling 166
knuckles, displayed 333
Konopacki, Allen 167
Koreans 326
Krauss, Robert 289–90

Labour Party 152
Lacey, Robert 199
Lamb, Charles 116–17
Larry King Live 62
laughter 88–9, 138, 164, 198,
  199–200, 235–6, 249
  in courtship 274–6
leaving tells 31
left-side advantage 174–5
legs 122–6, 191
  adjusting 292
  crossing 76–7, 226–7, 258
  emphasizing length 259–60
  spread apart 248
lekking 251–2
Lemmon, Jack 247
Lewinsky, Monica 136, 238,
  293, 294, 303
Lewis, Carl 239
Lincoln, Abraham 38, 128,
  134
lips
  biting 24–5, 239, 354
  parted 268, *270*
  pouting 255–6
  pursed 314–15
  and smiling 56–7
  thin 56
  touching 20
  see also mouth; smiling
listening 105–8, 112, 114–16,
  317–20

Lloyd George, David 152
local tells 26, 327
looking tells 67–70, 236–7
Lord of the Flies (Golding) 318
lordosis 260
love, symptoms of 279
lovers
  signals between 17, 276–9
  see also courtship signals
Lowen, Alexander 224–5
Lumley, Joanna 139
lying 20, 22, 284–306
  how to detect 305–6
  reasons for non-detection of
    286–90

MacArthur, General Douglas
  48, 172–4
Machiavelli, Niccoló, *The
  Prince* 135, 285
macho messages 42–4, 45
Macmillan, Harold 152, 160
macro-tells 17
Mahl, George 30
Major, John 150–1
Manchester United 240
Manes, Joan and Wolfson,
  Nessa 273
Mao Tse-tung, Chairman 168,
  176
Maori people 308
Margaret, Princess 207
Marx, Groucho 87–8
masking 296, 299
Massachusetts, University of
  284
mate-guarding, mate-retention
  280–1
meetings 164
memories, locked-up 29

men
  sexual signals by 248
  see also gender differences
menstrual cycle 252–3
micro-tells 17–20, 299–301,
  351
micromomentary expressions
  18, 33
Middlesex Hospital, AIDS
  clinic 209
Milgram, Stanley 235–6
mirroring 31–2
Mitchell, Leslie 159
Mitterrand, François 346
mixed messages 45–6
Monroe, Marilyn 247, 268,
  270
Moore, Monika 254, 276
Moore, Roger 88
Mossi, Emperor of 69–70
mouth 55, 237–40
  clamped 314–15
  cover 229, 292, *295*
  dry 238
  opening when smiling 138
  'oxbow' 136
  touching 292–3
  see also lips; smiling
moutza 323–4
multiple tells 350
Murphy, Sheila 353
muscles, tension 224–5
musculature 90–1, 133
Mussolini, Benito 128

nail-biting 28, 239–40
name-dropping 117–18
names 186–9
Napier, John 352
Napoleon I, Emperor 26–7, 128

narrow-casting 252
nasal fold wipe 212
Naunton, Sir Robert 201
neck-show 263, 264, *270*
negative emotions 296
negative statements 303
New Guinea 42, 151
New Zealanders 308
Nicolson, Harold 198
Nietzsche, Friedrich 70
Nixon, Richard 128–9, 131,
  153, *173*, 174, 176, 237,
  303
Norwegians 326
nose, touching 289, 293–4,
  305
Nott, John 160–1
Nottingham Forest football
  club 324

obedience experiments 235–6
observation, failure of 349
Obsessive Compulsive
  Disorder 279
offensive tells 147–54
Oprah Winfrey Show 182–3
oral phase 339
orbicularis oculi muscles 91,
  234
other-promotion 99
outlining 302
overlap talk 104–5, 108–10,
  318
overlook tell 56
ownership signals 281

parallel stance 41, 123
paralysis, hysterical 28
Parker, Bonnie 51
parting 189–95

party insults 152
patting on back 21, 65, 181–2
Paxman, Jeremy 160, 161
pecking order 37
Peel, Robert 152
phallic displays 42–4
phallic symbolism 337
phantom friends 147
Philip, Prince, Duke of
    Edinburgh 196, 198, 199,
    204, 208, 218
phobias 28–9
phoney insults 153
Pinocchio syndrome 293
pitch, vocal 62–5
play 249
play face 88–9, 138
Plutarch 26
poker 13–14, 354–6
politics 127–162
    and handshakes 172–9
    insults 151–4
    interviews 154–62
polygraph lie detector 289
Pompidou, Georges 346
Portsmouth University 302
Portuguese 326
possessiveness 280–1
post-interpretations 120
posture 38–9, 122–6, 224–7
    changing 225, 248, 258
    matching 276–8, 352
    mismatching 278
pouch posture 205
pouting 255–6
power 172–9
power grips 329–30
pre-apologies 120
pre-interpretations 119–20
precision grips 322, 329–30

predictive tells 31–3
Presley, Elvis 176
pretzel posture 226–7
prodding 149
promenading 251–3
promotion tells 257
pronouns 117
Provine, Robert 199, 274, 275
public speaking 242
    see also politics
punching 149
put-downs 280
put-offs 257, 276
Putin, Vladimir 56–7

Quayle, Dan 62
questions 107
    closed and open 154–5
    methods of dodging 155–7
quick-step 260–1

Rabin, Yitzhak 177–9
Rathbone, Basil 88
Rather, Dan 160
Reagan, Nancy 145, 147
Reagan, Ronald
    Ford on 153
    head-twist 27, 138–9
    health 128, 129
    and Nancy 145
    popularity 134
    smiles 137, 147
    voice 139, 140
    walking style 132, 133
    waving 147
recognition 164–5, 189
    failure of 349
Reich, Wilhelm 224
rejection signals 276, 278, 294
relationship signals 191

relaxation 46, 69
release pat 21, 181–2
relic tells 60, 326
retreat tells 33
Ricks, Christopher 94
ring, playing with 30
ritualization 52
Robinson, Anne 56
Roosevelt, Franklin D. 128, *344*, 345
Rounders 14
royalty 196–218
Rubens, Peter Paul 245
Russians 311, 326
Rutgers University 293

Samuel, Herbert 152
Scandinavians 313
scanning 251
Scheflen, Albert 114
Schopenhauer, Arthur 351
scissors stance 76, 124–5, 226
scowling 353
scratching 149–50
scrotch 43
Seaford, Henry 314–15
secret societies 17–18
self-comforting tells 77–9, 226–9, 338
self-deprecation 99–100
self-directed behaviour 228
self-disclosure 273
sensory modalities 53
sentence, end of 112
separation 189–90
sexual characteristics
    secondary 244–8, 256, 336
    tertiary 248
sexuality 215, 244–83
    availability 249–53

dominant faces and 54
Seymour, Jane 315
Shakespeare, William 321
Shaw, George Bernard 227
Sherlock Holmes stories 351–2
shibboleths 307–9
shoulders
    lift *270*
    lowering 301
    raising 73, 74–5, 264
shrugging 25, 72–5, 83, 111, 320
signature tells 25–7, 87–8, 138–9, 161, 200, 215–16, 355–6
    see also trademark tells
Simons, Daniel and Levin, Dan 348–9
Simpson, Wallis (later Duchess of Windsor) 202
sitting 38, 40–1, 44–6, 76–7
size 16–17
smaller, looking 75–6
smiling 25–6, 55–7, 88–93, 137–9, 164, 353
    anxiously 234–5
    clamped smiles 57
    closed-mouth 178
    Diana's smiles 215
    dipped 214–15
    drop-jaw smiles 137–8
    Duchenne smiles 90–1
    false 91–3, 297–8, 300
    gender differences 92–3
    and nationality 314–15
    open-mouthed 164
    pursed 214, 217
    sealed and clamped 57, 138
    as sexual approach 256
    as sign of lying 289, 297–8

Spencer smile 214, 217
symmetry 298
turn-away smiles 215–16, 267
types of 137–8, 214–15
upward 354
smoking 240, 328–46
background 355
and breast-feeding 339
and courtship signals 336–7
and mood 343–6
and personality 340–3
topography of 328–9, 341–2
see also cigarettes
smooth transitions 104, 111
smugglers 301
softeners 119–20
Some Like It Hot 247
South Africa 64
Southgate, Gareth 230–1
space, use of 260–1
Spaniards 311, 325–6
speech melody 112
Spencer, Earl 217
standing tells 41–4, 76, 249
Stanford University, California 55
startle response 73
state anxiety 219
stealth tells 20–1, 182, 293
step postures 44–5
Stephanopoulos, George 177–8
Stern, John 237
Stevenson, Adlai 153
Stone, Sharon 258
stotting 262
straddle stance 41–2, 49, 124
straight-leg postures 44–5
strobe glance 254

stupidity insults 153
stuttering 241–2
Stylistics 64
submission 36–7, 46, 71–103, 172, 249
supernormal stimuli 86
substitution tells 77–8
swallowing 238–9
sweating 21, 23, 28, 221–2, 289, 350
Swedes 317, 326

table, sitting around 40–1
table manners 309
talk 61–2, 104–26, 240–3
and blood flow to brain 316
in courtship 272–4
and lying 302–6
and nationality 307–10
pausing 241, 289, 304–5
speed 241, 289, 304
tall tells 37–9
Taylor, Elizabeth 62
teasing 280
teeth 54, 60
tell blindness 349–51
telleology 350–2
tell-suppressing tells 25, 242–3
tell-tales 347–56
tells, defined 14–17, 354–5
tense, past 304
tension release tells 301
Tenzing Norgay 313
termination signals 182, 320
territorial tells 39–41
Texas, University of 245
Thackeray, W.M. 340
Thatcher, Margaret 27, 114, 117, 140, 143, 148, 156, 158–9, 161, 300–1

thighs, pressed together 226
threat displays 32, 59–60, 280–1
threshold settings 288
threshold tells 217–18
thumb, sucking 229
thumbs-up gesture 323
tics 28
tie signs 281
tie tidy 217–18
tie tuck 212, 213, 218
Tiedens, Larissa 55
time-locked tells 28–9
time-shifted tells 29–30
tongue flick 97–8
tongue show 96–7
torso 123
touching 269–72
  controlling 320
  objects 228–9, 271–2
  others 65–6, 77–8, 98–9,
    205–10, 228, 271, 281
  self 77–9, 227–8, 269, 289,
    338
Townsend, Group Captain
  Peter 207
trademark tells 26–7, 56, 227,
  239
  see also signature tells
trait anxiety 219–20
transfix 114
transitional objects 338
transition tells 164–6
transposed tells 27–30
A Treatise of Daunces 321
Truman, Bess 145
Truman, Harry S 145, 172–4
tucked postures 44–5
Turks 309
turn-taking in conversation
  104–17, 159, 318–20

Tyson, Mike 169

Ukrainians 325
undiscovered tells 16
unintention display 106–7,
  125, 227
United Nations 177
United States of America 121,
  177, 326–7, 354
  see also Americans
universal tells 327
University College, London
  266
unprincipled insults 153
unqualified insults 153
Uppsala University 353
urination 227

V-signs 324–5
Van Cleef, Lee 55
vasoconstriction 293
Victoria, Queen 202
Victorians, and blushing 94–5
Virginia 314–15
  University of 286
visual dominance 68–70
voice 62–5, 139–41, 240–3
  breathiness 139–40
  pitch 24, 240–1, 272–3, 305
  volume 241, 252, 272
Vrij, Aldert 302

waistcoat, hand in 26–7
Wake Island 172
walking 131–5, 259–60, 262–3
  physical contact while 281
Washington, George 27, 134,
  285
Washington University, St
  Louis 237

Watergate affair 136, 237, 303
waving 147, 164, 354
Wayne, John 64, 346
The Weakest Link 56
Webster, Stephen 62
Weinstein, Eugene 119–20
Welsh 313
whispering 140
Wilde, Oscar 334
William, Prince 209, 210,
   211, 216–18
Wilson, Harold 131–2
Winfrey, Oprah 182–3
withdrawal 189–90, 194–5
women
   and menstrual cycle 252–3
   sexual signals by 246–83

   see also gender differences
word choice 303

Yale University, obedience
   experiments 235–6
yawning 32, 58–60, 276
   types of 58–9
yo-yo phenomenon 193–4
York University 155
youth displays 255

Zajonc, Robert 316, 353
Zeldin, Theodore, *The French*
   311, 315
zygomatic major muscles
   90–1, 235

A SELECTED LIST OF RELATED TITLES
AVAILABLE FROM BANTAM BOOKS

THE PRICES SHOWN BELOW WERE CORRECT AT THE TIME OF GOING TO PRESS. HOWEVER TRANSWORLD PUBLISHERS RESERVE THE RIGHT TO SHOW NEW RETAIL PRICES ON COVERS WHICH MAY DIFFER FROM THOSE PREVIOUSLY ADVERTISED IN THE TEXT OR ELSEWHERE.

81440 0	THE ART OF EFFORTLESS LIVING	Ingrid Bacci	£7.99
81486 9	EMOTIONAL YOGA	Bija Bennett	£10.99
81354 4	THE BOOK OF ANSWERS	Carol Bolt	£9.99
34539 7	HANDS OF LIGHT	Barbara Ann Brennan	£19.99
81367 6	PERFECT HEALTH	Deepak Chopra	£12.99
81563 6	YOUR HANDS CAN HEAL YOU	Master Stephen Co	£10.99
81547 4	SETTING YOUR HEART ON FIRE	Raphael Cushnir	£7.99
81366 8	AWAKENING THE BUDDHIST HEART	Lama Surya Das	£8.99
81564 4	A TRAVEL GUIDE TO HEAVEN	Anthony Destefano	£7.99
81615 2	EXPECT A MIRACLE	Kathy Freston	£7.99
81323 4	THE JOURNEY TO YOU	Ross Heaven	£7.99
81666 7	THE PRESENT	Spencer Johnson	£9.99
81496 6	ZEN AND THE ART OF FALLING IN LOVE	Charlotte Kasl	£6.99
50544 0	THE WHEEL OF LIFE	Elisabeth Kubler-Ross	£8.99
81526 1	THE SOUL OF SEX	Thomas Moore	£7.99
50527 0	ANATOMY OF THE SPIRIT	Caroline Myss	£8.99
50592 0	ANAM ĊARA	John O'Donohue	£8.99
81347 1	STAYING SANE	Raj Persaud	£8.99
40902 6	THE CELESTINE PROPHECY	James Redfield	£7.99
81371 4	LIFE MAKEOVERS	Cheryl Richardson	£7.99
81325 0	MIND SCULPTURE	Ian Robertson	£7.99
81364 1	THE MILLIONAIRE MIND	Thomas J. Stanley	£8.99
81565 2	THE NAKED LEADER	David Taylor	£7.99
81380 3	SHAMAN, HEALER, SAGE	Alberto Villoldo	£8.99
81595 4	POLAR BEAR PIRATES	Adrian Webster	£6.99
81427 3	UNCONDITIONAL SUCCESS	Nick Williams	£7.99
81545 8	EVERYDAY GRACE	Marianne Williamson	£9.99
81492 3	HUMAN INSTINCT	Robert Winston	£7.99
40397 4	THE FRAGRANT PHARMACY	Valerie Ann Worwood	£9.99
81590 3	THERE MUST BE MORE THAN THIS	Judith Wright	£7.99

All Transworld titles are available by post from:
Bookpost, PO Box 29, Douglas, Isle of Man, IM99 1BQ
Credit cards accepted. Please telephone 01624 836000,
fax 01624 837033, Internet http://www.bookpost.co.uk
or e-mail: bookshop@enterprise.net for details.
Free postage and packing in the UK. Overseas customers: allow
£2 per book (paperbacks) and £3 per book (hardbacks).